PRAYERSCRIPTS

SCRIPTURES & PRAYERS FOR
OVERCOMING THROUGH THE BLOOD

60 DAYS OF PRAYERS FOR CLAIMING YOUR BLOOD-BOUGHT INHERITANCE

CYRIL OPOKU

Scriptures & Prayers for Overcoming Through the Blood: 60 Days of Prayers for Claiming Your Blood-Bought Inheritance

© 2025 Cyril Opoku. *PrayerScripts*. All rights reserved.

No part of this publication may be reproduced, stored in a retrieval system, or transmitted in any form or by any means—electronic, mechanical, photocopy, recording, or otherwise—without the prior written permission of the publisher, except in the case of brief quotations used in reviews, articles, or devotionals.

Published by *Quest Publications*

ISBN: 978-1-988439-75-4

Cover design by *Quest Publications (questpublications@outlook.com)*

Unless otherwise indicated, all Scripture quotations are taken from the World English Bible WEB, which is in the public domain. For more information, visit: www.worldenglish.bible

This book is a work of devotional encouragement and prayer. It is not intended to replace biblical study, pastoral counsel, or professional therapy.

Printed in the United States of America.

First Edition: August 2025

For more books like this, visit *PrayerScripts:* https://prayerscripts.org

Contents

Preface .... *xix*
Introduction .... *xxi*
How to Use This Book .... *xxiii*

DAY 1 .... **XXIV**
    Redeemed by the Blood of Jesus 1
    Divine Protection Through the Blood 2
    Overcoming Satan by the Blood 3
    Healed by His Wounds 4
    Christ Became Poor for Me 5
    Peace Purchased at the Cross 6

DAY 2 .... **8**
    Justified From All Wrath 8
    Marked by the Blood at Home 9
    Victory Over Destruction and Judgment 10
    Wholeness Through His Stripes 11
    Blood-Purchased Kingship 12
    Inner Peace, My Right in Christ 13

DAY 3 .... **15**
    Cleansed and Walking in Light 15
    Preserved From the Destroyer 16
    Triumphant Exposure of Demonic Forces 17
    Jesus Carried Our Sickness 18
    Heirs of the Kingdom 19
    Peace with God Through Justification 20

DAY 4 .... **22**
    Freed from Shame and Filth 22

Faith in the Blood's Power 23
More Than a Conqueror 24
Covered From Every Plague 25
Curse of Lack Broken 26
The Blood Silences Separation Anxiety 27

DAY 5 28

Purged for Pure Service 28
Life Flows in the Blood 29
Freedom from Every Prison 30
Vitality Through the Blood 31
Redeemed from Poverty 32
Paid-in-Full Peace for My Soul 33

DAY 6 34

Rescued from Darkness into Light 34
Grateful for the Shed Blood 35
Canceling Every Weapon by the Blood 36
Cleansed to Serve Again 37
Eternal Inheritance Secured 38
Peace in a Clean and Healed Conscience 39

DAY 7 40

Boldness to Enter God's Presence 40
Covered by the New Covenant 41
The Blood-Stained King Leads My Victory 42
Healing Every Disease 43
Qualified for Provision 44
The Peace of Being Fully Cleansed 45

DAY 8 46

Covenant of Forgiveness Sealed 46

Spared from Wrath 47
Destroying Death and Fear Through the Cross 48
Nourished by His Blood 49
Peace Purchased for Provision 50
Walking Daily in Cleansing Peace 51

DAY 9 52

Life-Giving Blood for My Family 52
Entering the Place of Refuge 53
Blood-Wrought Destruction of Satan's Works 54
Overcoming Affliction and Torment 55
Justified to Prosper 56
Peace Through Forgiveness 57

DAY 10 58

Without Blood, No Forgiveness 58
The Blood Speaks a Better Word 59
Declaring Satan Crushed Underfoot 60
Yahweh Who Heals Me 61
Kingly Abundance Released 62
Peace in Chaos from Faith in the Blood 63

DAY 11 64

Washed Whiter Than Snow 64
The Blood Speaks Protection 65
Victory Through Blood-Bought Belonging 66
Sanctified by His Blood 67
Boldly Accessing Heavenly Resources 68
Calm Confidence in God's Presence 69

DAY 12 71

The Lamb Who Bore It All 71

v

Overcoming by the Blood 72
Eternal Redemption, Unshakable Victory 73
Faith's Touch Draws Healing 74
Accessing Divine Favor and Connection 75
Hearing the Voice of Peace 76

DAY 13 78

The Blood On Our Doorposts 78
The Blood Silences Vengeance 79
Freedom from Generational Curses 80
Sprinkled and Washed Clean 81
Prosperity Is My Covenant Portion 82
Peace Through Resurrection Power 83

DAY 14 84

Healed Through His Wounds 84
Sprinkled for Safety and Sanctification 85
Delivered from Strong Enemies 86
Peace Through His Blood 87
Standing on Better Promises 88
Peace in Full Redemption 89

DAY 15 90

Faith in the Blood Alone 90
Covenant Blood Breaks All Prisons 91
Warfare by the Blood, Not Flesh 92
Washed from Sin's Decay 93
No Lack in My Life 94
A Renewed Mind for Peace 95

DAY 16 96

Precious Blood, Priceless Ransom 96

    Anchored in an Eternal Covenant 97
    Washed and Empowered to Prevail 98
    Healing the Brokenhearted 99
    Generational Blessing by the Blood 100
    Peace as My Inheritance 101

DAY 17 102
    Set Apart By His Blood 102
    Washed and Kept by the Blood 103
    Victory in My Redeemed Identity 104
    Identity Justified by the Blood 105
    Let the Blood Speak Increase 106
    Perfect Peace in Trust 107

DAY 18 108
    Completely Washed And Restored 108
    Washed and Guarded in Spirit 109
    Justified and Saved from Wrath 110
    Restored Like a Child Again 111
    Power to Produce Wealth 112
    Peace Guarding My Emotions 113

DAY 19 114
    Robes Washed In The Blood 114
    Blood-Cleansed and Enemy-Proofed 115
    Perfected to Walk in Authority 116
    Freedom from Pain and Limits 117
    Abundant Life Over My Finances 118
    Sanctified in the Peace of the Blood 119

DAY 20 120
    Forgiven And Forever Free 120

- Renewed in Covenant Safety 121
- Pushing Back Every Adversary 122
- Healing from Gethsemane's Blood 123
- Justified to Receive God's Best 124
- Peace in God's Holy Presence 125

DAY 21 126
- Sins Cast into the Sea 126
- Protected From Sickness and Affliction 127
- Standing in Blood-Bought Authority 128
- Mercy for Every Weak Moment 129
- Heir, Not a Beggar 130
- Peace as My Warfare Weapon 131

DAY 22 133
- Blotted Out and Made New 133
- Purity That Disarms the Accuser 134
- Equipped by Covenant Blood 135
- Healing by Atonement's Power 136
- Drinking from the Covenant Cup 137
- Anchored in Christ's Finished Peace 138

DAY 23 139
- No More Condemnation 139
- Covered by Psalm 91 Protection 140
- Warring From Peace, Not Panic 141
- Healing from Heaven's Tree 142
- The Blood on Our Door 143
- Resting in the Unshakable Covenant 144

DAY 24 145
- Righteous By His Blood 145

Secured As God's Protected Property 146
Cleansed to Serve in Power 147
Speedy Healing by Covenant Blood 148
God Delights in My Prosperity 149
The Peace of His Lifted Face 150

DAY 25 151

Washed And Renewed 151
Hidden In Christ Through Communion 152
Victory by Daily Sprinkling 153
Deliverance from Demonic Oppression 154
Double for My Shame 155
Peace as My Divine Blessing 156

DAY 26 157

Living By Faith In The Blood 157
Mercy Prevails Over Judgment 158
Maintaining Victory Through Purity 159
Wholeness in Ear, Hand, and Foot 160
Calling Provision into Being 161
The Blood Speaks Peace 162

DAY 27 163

Hearts Sprinkled Clean 163
Blood Disarms Death and Hell 164
Gratitude for Constant Victory 165
Health Through the Sanctified Sacrifice 166
Cleansed for Covenant Access 167
Grace and Peace Through the Cross 168

DAY 28 169

Crucified With Christ 169

Victory Over Every Demonic Force	170
Blood Power to Trample Darkness	171
Quickened by the Spirit of Life	172
Eternal Redemption, Eternal Provision	173
The Life of Peace in the Blood	174

DAY 29 175

Life Through Communion	175
God Is On Our Side	176
Trusting the Lamb to Win	177
Washed from Sickness Residue	178
Abundance by Covenant Right	179
Living in Kingdom Peace	180

DAY 30 181

Cleansed By Living Water	181
Angelic Protection Activated by Blood	182
Freedom from Sin's Dominion	183
The Blood-Covered Word Heals	184
Bound by the Blood to Provide	185
Sanctified by the God of Peace	186

DAY 31 187

Bought And Paid For By His Blood	187
Marked for Divine Purpose	188
Flood-Resistant Standard Raised	189
Healing That Touches Generations	190
Multiplied Through Covenant Obedience	191
Rest in the Shadow of the Cross	192

DAY 32 194

Gratitude for Christ's Mercy Seat Work	194

Blood-Covered Senses for Discernment 195
Victory Over the World's Storms 196
Rising into Blood-Righteous Healing 197
Overcoming Financial Warfare 198
Covered in Peaceful Protection 199

DAY 33 200

Deep Cleansing And Restoration 200
Sealed from Harm and Judgment 201
Let the Blood Fight 202
Blood-Anointed for Preservation 203
No Sorrow in My Blessing 204
Pardon That Calms the Soul 205

DAY 34 206

Rejoicing In Erased Records 206
Exempt by the Mark of Blood 207
Trust in Blood, Not Strength 208
Healing from Sin's Root 209
Supernatural Provision Without Currency 210
Breaking the Curse's Grip 211

DAY 35 212

Walking in the Power of the Covenant 212
Covenant Blood Establishes My Shield 213
Boldness Granted by Blood Access 214
No Plague Near Our Dwelling 215
Satisfaction in Every Famine 216
Freedom from the Inner Prison 217

DAY 36 218

Embracing the Blood Fountain 218

    Engraved in God's Hands 219
    Life Declared Over Death Threats 220
    Let the Blood Speak Healing 221
    Overflow in All Things 222
    Healing for the Broken Heart 223

DAY 37 224
    Thanksgiving for Blessed Pardon 224
    Untouchable Under Blood Protection 225
    Blood-Cries for Vengeance 226
    Sustained on the Sickbed 227
    No More Guilt, Only Grace 228
    Peace in Reconciliation 229

DAY 38 230
    Receiving God's Full Forgiveness 230
    The Blood Silences Every Accuser 231
    Covenant Rights Deployed 232
    Flesh Like a Child's 233
    Abrahamic Wealth Flows to Me 234
    Cleansed from Guilt's Grip 235

DAY 39 236
    Joy in Divine Forgiveness 236
    Renewed Covering by Atoning Blood 237
    Superior Voice of Jesus' Blood 238
    Look and Live 239
    Equipped for Prosperity 240
    Peace as God's Purchased Possession 241

DAY 40 242
    Freedom From Legal Accusations 242

    Hedge of Protection by the Blood 243
    Christ, Warrior in Blood 244
    Health and Prosperity by Blood 245
    My Year is Crowned 246
    Peace in the Family Circle 247

DAY 41 248
    Declaring Jesus As Savior 248
    Walk in Strength and Wholeness 249
    Rebuking the Accuser Through Blood Authority 250
    Immediate Healing by Contact 251
    Days in Prosperity, Years in Pleasure 252
    Peaceful Life Through Righteous Blood 253

DAY 42 254
    Christ Our Ransom 254
    Cancel Every Weapon Formed 255
    Refusing the Thief Access Through the Blood Wall 256
    Healing Answer to My Prayer 257
    Prosper in All You Do 258
    Hope and Peace 259

DAY 43 260
    God's Mercy Not Based on Merit 260
    God's Army, Fearless and Ready 261
    Canceling Guilt and Shame in Spiritual Warfare 262
    Protection for Bones and Core 263
    Open the Windows of Heaven 264
    Channel of Peace 265

DAY 44 266
    Returning to the Father Through Grace 266

- Blood Routes Every Attack.. 267
- Letting the Blood Speak Over Conflict and Accusation......... 268
- Total Removal of All Sickness 269
- Freedom from Financial Captivity 270
- Peace with Enemies... 271

DAY 45 272
- Bold Declaration of Forgiveness 272
- The Blood Fights My Battles... 273
- Letting God Fight Your Spiritual Battles 274
- Cleansed in Every Dimension... 275
- Treasures in Secret Places... 276
- The Ruling Peace of Christ's Blood....................................... 277

DAY 46 278
- Worship From a Forgiven Heart.. 278
- Blood Cries for My Justice.. 279
- Declaring Your Identity as an Overcomer 280
- Faith Unlocks Healing Power.. 281
- Whatever I Do Will Prosper.. 282
- Peace Through Obedience by Grace..................................... 283

DAY 47 284
- Calling on God's Forgiving Nature 284
- Victory in the Garden of Agony.. 285
- Seated in Victorious Authority with Christ 286
- Signs and Wonders Through Blood...................................... 287
- Life More Abundantly... 288
- Set Apart from Emotional Chaos.. 289

DAY 48 290
- Confession That Leads to Mercy... 290

Permanent Deliverance by the Blood 291
My Victory Is Sealed 292
Long Life Through the Blood 293
You Alone Are the Source 294
Peace in Knowing Sin Has Been Removed 295

DAY 49 ..... **296**
Atonement Fulfilled in Christ 296
The King in Blood-Soaked Glory 297
Built as an Unshakable Pillar 298
Health from the Blood-Soaked Word 299
Expecting Every Good Thing 300
Receiving the Mind of Christ 301

DAY 50 ..... **302**
Salvation Through Confession and Belief 302
Fire-Walled by the Blood 303
Sanctified for Dominion 304
God's Personal Healing Vow 305
No Good Thing Withheld 306
A Calm Life Through Christ's Presence 307

DAY 51 ..... **308**
Living In Covenantal Pardon 308
Kept From All Harm 309
Weapons of Praise and Blood 310
Healing in Consecrated Spaces 311
Blood-Mark on My Labor 312
Peace Sealed by the Blood 313

DAY 52 ..... **315**
Appeal to God's Mercy 315

    Marked With Christ's Ownership 316
    Victory Over the End-Time Beast 317
    Healing Mercy Answers My Cry 318
    Honoring the Blood Guarantee 319
    Grace to Live Peaceably 320

DAY 53 .... **321**
    Heart-Level Repentance 321
    Redeemed and Hidden by Blood 322
    I Will Not Die But Live 323
    You Alone Heal and Preserve 324
    Treasured and Positioned by Favor 325
    Rescued from Inner Turmoil 326

DAY 54 .... **327**
    Jesus, Our Intercessor When We Fall 327
    Covered by Divine Surveillance 328
    The Lord is My Man of War 329
    Restored From Long-Term Affliction 330
    Overtaken by Covenant Blessings 331
    Surrendering to Peace 332

DAY 55 .... **333**
    Silencing Guilt and Accusation 333
    Jesus Keeps What's Entrusted 334
    Covered Courage Under Covenant 335
    Freedom From Every Infirmity 336
    Taught to Profit by the Lord 337
    Peace Through the Living Word 338

DAY 56 .... **339**
    Coming Boldly for Mercy and Grace 339

Shielded from End-Time Calamity 340
　　Faith in the Blood Prevails 341
　　Restoration of Soul and Spirit 342
　　God's Investment Must Prosper 343
　　Cleansed for Mental Stability 344

DAY 57 345
　　Redeemed From Judgment 345
　　Guarded from Satanic Ambush 346
　　Freedom Through the Blood's Law 347
　　Living in a Healing Atmosphere 348
　　Barns Filled, Vats Overflowing 349
　　Healing from Emotional Pain 350

DAY 58 351
　　Complete Salvation In Christ 351
　　Standard Against Flood Attacks 352
　　Trained Hands, Blood-Anointed Warfare 353
　　Sickness Taken from Among Us 354
　　Increase Upon Increase 355
　　Peace and Righteousness United 356

DAY 59 357
　　Christ Came to Save, Not Condemn 357
　　Shielded by God Himself 358
　　Final End to All Trouble 359
　　Healing to the Uttermost 360
　　Harvest from Blood-Bought Seed 361
　　Walking in the Gospel of Peace 362

DAY 60 363
　　Praise For National and Personal Pardon 363

The Blood, My Stronghold	364
Inheritance of the Overcomer	365
Healing Through Faith and Blood	366
Final Inheritance, Fully Secured	367
Resurrection Peace Every Day	368
Epilogue	*369*
Encourage Others with Your Story	*370*
More from PrayerScripts	*371*

Preface

"And they overcame him by the blood of the Lamb, and by the word of their testimony..." — Revelation 12:11 (KJV)

The blood of Jesus is not just a theological truth—it is the believer's battlefield advantage. Through the Blood, you are pardoned from sin's guilt, protected from the enemy's attacks, empowered to prevail in every battle, preserved in health and wholeness, prospered in every good work, and anchored in the peace of God that cannot be shaken.

This book is a distillation of six powerful prayer journeys—each one focused on a distinct covenant blessing secured by Christ's sacrifice. For the first time, *Pardon Through the Blood*, *Protection Through the Blood*, *Prevail Through the Blood*, *Preservation Through the Blood*, *Prosperity Through the Blood*, and *Peace Through the Blood* have been brought together into one strategic daily weapon for victorious living.

Every page is saturated with Scripture and forged in the fire of prayer. These are not casual words; they are Spirit-led declarations meant to dismantle strongholds, silence the accuser, and release God's covenant promises over your life. As you go through each day, expect transformation. Expect breakthrough. Expect to see the Blood of Jesus at work in ways you've never imagined.

The battle is real, but so is your victory. And the Blood still speaks.

Overcoming through the Blood,
Cyril O.
Illinois, August 2025

Introduction

What if the one thing you've been missing in your spiritual battles is the very thing that guarantees your victory?

Too often, believers try to fight life's battles in their own strength—striving harder, praying longer, reading more, yet still feeling overwhelmed, defeated, or weary. But God never intended for you to fight in your own power. He has already given you the ultimate weapon: the Blood of Jesus.

This is more than a symbol of forgiveness. It is a living covenant that covers every area of your life—your past, your present, and your future. The Blood doesn't just cleanse; it protects, empowers, heals, prospers, and secures you in supernatural peace.

In *Scriptures & Prayers for Overcoming Through the Blood*, you will embark on a 60-day journey that combines the life-giving truths from six transformative books into one powerful manual for victory. Each day's PrayerScript draws from a different facet of the Blood's covenant power—so you're not just praying in one area of breakthrough, but in all six covenant dimensions of God's promise:

- **Pardon** — Total forgiveness and freedom.
- **Protection** — Living untouchable under Christ's covering.
- **Prevail** — Spiritual mastery over the enemy.
- **Preservation** — Divine healing and wholeness.

- **Prosperity** — Unlocking Heaven's wealth and increase.
- **Peace** — Unshakable rest in God.

By the end, you won't just know about the Blood—you'll live in its reality.

If you are tired of living under attack, weighed down by guilt, or tossed by fear, this book is your war cry. It is your reminder that you have been purchased at a price, armed with a covenant, and called to live as more than a conqueror.

How to Use This Book

This book is designed to be more than just read—it's meant to be prayed, spoken, and lived.

Each day, you'll encounter a blood-related Scripture, a themed prayer focus, and a prophetic prayer declaration. These prayers are intentionally crafted to help you and your family receive and walk in the full covenant rights Christ purchased for you through His blood. The goal is not religious routine, but *spiritual renewal*.

Here's how to make the most of each entry:

1. **Set a Consistent Time** — Treat this as a daily spiritual appointment with God. Whether morning or night, guard the time fiercely.
2. **Read the Scripture First** — Let the Word of God renew your mind before you speak a single prayer. The verses selected are your foundation and legal standing in the spirit.
3. **Pray Aloud** — These PrayerScripts are meant to be spoken, not just read silently. Declare the words over yourself, your family, your children, and your legacy. Declare them with faith, conviction, and expectation. Your voice matters in the spiritual realm.
4. **Engage Your Heart** — Don't just repeat words; align your faith with what you are declaring. Picture the truth of God's promises being activated in your life.
5. **Journal Breakthroughs** — Keep a record of what God does as you pray. The Blood will work in ways

you may not expect—healing relationships, opening doors, breaking cycles, and lifting burdens.
6. **Repeat as Needed** — This is not a one-time journey. You can revisit these prayers whenever you need a renewed encounter with the power of the Blood.

You can use this book over 60 days, revisit specific themes weekly, or allow the Spirit to lead you day by day. However you move through it, do so with faith—believing that the blood still speaks.

DAY 1

PARDON

REDEEMED BY THE BLOOD OF JESUS

> "In him we have our redemption through his blood, the forgiveness of our trespasses, according to the riches of his grace."
> — Ephesians 1:7 WEB

O Redeemer of my soul, I boldly stand in the assurance that I have been purchased and pardoned by the blood of Jesus. I do not come by works or by merit, but by the riches of grace that have been poured out for me and my household. I declare that Your mercy has triumphed over judgment, and Your forgiveness has silenced every accusation. Through the blood, I have been brought near—cleansed, accepted, and beloved.

Father, I apply this redemption to every failure, secret struggle, and generational stain that has plagued my life or family line. Let the blood that speaks better things than judgment echo through the foundations of our history, and silence every voice of condemnation. Let cycles of guilt and shame break now under the weight of divine mercy. I declare that my lineage is free—my children and descendants walk in holy liberty.

Because of the blood, I decree that no stain remains. We are redeemed from bondage, delivered from darkness, and restored to our rightful inheritance in You. The blood has spoken, and the verdict is final: we are forgiven, cleansed, and forever Yours.

In Jesus' name, Amen.

PROTECTION

DIVINE PROTECTION THROUGH THE BLOOD

> "When I see the blood, I will pass over you. No plague will be on you to destroy you."
> —Exodus 12:13 WEB

O God of my refuge and strong defense, I stand under the eternal banner of the blood of Jesus! As You once passed over the homes of Israel, so today I declare that Your covenant blood covers me and my entire household. Let every plague, disaster, and demonic intrusion be halted at the threshold. The destroyer will not cross the line drawn by the Lamb's blood.

By faith, I mark the lintels of my life with the blood of Christ. Over my children, over my spouse, over our home and possessions—I decree divine exemption. Though chaos surrounds the nations, the blood marks us as untouchable. Our dwelling becomes holy ground, invisible to the plans of death and destruction.

Father, thank You that the blood still speaks. It cries out for mercy over judgment, for deliverance over destruction. Your covenant is unbreakable, and through Jesus, I am sealed, safe, and sheltered. I rejoice in this divine Passover—this spiritual security that no enemy can penetrate.

Let this blood shield continue night and day. I decree angelic protection, Holy Spirit fire, and divine peace in every room and every journey. In Jesus' name, Amen.

PREVAIL

OVERCOMING SATAN BY THE BLOOD

> "They overcame him because of the Lamb's blood and the word of their testimony."
> —Revelation 12:11 WEB

O Lord of Glory, by the eternal power of the blood of the Lamb, I rise today in holy defiance against every demonic resistance. I declare: by the blood, I overcome every satanic accusation, every lying spirit, every generational curse, and every voice of the accuser. Your blood speaks louder than any condemnation. Your blood testifies of my victory, my cleansing, and my right to stand as a son in the courts of Heaven.

By the blood of Jesus, I silence the adversary who wars against my soul and my household. I boldly proclaim that we are not victims—we are victors. The word of my testimony aligns with the testimony of Heaven: I am redeemed, washed, forgiven, empowered, and set apart for the glory of God. Every legal right the enemy has claimed over my family is revoked by the speaking blood of Jesus.

Father, let Your overcoming power rest upon my home. Let angels be released to enforce the covenant of victory You have established through the blood. Let no satanic surveillance, no hidden trap, and no witchcraft curse prevail against us. We overcome not by strength, not by strategy, but by the blood that has never lost its power.

In Jesus' name, Amen.

PRESERVATION

HEALED BY HIS WOUNDS

> "By his wounds you were healed."
> — 1 Peter 2:24 WEB

Righteous Redeemer, I lift my voice in bold faith, declaring that the wounds of Jesus speak healing over my life and my family. The blood that flowed from His lacerated body carries eternal power to reverse every sickness and dismantle every disease. By the finished work of Calvary, I proclaim healing as my covenant right.

Let the voice of His wounds echo through every system in my body—my blood, my bones, my organs, and every cell. I declare restoration from chronic afflictions, reversal of doctor's reports, and renewal in my joints, muscles, and mind. Let every spiritual root of infirmity be severed by the power of His suffering. I apply the virtue of the stripes He bore to every area of weakness and pain.

Over my household, I decree a divine alignment under the healing authority of the Blood. Let His wounds speak over every generational sickness and end cycles of pain. I declare supernatural immunity over my children, and restoration over every weary soul within my family.

We do not beg for healing—we receive it boldly through the eternal voice of the cross. We are the healed of the Lord, purchased and preserved by divine blood.

In Jesus' name, Amen.

PROSPERITY

CHRIST BECAME POOR FOR ME

> "For you know the grace of our Lord Jesus Christ, that though he was rich, yet for your sakes he became poor, that you through his poverty might become rich."
> — 2 Corinthians 8:9 WEB

Righteous Redeemer, I thank You for the lavish grace poured out through the blood of Your Son. I lift my voice in bold declaration: I refuse to live beneath the covenant that Christ has sealed with His blood. Jesus, though You were infinitely rich, You chose poverty—not for Yourself, but for me and my household. You took the full weight of lack, insufficiency, and deprivation so that I might step boldly into the abundance You secured.

By Your blood, I access every inheritance of prosperity—not just for survival but for divine flourishing. My hands are anointed to multiply. My work is blessed. I declare that financial barrenness is broken off me and my lineage. We will not toil under scarcity when the blood has spoken better things for us.

Lord, let the evidence of Your sacrifice manifest in my daily provision. Let there be a shift in my bank accounts, my business, my stewardship, and my legacy. I speak divine prosperity over my family. We receive what the cross purchased—nothing lacking, nothing broken.

In Jesus' name, Amen.

PEACE

Peace Purchased at the Cross

> "Having made peace through the blood of his cross..."
> — Colossians 1:20 WEB

O Prince of Peace, I lift my heart to You in holy gratitude, for Your blood has spoken a better word over my life and my household. At the cross, You did not merely purchase my pardon—you secured my peace, a covenant peace that storms cannot steal and enemies cannot overthrow. I declare over my mind, my emotions, and my relationships: the peace of God, bought with the crimson price, rules here.

Lord Jesus, let the power of Your blood silence every voice of fear, unrest, and confusion. May Your peace flow like a river through my home, calming anxious hearts, soothing wounded spirits, and knitting us together in Your unfailing love. Let every spiritual storm dissipate under the weight of this covenant truth: I am reconciled to God, and therefore, I am secure.

I stand in the unshakable reality that my peace is not fragile or circumstantial—it is anchored in the finished work of the cross. Every dark cloud of strife must part, for the blood has decreed my wholeness. I embrace this peace for me, my family, and generations to come.

In Jesus' name, Amen.

DAY 2

PARDON

Justified From All Wrath

> "Much more then, being now justified by his blood, we will be saved from God's wrath through him."
> — Romans 5:9 WEB

Righteous Judge and Merciful Savior, I stand today not in fear but in boldness, because I have been justified by the precious blood of Jesus. The wrath that was due me and my family has been turned away—not by pleading, but by the poured-out sacrifice of the Lamb. The blood has settled every legal case brought against me in the courts of Heaven, and I am declared righteous in Your sight.

I lift my voice and declare over my family: no wrath, no curse, no judgment shall overtake us, for the blood has covered us fully. The accusations of the enemy hold no power; the shame of past sins no longer sticks to our name. Because of this divine justification, peace is our portion and reconciliation is our inheritance. The blood speaks innocence over our household.

We shall not live under torment or spiritual backlash, but walk in the confidence of those who are covered, justified, and secured by Christ. The blood is our refuge, and its voice shields us from every storm of divine wrath or human attack. We live in the shelter of mercy. In Jesus' name, Amen.

PROTECTION

MARKED BY THE BLOOD AT HOME

> "They shall take some of the blood and put it on the two door posts..."
> —Exodus 12:7 WEB

Heavenly Father, I stand today as a priest over my home, declaring that the blood of Jesus marks our doorposts. As it was in Egypt, so let it be now—our house is a house of protection because of the precious blood. No spirit of fear, infirmity, or destruction shall cross the boundary of Your covering.

I spiritually apply the blood to every entrance—physical and spiritual. I apply it to our hearts, minds, and bodies. Over my children's bedrooms, over our comings and goings, over the foundation and roof—I decree this house belongs to the Lord. Let the blood be our wall of fire and our canopy of peace.

Lord, we are not covered by human effort, but by divine covenant. What You see, You honor, and where You see the blood, You deliver. I lift my hands in faith and declare: not one life in this house will be lost; not one destiny will be cut short. We are hidden under the shadow of Your wings.

Thank You, Jesus, for the blood that was shed and still speaks. We welcome Your presence and expel every darkness. Our home is a tabernacle of glory. In Jesus' name, Amen.

PREVAIL

VICTORY OVER DESTRUCTION AND JUDGMENT

> "The blood shall be to you for a token... when I see the blood, I will pass over you."
> —Exodus 12:13 WEB

O Mighty Deliverer, I plead the blood of Jesus over my life, my children, my household, and all that concerns me. Let the blood be a divine mark upon our doorposts and our destiny. Let every angel of death, every storm of judgment, every plague of destruction pass over us. Because of the blood, we are exempt, we are protected, we are sealed.

Your blood is our shield and our refuge. I declare that calamity will not visit our dwelling, nor will sudden disaster take us unaware. I command premature death, terminal affliction, and every orchestrated tragedy to scatter by the power of the blood. Let the enemy see the crimson covering and retreat in terror. Let the destroyer recognize the mark and flee in confusion.

Father, preserve us not just from what we see, but from the unseen evil lurking in the shadows. Let Your covenant of preservation wrap around our family like fire. May the blood of the Lamb keep our borders secure and our minds at peace, even in a world of chaos.

In Jesus' name, Amen.

PRESERVATION

Wholeness Through His Stripes

> "...he was pierced... and with his stripes we are healed."
> — Isaiah 53:5 WEB

Holy Deliverer, I rise in the authority of the Suffering Servant, whose back was shredded so mine could be restored. You were pierced for my rebellion, crushed for my guilt, and whipped so that I could be made whole. By Your agony, my healing is sealed.

I stand under the flow of Your covenant blood and claim wholeness in every realm—physically, emotionally, and spiritually. Let the stripes You bore destroy every root of trauma, every affliction that lingers, and every diagnosis that dares to rise against Your finished work. I declare that healing is not delayed—it is now.

Father, for my family, I invoke divine health over every member. I rebuke hereditary disorders, lingering symptoms, and invisible torments. By Your stripes, we walk in wholeness, clarity of mind, soundness of heart, and strength of body. Where fear tried to lodge, let healing rush in like a flood.

The punishment that brought me peace fell upon You, and by that sacrifice, I call our bodies blessed, our minds sound, and our futures secured in health.

In Jesus' name, Amen.

PROSPERITY

BLOOD-PURCHASED KINGSHIP

> "They sang a new song, saying, 'You are worthy to take the book and to open its seals: for you were killed, and bought us for God with your blood out of every tribe, language, people, and nation, and made us kings and priests to our God; and we will reign on the earth.'"
> — Revelation 5:9-10 WEB

Holy Lamb of God, You were slain, and with Your precious blood, You bought my family and me out of obscurity into royalty. I rise in prophetic understanding today: we are no longer bound, nameless, or without inheritance. We are blood-bought royalty. Dominion runs in our spiritual DNA.

Because You have made us kings and priests, we walk with authority. I decree that everything attempting to enslave us financially must bow to the voice of the blood. You didn't just save us for heaven—you crowned us to reign on earth. Every system, environment, and economic realm must now yield to the kingly anointing You placed on our lives.

Let our decisions be bathed in wisdom. Let our resources multiply supernaturally. Let our influence stretch wide, and our impact go deep. I call forth the manifestation of divine rulership in my family, in our finances, and in our fields of influence. We reign—not by pride, but by purchased right.

In Jesus' name, Amen.

PEACE

INNER PEACE, MY RIGHT IN CHRIST

> "Being justified by faith, we have peace with God…"
> — Romans 5:1 WEB

Faithful Father, I boldly declare that I have been justified through faith in the Lord Jesus Christ. This is not a temporary verdict but an eternal decree, and with it comes the peace that flows from being in right standing with You. No guilt, shame, or accusation can overthrow this peace, for it is my covenant right in Christ.

Let this divine peace flood my inner being and the atmosphere of my home. Lord, drive out the unrest that seeks to lodge in our minds and emotions. Replace every burden with the ease of Your presence, every tension with the stillness of Your Spirit. Let the peace of God be the air my family breathes, the shield around our hearts, and the foundation under our feet.

I proclaim that our peace is not subject to the shifting sands of life's pressures. It is rooted in Christ's unchanging love and the eternal verdict of "justified." This peace guards us, strengthens us, and guides us into every good work You have prepared. We receive it now as our portion.

In Jesus' name, Amen.

DAY 3

PARDON

CLEANSED AND WALKING IN LIGHT

> "But if we walk in the light as he is in the light, we have fellowship with one another, and the blood of Jesus Christ, his Son, cleanses us from all sin."
> — 1 John 1:7 WEB

Light of the World, I come into the brilliance of Your presence, leaving every hidden place behind. I declare that my life and my family are aligned with truth, transparency, and the purifying fellowship of Your Spirit. Because of the blood of Jesus, we are not stained by sin, but daily washed and renewed.

Father, I receive the continual cleansing that flows from the cross—cleansing of thoughts, words, and actions. Let the blood purify our conscience, reset our desires, and bring us into a holy rhythm of righteousness. I break every power of habitual sin and secret darkness; let Your blood flood the deepest recesses of our hearts and drive out all impurity.

Because of the blood, we walk in unity—no strife, no bitterness, no walls of division. Let Your peace govern our relationships. Let fellowship flourish where there was once isolation. Our home shall be a sanctuary of light, love, and truth, all held together by the cleansing power of the blood. In Jesus' name, Amen.

PROTECTION

PRESERVED FROM THE DESTROYER

> "...Yahweh will pass over the door, and will not allow the destroyer to come..."
> —Exodus 12:23 WEB

Mighty Deliverer, You are the God who forbids the destroyer! You set a blood boundary over Israel, and today I decree that the same blood line surrounds my life, my family, and my legacy. You do not permit destruction where the blood has been applied, and I boldly invoke that protection now.

By the authority of Jesus' sacrifice, I cancel every plan of premature death, disaster, and demonic ambush. The destroyer may prowl, but he will not prevail. I declare divine interruption to every curse, accident, disease, or snare meant to devour us. The blood is our legal defense, and heaven enforces it.

Let every evil spirit be turned away at the sight of the blood. Let angelic warriors surround our family gates, enforcing divine restraint. What was sent to harm us shall pass over, and what was aimed at us shall be reversed. I plead the blood over our vehicles, our decisions, our relationships, and every new season.

We walk forward in holy confidence, not in fear. God has passed over, and the enemy must pass by. Thank You for this hedge of grace. In Jesus' name, Amen.

PREVAIL

TRIUMPHANT EXPOSURE OF DEMONIC FORCES

> "He made a show of them openly, triumphing over them in it."
> —Colossians 2:15 WEB

Captain of Heaven's Hosts, I stand under the banner of Your blood-stained triumph. You disarmed every principality, stripped every demon of power, and paraded them in open shame through the cross. Let that same triumph manifest in my life today. Let every hidden plot, secret scheme, and cloaked curse be exposed and dismantled.

In the authority of the blood, I declare that no power of darkness shall operate undetected in my home. Every monitoring spirit is blinded, every manipulative spirit is bound, and every force of sabotage is scattered. Let the fire of the blood uncover what's been lurking, and let Heaven's judgment fall swiftly upon every demonic agent assigned to my family.

I will not live in fear. I will not dwell in defeat. The blood of Jesus has secured my victory and broken the enemy's teeth. I walk in the light of revelation and the confidence of triumph. Every altar raised against us is burned. Every chain is shattered. Every shadow is dispelled. My family is surrounded by glory, and hell's power is made powerless.

In Jesus' name, Amen.

PRESERVATION

JESUS CARRIED OUR SICKNESS

> "...He took our infirmities and bore our diseases."
> — Matthew 8:17 WEB

Great Burden-Bearer, I worship You for the mystery of mercy that took my afflictions upon Your own flesh. You did not ignore my sickness—you carried it. You bore the weight of every disease I would ever face. You wore the pain I could not carry.

Today, I honor Your sacrifice by refusing to carry what You already bore. I declare that every infirmity, from chronic fatigue to internal disease, must bow to the One who took my place. I lift off the burden of anxiety, depression, and unrelenting pain, and I lay it on the shoulders of my Savior, who bore it already.

Over my family, I decree divine freedom from inherited conditions, hidden viruses, and persistent infections. I thank You, Lord, that You bore every disease that tries to afflict my children, spouse, parents, and loved ones. What You carried cannot remain on us. What You bore must now leave.

We walk forward healed and unburdened, because You took it all. The cross was enough, and the Blood still speaks.

In Jesus' name, Amen.

PROSPERITY

HEIRS OF THE KINGDOM

> "...and if children, then heirs—heirs of God and joint heirs with Christ..."
> — Romans 8:17 WEB

Abba Father, I step into the full understanding of my place in You. I am not an outsider—I am a rightful heir. Through the blood of Jesus, I've been adopted, accepted, and enthroned as a co-heir with Christ. What belongs to Him is now mine—not by merit, but by covenant.

I activate my inheritance today. I will not live as though I am fatherless, landless, or abandoned. I lay claim to spiritual, emotional, and financial wealth that flows from being joined to Christ. The same favor that surrounds Him now surrounds me. The same supply that sustains heaven now sustains my household.

Father, teach me to walk in my inheritance with boldness, with humility, and with clarity. Let my family come into full awareness of what we possess in You. Let generational lack be broken, and generational wealth—righteous wealth—begin to rise. We walk as joint heirs, knowing that no good thing will You withhold.

In Jesus' name, Amen.

PEACE

Peace with God Through Justification

> "Much more then, being now justified by his blood…"
> — Romans 5:9 WEB

Righteous Judge, I stand under the covering of the blood that justifies. You have pronounced me righteous, not by my deeds, but by the perfect sacrifice of Jesus Christ. Because of this, I have peace with You—a peace that banishes every fear of judgment and reconciles my heart to Yours.

Let the power of justification through the blood saturate my soul and my family's life. Wash away every lingering shadow of condemnation, every whisper of inadequacy, and every lie of the enemy that seeks to steal our rest. Let this peace anchor us in the certainty that we are loved, accepted, and secure in Your presence.

Lord, I receive this blood-bought peace as a shield for my home. May it guard our minds in anxious moments, protect our hearts from offense, and knit our relationships together in grace. This is the heritage of the justified: peace with God and wholeness in every part of life. I claim it for me and my household.

In Jesus' name, Amen.

DAY 4

PARDON

FREED FROM SHAME AND FILTH

> "To him who loves us and washed us from our sins by his blood..."
> — Revelation 1:5 WEB

O Faithful and True, how marvelous is Your love, that You would reach into the depths of my guilt and wash me clean. I declare that Your blood has not just covered my sins but has removed them, washed them away like stains from a garment. I am not who I was—my identity is no longer tethered to my failures.

By the authority of Your blood, I break the hold of shame, regret, and condemnation over myself and my family. Every memory that accuses, every whisper of the past that seeks to haunt—be silenced now by the blood. I decree emotional healing over our minds, restoration over our names, and dignity over our destiny.

We are loved, washed, and welcomed. Because of the blood, I lift my head high and lead my household in the assurance that we are clean, consecrated, and called. What once defiled us no longer defines us. We have been made new, and nothing shall separate us from Your love. In Jesus' name, Amen.

PROTECTION

FAITH IN THE BLOOD'S POWER

> "By faith he kept the Passover and the sprinkling of the blood…"
> —Hebrews 11:28 WEB

Almighty God, today I rise in faith—faith in the eternal power of the blood of Jesus. Just as Moses believed and obeyed, so I too embrace the covering of the blood over my household. This is not superstition—it is covenant. This is not ritual—it is relationship.

By faith, I sprinkle the blood upon my family: over my spouse, my children, and our generations to come. I reject fear and stand in holy boldness. Let every spirit of judgment, disaster, and destruction be turned back by reason of the blood. No wrath shall come near our borders, for we live beneath the shadow of the Almighty.

Teach me to walk daily in this faith—to speak it, declare it, and enforce it. Let my home be a testimony of the power of covenant obedience. May my life honor the sacrifice of Christ as I trust in Your preserving grace.

Father, let this Passover faith ignite in my children and echo through every generation. The blood speaks louder than accusation, sin, or fear. I trust in Your word and rejoice in Your mercy. In Jesus' name, Amen.

PREVAIL

More Than a Conqueror

> "No, in all these things, we are more than conquerors through him who loved us."
> —Romans 8:37 WEB

Abba Father, through the blood of Jesus, I rise in boldness and declare: I am not merely surviving—I am more than a conqueror. My victories are not accidental; they are intentional, purchased by divine blood and sealed in covenant love. My family and I walk in supernatural triumph over every battle that rages.

We are not defined by setbacks. We are empowered by resurrection. Every hardship is turned into a stepping stone, and every trial births new glory. By the blood of Jesus, we ascend above fear, limitation, and loss. Our identity is victory, and our legacy is dominion. Nothing can separate us from this love that causes us to win every time.

Lord, let this conquering anointing rest on my household. Let my children carry this mantle. Let every enemy bow to the force of covenant love wrapped in blood. Let generational victory be our portion, and let our story echo the testimony of Heaven: they overcame through Christ who loved them.

In Jesus' name, Amen.

PRESERVATION

Covered From Every Plague

"...when I see the blood... no plague will be on you..."
— Exodus 12:13 WEB

Covenant-Keeping God, I plead the blood of Jesus over my home, my family, and every space we inhabit. Just as You passed over the households marked by blood in Egypt, I decree that every plague, virus, or outbreak must pass over us now.

The blood on the doorposts of my life is not symbolic—it is divine insurance. I declare that no evil shall enter, no pestilence shall touch, and no contagious affliction shall prevail. Whether seen or unseen, natural or engineered, every disease must bow to the superior covenant of protection in Christ's blood.

Over my family, I release divine exemption from outbreaks, epidemics, and strange infirmities. I apply the blood to every room, every vehicle, every place of work and school. We are hidden in Christ, and shielded by what speaks louder than death—His blood.

Let angels stand guard as divine enforcers. Let the destroyer see the blood and flee. We live untouchable, because we are blood-marked.

In Jesus' name, Amen.

PROSPERITY

Curse of Lack Broken

> "Christ redeemed us from the curse of the law, having become a curse for us... that the blessing of Abraham might come on the Gentiles through Christ Jesus..."
> — Galatians 3:13-14 WEB

O Blood Redeemer, I thank You that the curse has been shattered by the cross. You became the curse so I could carry the blessing. The generational strongholds of lack, limitation, and financial despair are demolished because of what You bore on that tree.

I claim the blessing of Abraham today—not in theory, but in full experience. I declare that my family is blessed going out and coming in. Our baskets overflow. Our barns are full. What once drained us now multiplies in our hands. The blood has reversed every word, pattern, and cycle of poverty.

Let the evidence of divine reversal show up in our finances, in our real estate, in our ideas, in our giving. I walk in covenant prosperity because You carried the weight of my insufficiency. I declare the curse is not just broken—it is forbidden from reattaching itself. The blessing rests on us.

In Jesus' name, Amen.

PEACE

THE BLOOD SILENCES SEPARATION ANXIETY

> "But now in Christ Jesus you who once were far off are made near in the blood of Christ. For he is our peace..."
> — Ephesians 2:13-14 WEB

Covenant-Keeping God, I rejoice that by the blood of Jesus, I am no longer far from You. The distance sin created has been forever closed, and in its place stands a bond of unbreakable nearness. You Yourself are my peace, and I rest in Your presence.

Lord, silence every fear of abandonment, rejection, and isolation in my life and my family. Let the power of the blood speak louder than the voices that say we are alone. Surround our hearts with the tangible reality of Your nearness. Let my home be a dwelling place for Your peace, where no spirit of separation or division can find entrance.

I declare that the blood of Christ has brought us near, not just to You but to one another. In this nearness, there is healing for wounds, restoration for broken connections, and strength for the journey ahead. Your peace is not distant—it is here, alive, and reigning in our midst.

In Jesus' name, Amen.

DAY 5

PARDON

PURGED FOR PURE SERVICE

> "How much more will the blood of Christ... cleanse your conscience from dead works to serve the living God?"
> — Hebrews 9:14 WEB

O Living God, I thank You for the blood of Your Son that not only forgives but transforms. I stand today, fully aware that Your blood has gone beyond surface cleansing—it has reached the core of my conscience. I am no longer bound to perform or strive for Your approval; the blood has freed me to serve You in spirit and in truth.

I renounce every dead work, every empty ritual, every legalistic attempt to earn Your favor. By the blood, I am delivered from guilt-driven religion and brought into peace-filled relationship. Let my heart beat in rhythm with grace. Let my family serve not out of fear but from love ignited by redemption.

Because of the blood, our service shall be joyful, Spirit-empowered, and fruitful. We are cleansed for purpose, purified for assignment, and prepared for glory. I decree a household of servants who live to make Your name known, unburdened by the weight of yesterday. In Jesus' name, Amen.

PROTECTION

LIFE FLOWS IN THE BLOOD

> "...the life of the flesh is in the blood..."
> —Leviticus 17:11 WEB

Lord of Life, I honor the power of the blood that was shed for me and my family. Your Word declares that life itself flows through the blood—and I decree that the life of Jesus now flows through every fiber of our being. Let sickness be driven out. Let vitality, wholeness, and divine strength be restored.

I proclaim that the blood of Jesus cancels every assignment of premature death. It renews our health, fortifies our minds, and saturates our home with vitality. I declare that no weapon formed against our bodies shall prosper. Let the blood speak healing over chronic conditions, inherited afflictions, and silent attacks.

Father, I receive the supernatural life that flows from Your Son's veins. I call it into my bloodstream, my organs, my immune system, my thoughts. I speak it over my family members—from the youngest to the oldest. Where there was weakness, let there now be strength. Where there was anxiety, let peace reign.

Jesus, thank You for the blood that gives life more abundantly. We are not under the dominion of death but under the power of life. We rise and live by that blood. In Jesus' name, Amen.

PREVAIL

Freedom from Every Prison

> "Because of the blood of your covenant, I have set your prisoners free."
> —Zechariah 9:11 WEB

O Covenant-Keeping God, I lift my voice in freedom's cry, for the blood of Jesus has broken every chain. I decree that no prison—mental, emotional, spiritual, or generational—can hold me or my family captive. By the covenant blood, I proclaim: we are the liberated of the Lord.

Every confinement the enemy erected—bondage to fear, cycles of poverty, addiction, depression, or spiritual stagnation—is shattered now by the power of covenant. I speak to every prison door and command it to open. I call my family out of places of shame, delay, and spiritual dryness. We are not prisoners of our past—we are covenant sons and daughters of freedom.

Father, thank You for remembering the blood and acting in our defense. Let angels be dispatched on our behalf to bring us out with a strong hand. We are no longer limited. We are no longer silenced. Our feet are free to dance, our voices free to prophesy, and our hands empowered to build. We are the redeemed, and we walk in holy liberty.

In Jesus' name, Amen.

PRESERVATION

VITALITY THROUGH THE BLOOD

> "The life... is in the blood..."
> — Leviticus 17:11 WEB

O Living God, I honor the sacred mystery of the blood that gives life. I declare that divine life flows through me because of the blood of Jesus. Not just existence, but vitality—spiritual energy, physical strength, emotional stamina, and mental clarity—are mine by the covenant of life in the blood.

I receive renewal in every cell and organ. Let tired blood be revitalized, weak hearts be strengthened, and aging bodies be infused with new strength. I call forth youth-restoring power through the veins of my household. We shall not wither in our prime. We shall flourish, because the blood of Jesus flows through our spiritual DNA.

Let every dormant gift be awakened. Let life overcome lethargy. I cancel the agenda of premature death, and I decree that life and vitality reign in my body and my family line. The life of God courses through us, sustaining, preserving, and refreshing us daily.

Because of the blood, I declare: we shall live and not die. We are full of life from the throne of God.

In Jesus' name, Amen.

PROSPERITY

Redeemed from Poverty

> "In him we have our redemption through his blood, the forgiveness of our trespasses, according to the riches of his grace."
> — Ephesians 1:7 WEB

Mighty Redeemer, I thank You for the wealth of grace that flows from Your blood. This is not cheap grace—it is rich, weighty, and overflowing. Through that blood, I've been bought back from every form of bondage—including financial affliction and poverty.

Redemption means my debt is canceled. Redemption means my dry seasons have an expiration date. I decree that my household walks in redeemed economics—where heaven governs our increase. We are no longer under financial oppression. The blood has paid our ransom and secured our release.

Let the riches of Your grace be evident in every area of our lives. Let favor rest on our work, our hands, and our hearts. Let doors open not by manipulation but by the mystery of blood redemption. We are not broke; we are blood-bought and abundantly supplied.

In Jesus' name, Amen.

PEACE

PAID-IN-FULL PEACE FOR MY SOUL

> "...the chastisement of our peace was on him..."
> — Isaiah 53:5 WEB

Lamb of God, I worship You for taking upon Yourself the chastisement that purchased my peace. Every stripe, every wound, every moment of suffering was the price for my wholeness—and You paid it in full. I will not accept anything less than what You died to give me.

Let this paid-in-full peace govern my soul and my household. Where there has been turmoil, let there now be rest. Where there has been fear, let there be faith. Let my mind be still, my emotions be steady, and my relationships be clothed in harmony because of what You endured for me.

I declare that no storm will override the peace secured by Your sacrifice. My family walks in the freedom of a soul unshaken by the enemy's lies. This peace is our legal inheritance, and we receive it with gratitude and boldness, knowing it cost You everything.

In Jesus' name, Amen.

DAY 6

PARDON

RESCUED FROM DARKNESS INTO LIGHT

> "In whom we have our redemption, the forgiveness of our sins."
> — Colossians 1:14 WEB

Rescuing King, I exalt You for the blood that tore me from the grip of darkness and brought me into the light of forgiveness. I was once imprisoned by guilt and shame, but now I live in liberty. My family and I have been transferred—we no longer live under the domain of the enemy.

The blood of Jesus has paid our ransom. I speak it over every pattern of failure, every generational grip of sin, every spiritual stronghold: you have no hold. We are forgiven, and forgiveness is our banner. I declare that no darkness shall prevail over this household, because the blood has marked our doorway.

Let Your light invade our minds, our emotions, our children's destinies. I speak breakthrough where there's been bondage, clarity where confusion reigned, and holiness where impurity once ruled. We walk in redemption power, fearless and forgiven.

In Jesus' name, Amen.

PROTECTION

Grateful for the Shed Blood

> "...without shedding of blood there is no remission."
> —Hebrews 9:22 WEB

Righteous Judge, I come today not by my own merits but by the blood of Jesus that was shed once for all. Thank You for the sacrifice that broke the curse and silenced the wrath that once stood against me. I am no longer condemned—I am covered, cleansed, and consecrated by the blood.

That blood purchased my pardon and my peace. It brought my family into covenant, and it keeps us from destruction. I declare that by this blood, we are rescued from every cycle of sin, shame, and suffering. No judgment shall land where the blood has been applied.

Lord, I rejoice in the mercy that flows from the altar of Christ. I plead that mercy over my household, over my past, over every legal accusation in the realm of the spirit. Let that crimson stream drown every claim of the enemy.

You have made a way through sacrifice, and I say yes to it. Thank You, Jesus, for shedding Your blood for me. I will never take it lightly. I honor it. I apply it. I trust it. In Jesus' name, Amen.

PREVAIL

Canceling Every Weapon by the Blood

> "No weapon that is formed against you will prevail."
> —Isaiah 54:17 WEB

Holy Defender, I stand in the shadow of Your blood and decree that no weapon forged against me or my family shall succeed. Whether visible or invisible, old or new, carnal or spiritual—every weapon is canceled now by the power of the cross. Your blood speaks a better word than the weapons of the enemy.

Every arrow launched in the night, every word curse spoken in secret, every satanic projection or hex has no power over me. I return every evil assignment to the sender. I raise the blood as my banner and declare that I am immune, my family is fortified, and our lives are shielded. No demonic device shall prosper. No adversarial plan shall unfold.

Let every trap set for our downfall become a snare for those who set it. Let every lie be exposed. Let every backlash be reversed. I rest under the divine guarantee of preservation, for the blood of Jesus secures my safety and silence every tongue that rises in judgment.

In Jesus' name, Amen.

PRESERVATION

CLEANSED TO SERVE AGAIN

> "...cleanse your conscience... to serve the living God?"
> — Hebrews 9:14 WEB

Holy Purifier, I come boldly to the blood that doesn't just heal my body but cleanses my conscience. Wash me deep within. Let the blood of Jesus silence every accusing voice, erase every condemning memory, and restore the joy of clean living.

I reject the torment of past regrets and paralyzing guilt. I declare that my inner man is being restored. Depression flees. Anxiety dissolves. Trauma is uprooted. My mind is no longer clouded by shame—I am washed by better blood. My spirit is free to serve again, with boldness, with clarity, with holy purpose.

Lord, for my family, let generational shame be broken. Let the memories that torment and the pain that cripples be swept away in the flood of Jesus' blood. May we arise from the ashes of internal battles, whole and fearless.

We are no longer bound by what was. We are raised to serve the living God, whole and clean.

In Jesus' name, Amen.

PROSPERITY

Eternal Inheritance Secured

> "For this reason he is the mediator of a new covenant, since a death has occurred for the redemption... so that those who are called may receive the promise of the eternal inheritance."
> — Hebrews 9:15 WEB

Everlasting Mediator, thank You for dying my death and securing my future. You gave everything so I could gain everything in Your name. Your blood did not just purchase momentary help—it sealed the promise of an eternal inheritance for me and my family.

I walk in this new covenant with confidence. I do not waver, doubt, or shrink back. My inheritance is sure. I decree lasting abundance in my life—not based on market trends but on covenant truth. I lay claim to the lands, the legacy, and the provision You designed for me.

Father, I align my thoughts, decisions, and actions with this eternal wealth. Let my family prosper not only materially but generationally. Let our wealth be rooted in righteousness. May our storehouses never run dry. Our portion is eternal, and our Provider is unchanging.

In Jesus' name, Amen.

PEACE

Peace in a Clean and Healed Conscience

> "...how much more will the blood of Christ... purge your conscience from dead works to serve the living God?"
> — Hebrews 9:14 WEB

Holy Redeemer, I thank You for the blood of Jesus that not only washes away my sins but cleanses my conscience. You have lifted the heavy weight of guilt and replaced it with the lightness of peace. I am free to serve You with a heart unburdened and a mind at rest.

Lord, let this cleansing reach into every corner of my soul and into the hearts of my family. Heal the hidden wounds, silence the accusing memories, and uproot the seeds of shame. Let us stand before You with clear consciences, fully persuaded that we are accepted in the Beloved.

May this peace flow into our daily lives, making service to You a joy and not a duty, and relationships a blessing and not a strain. Let the atmosphere of our home reflect the purity of a conscience cleansed by the blood—light, open, and full of Your glory.

In Jesus' name, Amen.

DAY 7

PARDON

BOLDNESS TO ENTER GOD'S PRESENCE

> "Having therefore, brothers, boldness to enter into the holy place by the blood of Jesus..."
> — Hebrews 10:19 WEB

Holy God, because of the blood of Jesus, I come boldly—not timidly—into Your presence. I do not shrink back, for the veil has been torn, and the invitation extended. The blood has granted access to You, and I bring my family into this holy place with me.

I apply this blood-bought boldness to every prayer I utter, every request I make, and every mountain I face. Let fear and inferiority be silenced now. Let my children know the nearness of Your glory. Let our home be a dwelling place of divine communion, where intimacy with You is not occasional but continual.

No more distance, no more striving. The blood has qualified us. I declare that my family lives under an open heaven, and our prayers rise with confidence, reaching the very heart of God. We are not castaways—we are covenant children.

In Jesus' name, Amen.

PROTECTION

Covered by the New Covenant

> "This is my blood... poured out for many for the remission of sins."
> —Matthew 26:28 WEB

Covenant-Keeping God, thank You for the blood of the new covenant that was poured out for my freedom. What the law could not do, the blood has done. I declare that my family lives under a better covenant—ratified not by goats or bulls, but by the Lamb of God Himself.

I receive that covering with deep reverence. Let this blood speak forgiveness, protection, and reconciliation over my home. Let the terms of the new covenant—life, health, peace, and protection—be enforced in every area of our lives. We are not vulnerable; we are blood-covered.

Lord Jesus, as You lifted that cup at the Last Supper, You declared the beginning of a new era. I enter into that era now. Let old curses break. Let fear flee. Let generational bondage be uprooted by the covenant bloodline I now belong to.

I will walk boldly as a child of this covenant. The blood has secured my family's destiny and sealed our access to divine protection. We rest under its banner. In Jesus' name, Amen.

PREVAIL

THE BLOOD-STAINED KING LEADS MY VICTORY

"He is clothed in a garment sprinkled with blood."
—Revelation 19:13 WEB

Jesus, Mighty Man of War, You ride in majesty, clothed in blood and crowned with glory. You are not just my Savior—you are my conquering King. I see You go before me, Your blood-covered robe declaring every battle won. You are leading my family into victories we did not earn but were bought by Your blood.

Let the fragrance of triumph saturate my home. Let every step we take be under Your command. We will not move in fear; we will follow the Blood-Stained One. Your blood makes the crooked places straight and levels every mountain of resistance. You have fought, and You have overcome. Now You lead us in a procession of glory.

Thank You, Lord, that I never fight alone. My enemies do not see me—they see You, the Commander of the Armies of Heaven. March ahead of us, Jesus. Lead us into unshakable peace, undeniable breakthroughs, and undeniable victories. With You as our King, we cannot lose.

In Jesus' name, Amen.

PRESERVATION

HEALING EVERY DISEASE

"...who heals all your diseases..."
— Psalm 103:3 WEB

Jehovah-Rapha, the One who heals completely and without limitation—I praise You for being faithful to heal not some, but all diseases. I declare that there is no name of sickness higher than the name of Jesus, no condition beyond Your blood's power.

I bring before You every known and unknown disease—autoimmune disorders, chronic ailments, viral attacks, pain without diagnosis. I command each one to bow under the authority of divine healing. I decree that You heal what doctors cannot, and You restore what time has damaged.

Let my family experience full-spectrum healing—mind, body, and emotions. Let there be testimonies of reversals and recoveries, of healing at the root. I trust Your covenant of mercy that renews our youth and refreshes our strength.

We bless You, Lord, for not just forgiving our sins, but also healing every disease. We walk in complete health under the shadow of Your wings.

In Jesus' name, Amen.

PROSPERITY

QUALIFIED FOR PROVISION

> "...giving thanks to the Father, who made us fit to be partakers of the inheritance of the saints in light; who delivered us out of the power of darkness, and translated us into the Kingdom of the Son... in whom we have our redemption, the forgiveness of our sins."
> — Colossians 1:12-14 WEB

Faithful Father, I rise with gratitude today, knowing I am no longer disqualified by sin, shame, or scarcity. Your blood has qualified me. You made me fit—not man, not my works. You pulled me out of darkness and placed me into the light of divine provision.

I am a partaker of the inheritance of the saints. That means lack cannot lay hold of me. It means insufficiency cannot have dominion over me. You have already delivered my family from the grip of financial darkness. I walk in newness of provision today.

I speak over my household: we are qualified to receive, qualified to build, qualified to inherit, and qualified to multiply. The blood has spoken for us, and we align ourselves with its voice. Our portion is not crumbs—it is covenant-level provision.

In Jesus' name, Amen.

PEACE

The Peace of Being Fully Cleansed

> "...to him who loves us, and washed us from our sins by his blood..."
> — Revelation 1:5 WEB

Faithful Savior, I lift my voice in gratitude to the One who loves me and has washed me clean in His blood. No stain remains, no record stands against me. Your cleansing is complete, and with it comes a peace that no defilement can disturb.

Lord, let this truth saturate my soul and my household. May we live in the liberty of the cleansed, free from the chains of shame and the burden of regret. Let our peace be deep, settled, and constant—rooted in the knowledge that we are spotless before You.

I declare that every lie of the enemy that tries to accuse us falls powerless at the mention of Your blood. We are loved, we are washed, and we are at rest in the assurance of our salvation. This peace reigns in our hearts and in our home, unshaken by past failures or present challenges.

In Jesus' name, Amen.

DAY 8

PARDON

COVENANT OF FORGIVENESS SEALED

> "For this is my blood of the new covenant, which is poured out for many for the remission of sins."
> — Matthew 26:28 WEB

Covenant-Keeping God, I honor the precious blood of Jesus, poured out not in part but in full for my sins. This is no ordinary promise—this is the eternal agreement signed in blood, guaranteeing that I am forever forgiven. No power in hell can revoke what You have sealed.

I apply this covenant over my family. Every iniquity is blotted out, every transgression erased, every hidden fault cleansed. Let generational burdens be broken by this blood. I speak mercy into my bloodline, forgiveness into our story, and healing into our soul. The curse is canceled. The debt is paid.

We are not bound to our past—we are bound to You. And this covenant will never be broken. I rejoice that Your blood has done what no man could do: secure my standing and guarantee my freedom.

In Jesus' name, Amen.

PROTECTION

SPARED FROM WRATH

> "We will be saved from God's wrath through him."
> —Romans 5:9 WEB

God of Mercy and Justice, I praise You for the cross that diverted wrath and poured out grace. You have not appointed me or my family to wrath, but to obtain salvation through Jesus Christ. I rejoice in this divine exemption—purchased by blood, sustained by love.

Let every whisper of condemnation be silenced. I am not under judgment, but under the blood. My children are not marked for disaster, but for destiny. I reject every voice that speaks doom, every scheme that predicts ruin. The blood shields us from deserved judgment and undeserved attacks.

Let the blood of Jesus speak over every court of accusation—human or spiritual. We are justified, redeemed, and declared righteous. The wrath of God has passed over us because Christ absorbed it fully. What a Savior! What a covenant!

We walk forward without fear. Your wrath is satisfied; Your mercy is extended. We live in that safety and declare it boldly. In Jesus' name, Amen.

PREVAIL

Destroying Death and Fear Through the Cross

> "Through death he might bring to nothing him who had the power of death..."
> —Hebrews 2:14 WEB

Death has lost its grip. Fear has lost its voice. O Risen Christ, You have crushed the one who held the power of death, and through Your blood, we no longer live under its shadow. I speak boldly over my life and my family: we shall live and not die. We shall flourish and not fade. The blood of Jesus has conquered every grave.

By Your sacrificial death, You disarmed the dominion of decay, disease, and despair. You canceled the fear of dying, the dread of disaster, and the anxiety of the unknown. The cross is my confidence, and the empty tomb is my testimony. The blood has sealed our victory and secured our preservation.

Let every spirit of fear be cast out now. Let every tormenting thought be silenced. Let the joy of salvation rise afresh in our hearts. We are not bound by the fear of what could go wrong—we are anchored in the blood that made all things right. Let our days be lengthened, our bodies be healed, and our peace be unshakable.

In Jesus' name, Amen.

PRESERVATION

Nourished by His Blood

"...unless you eat the flesh... and drink his blood..."
— John 6:53 WEB

Living Bread from Heaven, I come to feast on the mystery of Your broken body and poured-out blood. This is not ritual—it is divine communion. I eat of You and live. I drink of Your blood and thrive. I receive spiritual nourishment that no famine can touch.

Let divine substance replace weakness. Let heavenly strength flood my bones. I declare that I am sustained by more than food or medicine—I am sustained by You. Where malnutrition of the soul tried to set in, let the richness of Your life revive me.

For my family, I decree supernatural sustenance. We shall not faint under pressure or lack. We are fed daily by divine resources. We live off of the Bread of Life and the Cup of Salvation. Let every need be met, every hunger satisfied, every spirit strengthened.

In this covenant meal, we find wholeness. In this blood, we are nourished and never empty again.

In Jesus' name, Amen.

PROSPERITY

Peace Purchased for Provision

> "But he was pierced for our transgressions. He was crushed for our iniquities. The punishment that brought our peace was on him..."
> — Isaiah 53:5 WEB

Prince of Peace, I thank You for bearing the full burden of punishment so that I could live in divine peace. Not just peace in my heart—but peace in my provision. Your blood bought rest from financial torment, from anxiety over bills, and from the dread of insufficiency.

I embrace the peace that flows from the cross. No more striving. No more toiling under the pressure of lack. The blood has settled it. I will eat in plenty and be satisfied. My family will know what it means to lie down in green pastures, for the Shepherd has already paid the price.

Let tranquility flood our finances. Let harmony reign in our financial decisions. I declare that divine order, supernatural ease, and holy abundance rest upon my household. We are no longer scattered—we are settled, prospering in the peace that was purchased in blood.

In Jesus' name, Amen.

PEACE

Walking Daily in Cleansing Peace

> "...and the blood of Jesus Christ, his Son, cleanses us from all sin."
> — 1 John 1:7 WEB

Eternal King, I praise You for the ongoing, daily cleansing of the blood of Jesus. This is not a one-time work, but a continual flow that keeps me and my family pure, free, and at peace. Each step I take is under the covering of this cleansing river.

Lord, let this daily cleansing guard our hearts from the build-up of offense, bitterness, or regret. As You wash us anew each day, fill us with fresh peace—peace that flows unhindered because no sin is left to trouble our consciences. Let this be the rhythm of our home: walk in the light, receive the cleansing, live in the peace.

I declare that my household will not be weighed down by the residue of yesterday. The blood of Jesus cleanses today, tomorrow, and every day after. We will walk in this continual peace, free to love You and one another with unclouded hearts.

In Jesus' name, Amen.

DAY 9

PARDON

LIFE-GIVING BLOOD FOR MY FAMILY

> "For the life of the flesh is in the blood..."
> — Leviticus 17:11 WEB

Breath of Life, I give thanks for the living blood of Jesus, which has become the source of eternal life for me and my family. I declare that this blood is not symbolic—it is supernatural. It carries divine life into every fiber of my being.

I speak life over every dying place, every weary soul, every weakened body. Where depression once ruled, let the blood speak joy. Where fear once gripped, let courage arise. Where sickness lurked, let resurrection power flood in. Your blood is our life source—constant, eternal, and unstoppable.

Let our children live and not die. Let our legacy be marked by vitality, fruitfulness, and flourishing in spirit and soul. I cover my home with this living blood and declare: life flows here, and death has no dominion.

In Jesus' name, Amen.

PROTECTION

Entering the Place of Refuge

> "Having therefore boldness to enter… by the blood of Jesus…"
> —Hebrews 10:19 WEB

Holy Father, thank You for the blood that has torn the veil and opened the way. I come boldly—not timidly, not shamefully, but confidently—into Your presence. This is my refuge and strong tower. My family is safe when we dwell in Your presence.

By the blood of Jesus, we are not strangers but sons and daughters. We enter into safety, wisdom, and divine provision. Every time we pray, the door is open. Every time we call, You answer. Let this boldness rise in our hearts as a flame, burning away fear and condemnation.

May our home be filled with Your glory. Let Your sanctuary not be a Sunday place but a daily reality. I bring my family into the secret place, under the shadow of the Almighty. No evil shall befall us there. No storm can shake us there.

Thank You, Jesus, for giving us access through Your blood. We will abide in Your courts and rest beneath Your wings. In Jesus' name, Amen.

PREVAIL

BLOOD-WROUGHT DESTRUCTION OF SATAN'S WORKS

> "The Son of God was revealed... that he might destroy the works of the devil."
> —1 John 3:8 WEB

Mighty Destroyer of Darkness, I praise You for the unstoppable mission of Jesus—the annihilation of every satanic work. By Your blood, You have rendered every curse powerless, every bondage broken, every assignment dismantled. I declare: every work of the devil operating in my life and family is destroyed now.

By the power of the blood, I uproot every evil planting. Let every generational yoke, inherited weakness, or spiritual manipulation be consumed by fire. Let cycles of affliction be interrupted. Let witchcraft be dismantled. Let delay, barrenness, and stagnation be broken. I enforce the finished work of Calvary and drive out every work of darkness.

The blood of Jesus is my weapon. The blood is my defense. The blood is my victory. Father, arise and scatter every enemy of my soul. Let Your justice roll like thunder against every force that resists my destiny. We are free. We are whole. We are restored.

In Jesus' name, Amen.

PRESERVATION

Overcoming Affliction and Torment

"...overcame him by the blood of the Lamb..."
— Revelation 12:11 WEB

Mighty Warrior of Heaven, I rise in the power of the Lamb's blood. I declare war against every tormenting affliction, and I decree victory through the crimson flood. Satan is defeated, sickness is disarmed, and every demonic agenda is overturned by the blood of Jesus.

I overcome fear that grips the night. I overcome tormenting pain, affliction that cycles, and spirits that whisper lies. By the blood, I declare that my mind is protected, my emotions are shielded, and my soul is preserved. No harassment of hell shall remain.

Over my family, I enforce this overcoming power. I cancel night terrors, rebuke sudden afflictions, and drive out mental torment. The blood is our legal evidence—we overcome, we prevail, we stand victorious.

The accuser is silenced. The tormentor is cast down. We overcome by the blood.

In Jesus' name, Amen.

PROSPERITY

JUSTIFIED TO PROSPER

> "...being justified freely by his grace through the redemption that is in Christ Jesus, whom God set forth to be an atoning sacrifice through faith in his blood..."
> — Romans 3:24-25 WEB

Holy Justifier, You declared me righteous, not by merit but by blood. I receive the full weight of that justification today. I am not condemned, unworthy, or disqualified. I am justified to prosper, justified to increase, justified to walk in divine supply.

By faith in Your blood, I access my portion. I don't earn it—I believe for it. Every accusation that would block my blessing is silenced by the blood. Every guilt-ridden memory that speaks of disqualification is overruled. I am justified to rise.

Let that justification speak in business deals, in financial decisions, and in family wealth. Let it echo through every closed door and open the way. My family will prosper—not in arrogance, but in the humility of grace received through blood.

In Jesus' name, Amen.

PEACE

Peace Through Forgiveness

> "Blessed is he whose disobedience is forgiven, whose sin is covered."
> — Psalm 32:1 WEB

Merciful Father, I bless Your name for the joy and peace that come from being forgiven. My sins are not exposed for judgment—they are covered by the blood of the Lamb. This covering is my shelter, my safety, and my song.

Lord, let this forgiveness shape the atmosphere of my home. Where there is forgiveness, there is peace; where there is peace, there is unity; and where there is unity, Your presence dwells. Let the reality of covered sin free us from defensiveness, soften our words, and deepen our love for one another.

I declare that my family will not live under the weight of past failures. We are the blessed of the Lord—washed, covered, and at rest in His mercy. This peace is not fragile; it is built on the immovable truth of divine pardon.

In Jesus' name, Amen.

DAY 10

PARDON

WITHOUT BLOOD, NO FORGIVENESS

> "Without shedding of blood there is no remission."
> — Hebrews 9:22 WEB

Most Holy God, I acknowledge the unshakable truth: there is no forgiveness without the blood. Not one of my sins was excused—they were paid for. I worship You for the blood of Jesus, which did not overlook my sin but washed it away.

Let this truth saturate my soul and silence every lie of unworthiness. I do not earn Your mercy—I receive it, because the blood has been shed. Over my family I proclaim: no condemnation remains, no sin is left uncovered. The blood has made full remission. Our record is clean, and our hearts are free.

Thank You for the justice and mercy that met at the cross. I will never treat the blood lightly. It is my banner, my defense, my covering, and my peace.

In Jesus' name, Amen.

PROTECTION

THE BLOOD SPEAKS A BETTER WORD

> "...to the sprinkled blood that speaks better things..."
> —Hebrews 12:24 WEB

Lord of the Covenant, I tune my ears to the voice of the blood. Where sin cries for punishment, the blood cries for mercy. Where the enemy speaks guilt, the blood declares innocence. I stand today, not on my failures, but on the unchanging word of the sprinkled blood.

Let that voice be loud in my life, my family, and my future. Silence every whisper of accusation, every word curse, every verdict of destruction. Let the blood of Jesus be our advocate, our defender, and our banner. What it speaks, heaven honors.

Thank You for this divine language—better than vengeance, better than justice, better than fear. It speaks protection, pardon, and peace. I plead it over my household today. Let its sound be heard in the courtroom of heaven and in the warfare of earth.

We will not be shaken, for the blood still speaks. And what it says, we receive: mercy, deliverance, and divine covering. In Jesus' name, Amen.

PREVAIL

Declaring Satan Crushed Underfoot

> "The God of peace will quickly crush Satan under your feet."
> —Romans 16:20 WEB

O God of Peace, I stand in the authority of Your Word and declare: Satan is crushed under my feet. Every demonic influence that dared to rise against me and my family is now beneath us—trampled, silenced, and overthrown. The blood of Jesus has guaranteed this defeat.

Let the foot of peace grind the enemy's plots to dust. Let the roar of triumph echo through my home. What once rose to oppress us is now under divine judgment. Every serpent is bruised. Every scorpion is trampled. The blood is our covering, and the peace of God is our banner. We do not fight for victory—we enforce it.

Thank You, Lord, for making us carriers of dominion. Let my children walk in boldness. Let our legacy be marked by peace and authority. Satan has no stronghold left, no voice to speak, no place to operate. Under the power of the blood and under my feet—this is where he belongs.

In Jesus' name, Amen.

PRESERVATION

Yahweh Who Heals Me

"...I am Yahweh who heals you."
— Exodus 15:26 WEB

O Healing God, I lift my hands in faith to the One whose very name is Healing. You do not merely provide healing—You are Healing. Your name carries authority over disease, and Your covenant seals my restoration.

I declare Your name over my body—Yahweh-Rapha, reign here. I declare it over my bloodline—You are the Healer of generations. Let Your name shatter every opposing force of sickness. Let the healing flow from heaven meet every pain on earth.

I trust not in physicians alone, but in the God who formed every organ, who stitched every part in the womb, and who renews what has been damaged. Over my family, I lift up Your healing name. Let healing sweep through our home, uproot affliction, and plant longevity.

You are Yahweh who heals us—our portion, our shield, our restorer.

In Jesus' name, Amen.

PROSPERITY

KINGLY ABUNDANCE RELEASED

> "...to him who loves us, and washed us from our sins by his blood—and he made us to be a Kingdom, priests to his God and Father..."
> — Revelation 1:5-6 WEB

Majestic King, You have not only cleansed me—you have crowned me. Through Your blood, You established me and my family as a kingdom. No longer beneath, no longer outsiders—we operate in the abundance of royalty.

Let kingly provision flow through our lives. I decree we live above the systems of this world. We are not beggars—we are kingdom builders. Let priestly stewardship and royal abundance mark every financial endeavor we take.

I walk in wealth not for selfish gain, but for kingdom advancement. My household is blessed to be a blessing. We carry the dignity of kings and the devotion of priests. Through Your blood, the throne room has become our inheritance.

In Jesus' name, Amen.

PEACE

Peace in Chaos from Faith in the Blood

> "...whom God set forth to be an atoning sacrifice, through faith in his blood..."
> — Romans 3:25 WEB

Mighty God, I put my faith fully in the blood of Jesus. This blood is my anchor when the waves of life rise high, my shield when chaos rages around me. Because of this blood, I have peace that defies understanding and overrules fear.

Lord, in every situation that threatens my calm—whether in my mind, my emotions, or my relationships—let my faith in the blood speak louder than the storm. May my household be a place where the chaos outside cannot invade, for the peace within is guarded by divine covenant.

I declare that the blood of Jesus is my family's defense, our assurance, and our peace in every circumstance. We do not look to the instability of the world; we rest in the eternal stability of the cross. Our faith in the blood releases heaven's peace right here, right now.

In Jesus' name, Amen.

DAY 11

PARDON

WASHED WHITER THAN SNOW

> "Though your sins be as scarlet, they shall be as white as snow."
> — Isaiah 1:18 WEB

Merciful Father, I run into the arms of grace today, overwhelmed by the power of Your mercy and the cleansing blood of Jesus. Where my sin had stained me crimson, You have made me white as snow. I stand in awe that nothing in my past—no action, thought, or word—has been too dark for Your redemption. The blood has blotted out every stain and restored me to innocence.

Let this supernatural cleansing flow over my family. I bring before You the failures of generations, the hidden faults, and the repeated patterns that have bound us. Wash us, Lord—not only from what we've done but from what we've become. Purify our memories, our emotions, our identities. Let guilt fall off like chains. Let purity rise up like dawn.

I declare over my household: we are not marked by shame, but by grace. Not scarlet, but snow-white. Not stained, but sanctified. Let our lives testify to the transforming power of mercy. Because of the blood, we are made clean and made new. In Jesus' name, Amen.

PROTECTION

THE BLOOD SPEAKS PROTECTION

> "...to the sprinkled blood that speaks better things..."
> — Hebrews 12:24 WEB

Righteous Redeemer, I stand today under the power of the blood that speaks on my behalf. Your blood does not cry out for vengeance like Abel's, but proclaims mercy, protection, and deliverance over me and my family. I declare that no accusation, calamity, or destruction shall have the final word over our lives, for the sprinkled blood of Jesus declares a better report!

By the blood, I silence every voice of judgment, fear, or inherited destruction. Let every negative decree spoken over my household be revoked and overruled by the speaking blood of the Lamb. Father, may Your divine voice echo through the blood, cancelling every curse, breaking every agreement with harm, and surrounding us with angelic protection.

Let this better-speaking blood be a hedge around my mind, my dwelling, my loved ones, and our future. I resist the whisper of fear and stand in bold confidence that You are our Defender. The blood is speaking healing over our bodies, peace in our home, and safety in our journey.

I rest in the declaration of the blood: that I am covered, surrounded, and secure. Let it speak perpetually and powerfully over every area of my life. In Jesus' name, Amen.

PREVAIL

VICTORY THROUGH BLOOD-BOUGHT BELONGING

"You purchased us for God with your blood..."
—Revelation 5:9 WEB

Lord Jesus, Champion of my soul, I lift my voice with confidence, for I have been purchased by blood—set apart, owned by God, sealed with purpose. I am not the enemy's property. My family is not open territory. We belong to You, and that covenant ownership guarantees divine preservation. Let every spiritual trespasser be evicted now by the authority of Your blood.

We are blood-marked, Heaven-claimed, and hell-proofed. I declare that my life and lineage are under divine custody. No hex, no harm, no hidden plot can override the red seal of redemption. Because I belong to You, no enemy can possess what is Yours. Let every assignment against our minds, marriages, and mandates be canceled by ownership rights signed in blood.

Abba, let Your ownership manifest in protection, provision, and peace. Let angelic forces patrol what is Yours. Let the blood speak daily over my household that we are chosen, accepted, and defended. We are not orphans, we are heirs—kept by the covenant that cannot be broken.

In Jesus' name, Amen.

PRESERVATION

Sanctified by His Blood

> "...that he might sanctify... through his own blood..."
> — Hebrews 13:12 WEB

Holy Redeemer, I exalt You for the sanctifying power of Your precious blood. You did not merely cleanse me outwardly—you purified me wholly, setting me apart for divine wholeness. Through Your sacrifice outside the gate, You bore the weight of my contamination and released the healing current of sanctification upon my entire being.

Lord, I declare that every defilement in my life—spiritual, physical, or emotional—is now dissolved in the fire of Your blood. I renounce all unclean residue from trauma, sin, sickness, and generational oppression. My body is a temple, and by Your blood, it is sanctified, healed, and sealed for Your glory.

I lift up my family under the canopy of this sanctifying blood. May every member be purified in spirit, soul, and body. I declare divine health, holy appetites, and sanctified minds.

Let the same blood that saved us also preserve us from disease, disorder, and destruction.

We are set apart, consecrated, and healed through Your blood, Lord Jesus. Our lives are marked by wholeness and holy fire.

In Jesus' name, Amen.

PROSPERITY

BOLDLY ACCESSING HEAVENLY RESOURCES

> "Having therefore, brothers, boldness to enter into the holy place by the blood of Jesus,"
> — Hebrews 10:19 WEB

O God of all glory, I come today with boldness purchased by the priceless blood of Jesus! I do not approach You timidly or from a distance, but as one covered, cleansed, and consecrated by the blood of the Lamb. Through the torn veil, I step into the fullness of the heavenly storehouse, claiming every spiritual and material resource ordained for me and my family.

By this blood, I declare that I have unrestricted access to divine strategies, provision, wisdom, and answers. Every need I have is met not according to the world's economy, but by the riches of Your glory in Christ Jesus. Father, I refuse to live beneath what Jesus died to give me. Let the floodgates of provision be opened over my household. Let healing flow, let provision flow, let favor overflow, because I stand where only the blood can take me—before Your throne of grace and glory.

I boldly decree that no barrier, curse, or lack can deny me now. I access the treasury of heaven through this covenant of blood. My family and I walk in the overflow. We are blessed and not burdened, supplied and not struggling, in Jesus' mighty name.

In Jesus' name, Amen.

PEACE

CALM CONFIDENCE IN GOD'S PRESENCE

> "Let's draw near with a true heart in fullness of faith, having our hearts sprinkled from an evil conscience, and having our body washed with pure water."
> — Hebrews 10:22 WEB

O Faithful Father, I come boldly into Your presence today, knowing that the blood of Jesus has cleansed my conscience from every stain of guilt and fear. By that precious blood, my heart has been sprinkled clean, and my spirit now rises above the whispers of condemnation. I declare that my family and I are free to draw near to You with full assurance, unshaken and unafraid, for the peace of Your presence is our resting place.

Lord of Peace, the storms of doubt cannot stand before the calm of Your Spirit. You have silenced every accusation and replaced it with the stillness of Your love. In this sanctuary of grace, I declare over my household that we will walk in unbroken communion with You—confident, steadfast, and secure.

By the power of the blood, our minds are settled, our emotions are stilled, and our hearts are anchored in the knowledge of Your favor. I decree that the peace of God's nearness will be the atmosphere of our home, now and forever. In Jesus' name, Amen.

DAY 12

PARDON

THE LAMB WHO BORE IT ALL

"Behold, the Lamb of God, who takes away the sin of the world!"
— John 1:29 WEB

Jesus, Lamb of God, I behold You today with fresh wonder and profound gratitude. You carried my sins—all of them—not in part, but in whole. You bore the weight of my failures, the shame of my rebellion, and the wrath that should have been mine. Thank You for taking it all upon Yourself and setting me free.

I lift up my voice in thanksgiving for Your selfless love. You did not look away from my mess. You stepped into it, wrapped Yourself in humanity, and became my Substitute. For me, and for my family, You became the Lamb—the perfect sacrifice who ended the reign of sin with one final offering. No more striving. No more punishment. No more debt.

Today, I exalt You as our sin-bearer. May my home be filled with songs of gratitude and reverence for the Lamb. May we live in the freedom You've purchased and never take lightly the blood that was shed. Because You took away our sin, we will live in joy, liberty, and righteousness all our days. In Jesus' name, Amen.

PROTECTION

Overcoming by the Blood

> "They overcame him because of the Lamb's blood..."
> — Revelation 12:11 WEB

Champion of Heaven, I rise today clothed in victory through the blood of the Lamb. Every plan of the enemy is overthrown, every scheme is scattered, and every attack is dismantled by the power of Jesus' shed blood. The blood has already declared that I overcome—not by might, nor by power, but by the testimony of divine redemption!

I decree that my family is not a victim of fear, loss, or destruction. We overcome sickness, sudden disaster, generational bondage, and the arrows of darkness through the blood. No force from the pit of hell can withstand the authority and covering of the crimson flow that bought our freedom.

Let the overcoming power of the blood dismantle every spiritual ambush against us. Let it rise like a banner over our heads and a wall around our gates. I plead the blood over my marriage, my children, our finances, and our travels—over every entry point of our lives.

I walk boldly knowing that we are more than conquerors because of the blood. We do not fear tomorrow, for the blood has gone ahead and secured our victory.

In Jesus' name, Amen.

PREVAIL

Eternal Redemption, Unshakable Victory

> "...entered in once for all into the Holy Place, having obtained eternal redemption."
> —Hebrews 9:12 WEB

O Eternal Redeemer, I come boldly, declaring that Your blood has purchased an unbreakable redemption for me and my family. The work is done, the price is paid, and the access is permanent. I stand on this eternal ground where defeat cannot reach, and the grip of bondage cannot return. You didn't rent my freedom—you bought it forever.

Because of Your eternal redemption, I declare that cycles are broken, guilt is silenced, and access to the Holy of Holies is my daily reality. My victory is not seasonal. My preservation is not partial. Your blood secures us eternally. I renounce every voice that suggests otherwise. The past has no power, and the enemy has no claim.

Let the permanence of Your redemption govern every area of my life. Let no recurring defeat deceive me. Let the finality of the cross break every repetitive battle. We are the eternally redeemed, and we walk with heads high and hearts secured. Let this holy assurance preserve our steps in triumph.

In Jesus' name, Amen.

PRESERVATION

FAITH'S TOUCH DRAWS HEALING

> "A woman… touched the fringe of his cloak…"
> — Luke 8:43-44 WEB

Faithful Healer, I come boldly and reach out, like the woman who refused to let affliction define her future. I refuse to let prolonged sickness rule my body or dominate my family. I stretch forth my spirit and lay hold of the hem of Your healing garment, drawing from the eternal well of blood-bought power.

The flow of affliction ends now. I declare that my reach is met by Your restoration. Where doctors failed and time drained hope, Your presence releases instant reversal. I receive this touch as covenant activation. No sickness can resist the surge of life flowing from Your body into mine.

Lord, over my family I release this same desperate and determined faith. We reach beyond fear. We press through doubt. We lay hold of You, and healing manifests. Let the bleeding stop in every area of lack—emotionally, physically, and spiritually.

Our faith touches You today, Jesus—and power flows back. We are not castaways; we are covenant-healed.

In Jesus' name, Amen.

PROSPERITY

ACCESSING DIVINE FAVOR AND CONNECTION

> "But now in Christ Jesus you who once were far off are made near in the blood of Christ."
> — Ephesians 2:13 WEB

Righteous Redeemer, I thank You for bringing me near—not only to Yourself but also to divine opportunities, people, and places. By the blood of Jesus, the wall of separation is demolished, and I step into covenant favor. Where once I was distant from destiny helpers and divine doors, now I am brought near. My family and I are aligned with Your purposes and positioned for breakthrough relationships.

Father, because of the blood, every connection we need for our next level is drawn to us by divine magnetism. Let favor go before us like a shield. Bring the right voices, the right partnerships, the right opportunities at the right time. By the blood, we are no longer strangers or outsiders—we are heirs of divine access.

I decree open doors that no man can shut. I decree kingdom relationships that bless, elevate, and prosper. I declare that the blood draws mentors, investors, intercessors, and covenant allies into our orbit. We are no longer far—we are fully present in the flow of God's favor.

In Jesus' name, Amen.

PEACE

Hearing the Voice of Peace

> "I will hear what God, Yahweh, will speak, for he will speak peace to his people, his saints; but let them not turn again to folly."
> — Psalm 85:8 WEB

Prince of Peace, I still my heart before You, for the voice of the blood speaks louder than the noise of the world. Your Word declares that You speak peace to Your people, and I receive that promise over my life and my family today. Every anxious thought, every restless feeling, bows to the sound of Your calming voice.

Through the blood of Jesus, You silence the lies of the enemy and speak wholeness to our spirits. You remind us that we are Yours—redeemed, beloved, and safe in the shadow of Your wings. I decree that every member of my household will hear and obey the voice of the Lord, walking in wisdom and never returning to paths of destruction.

Your peace is not fragile; it is fortified by the eternal covenant of the cross. I declare that this peace will govern our decisions, shape our relationships, and preserve our unity. The blood has spoken, and we say "Amen" to every word of blessing and rest You release over us. In Jesus' name, Amen.

DAY 13

PARDON

THE BLOOD ON OUR DOORPOSTS

"When I see the blood, I will pass over you."
— Exodus 12:13 WEB

O Covenant-Keeping God, I plead the blood of Jesus over my life, over my household, over every doorway of our lives. Just as the Israelites marked their homes with lamb's blood for protection, I mark our family with the eternal blood of the Lamb of God. Let every judgment pass over us. Let every plague turn away.

Father, I decree divine exemption from destruction. We are not exposed to the wrath that sweeps the earth—we are covered. Let no disease, disaster, or demonic attack breach the boundary of Your covenant. The blood is our defense, our shield, our banner. It cries out "Mercy!" over our home, and You see it and honor it.

I declare that fear will not rule us, because the blood speaks louder than the threat. We are hidden under the shadow of the Almighty, covered in covenant and wrapped in redemption. Let angels encamp around us. Let peace dwell within our walls. Because of the blood, we are safe, spared, and sealed. In Jesus' name, Amen.

PROTECTION

THE BLOOD SILENCES VENGEANCE

> "...the voice of your brother's blood cries..."
> — Genesis 4:10 WEB

Merciful Judge of all the earth, I come under the covering of the blood that speaks louder than guilt, louder than vengeance, and louder than every cry of injustice. The blood of Jesus drowns out every voice seeking to destroy or accuse me and my family.

Where demonic accusations rise, where ancestral bloodshed cries out, where injustice tries to pass from generation to generation—I silence it now by the superior voice of Jesus' blood. Let every lingering vengeance, known and unknown, be hushed by the mercy cry of Calvary's flow.

Father, may Your courts be saturated with the sound of the blood that redeems, restores, and reconciles. I declare that the enemy has no legal ground against us, for the blood has satisfied every claim. My conscience is cleared, my lineage is purified, and my home is released from retaliation.

We dwell in peace, not punishment; in blessing, not backlash. Let this divine blood covering render every evil claim null and void, and establish a new legacy of protection and grace.

In Jesus' name, Amen.

PREVAIL

FREEDOM FROM GENERATIONAL CURSES

> "Christ redeemed us from the curse of the law…"
> —Galatians 3:13 WEB

Redeeming Savior, I lift a shout of victory, for every curse—spoken, inherited, or initiated—is broken by the power of Your blood. The curse of the law, the sentence of failure, barrenness, delay, and death has been reversed in full. My family and I are no longer bound by bloodline failures—we are grafted into a new lineage of blessing.

By the blood, I cut ties with every generational stronghold. I sever the cords of ancient altars and legal rights the enemy claimed. Every repetitive pattern ends now. I renounce the record of the past, and I embrace the liberty of the cross. The curse is broken; the blessing has begun. My children shall not carry what You carried away.

Preserve us in this new inheritance. Let the voice of redemption drown every whisper of condemnation. Let righteousness run in our bloodline. We are no longer victims of inherited failure—we are heirs of covenant favor. Let this truth echo in every corner of our family tree.

In Jesus' name, Amen.

PRESERVATION

SPRINKLED AND WASHED CLEAN

"...hearts sprinkled... bodies washed..."
— Hebrews 10:22 WEB

Cleansing High Priest, I thank You for the inner and outer sanctification that flows through Your blood. You have sprinkled my conscience and washed my body—healing me from the inside out. I no longer carry shame, filth, or the residues of sickness in my soul or my skin.

Let Your blood go deep—into my thoughts, my memories, my bloodstream, and my bones. I receive a pure conscience and a healthy body. Where the soul was infected, let healing flow. Where guilt tormented, let peace rule. Where affliction manifested, let strength return.

Lord, over my family I apply this cleansing flood. Let every household member be free from inner torment and physical illness. May our hearts be free from bitterness and our bodies from pain. The blood doesn't partially cleanse—it perfects and preserves.

We are washed in mercy and sprinkled with power. We draw near with full assurance, completely healed.

In Jesus' name, Amen.

PROSPERITY

Prosperity Is My Covenant Portion

> "Wealth and riches are in his house. His righteousness endures forever."
> — Psalm 112:3 WEB

Great Provider, I lift my voice in the authority of covenant. By the blood of Jesus, I claim what is rightfully mine—prosperity with purpose, increase with integrity, and wealth that brings You glory. You have declared that wealth and riches are not the pursuit of the wicked, but the inheritance of the righteous. I declare this over my household: wealth belongs here, and riches are established under the covering of Christ's righteousness.

By the blood, I release every financial breakthrough that has been delayed or stolen. Let the blessing rest in my house—not just in my hands, but in my legacy. I will use these resources to build, bless, and advance Your Kingdom.

I uproot every mindset of lack, poverty, and limitation. I plant the truth of Your Word in the soil of my faith: the righteous shall never beg bread. Let prosperity arise and be established, for the blood has signed my access. My family shall not live hand to mouth—we live from glory to glory and from overflow to overflow.

In Jesus' name, Amen.

PEACE

Peace Through Resurrection Power

> "Now may the God of peace, who brought again from the dead the great shepherd of the sheep with the blood of an eternal covenant, our Lord Jesus..."
> — Hebrews 13:20 WEB

God of Resurrection, I lift my voice in praise, for the same blood that sealed the eternal covenant is the blood that brought Jesus from the dead. That power is working in my life today to restore every peace I have lost. Where sorrow tried to linger, joy is breaking forth. Where confusion clouded my mind, clarity now reigns.

Great Shepherd, You lead my family beside still waters and restore our souls. The blood of the covenant has reclaimed what the enemy tried to steal—our calm, our unity, our hope. We are not bound to yesterday's losses, for resurrection life flows through us.

I decree that by the blood, every dead area in our relationships, emotions, and dreams comes alive again. The peace we walk in is not fragile, for it is rooted in the victory of the empty tomb. We rise today in boldness and serenity, knowing our lives are secured in Your covenant care. In Jesus' name, Amen.

DAY 14

PARDON

HEALED THROUGH HIS WOUNDS

"He was wounded for our transgressions…"
— Isaiah 53:5 WEB

Suffering Servant, I honor You for the stripes You bore and the wounds You endured for me and my family. You were crushed for what we did wrong—wounded so we could be healed, chastised so we could have peace. Every lash, every bruise, every drop of blood shouted love louder than our sin ever could.

Today, I apply the healing virtue of Your blood to our lives. Let healing flow into every sickness, every trauma, every place of brokenness. From the crown of our heads to the soles of our feet, let Your stripes bring restoration. Emotionally, mentally, physically—we receive the full benefit of Your suffering.

We will not live under the dominion of pain or shame. Because You were wounded, we are whole. Because You bled, we are healed. I declare over my family that sickness must bow, torment must flee, and peace must reign. We are the healed of the Lord—set free by the power of the Cross.

In Jesus' name, Amen.

PROTECTION

Sprinkled for Safety and Sanctification

"...sprinkling of the blood of Jesus Christ..."
— 1 Peter 1:2 WEB

Holy Father, today I receive a fresh sprinkling of the blood of Jesus upon myself and my household. I declare that this divine application separates us from destruction and sets us apart unto You. Let the blood sanctify our minds, seal our doors, and shield every vulnerable place in our lives.

Just as the Israelites applied the blood and the plague could not enter, I now sprinkle the blood over every room, every member of my family, and every part of our journey. Let our days be marked by divine exemption, and our nights by supernatural peace.

Sanctify our thoughts, our choices, and our desires. Cleanse us from the dust of the world and guard us against the contaminations of sin, compromise, and spiritual assault. May we walk in the holiness that brings preservation and the purity that invites Your favor.

As we are sprinkled daily, we are made ready and resilient—covered in grace, saturated in mercy, and immune to the reach of the wicked one.

In Jesus' name, Amen.

PREVAIL

DELIVERED FROM STRONG ENEMIES

> "He delivered me from my strong enemy…"
> —Psalm 18:17 WEB

Deliverer of Israel, I praise You, for Your mighty hand has lifted me from the grip of my fiercest enemies. I declare that every strong enemy—whether spiritual oppression, chronic sickness, tormenting fear, or human adversaries—is overthrown by the force of Your blood. My enemies are strong, but my God is stronger.

By the blood of Jesus, I break the teeth of every oppressor. I call down the judgments of Heaven against every power that has long resisted our advancement. Let hidden enemies be exposed and cast down. Let Pharaohs be drowned. Let Goliaths fall by divine precision. My family will no longer live under siege.

Father, be our defense and deliverance. Surround us with the fire of Your covenant. Where the enemy once had control, now let liberty reign. We walk out of every snare, every valley, every siege. The strong enemy has fallen, and our testimony will sing of Your power.

In Jesus' name, Amen.

PRESERVATION

Peace Through His Blood

> "…peace through the blood of his cross…"
> — Colossians 1:20 WEB

Prince of Peace, I declare that my mind, my emotions, and my household shall be governed by Your peace. Not the fragile peace of this world, but the unshakable peace that was secured through the blood of Your cross. I receive this peace now as healing balm over every storm within me.

Let every wave of anxiety, anger, grief, and confusion be stilled by the power of the blood. You have made reconciliation between heaven and earth, and I step into that divine harmony. I release every conflict, every torment, and every mental struggle into the cleansing flow of Calvary.

Over my family, I command peace. Let strife be silenced, fear be uprooted, and division be healed. Where there is tension, let unity be restored. Where there is inner chaos, let wholeness arise. Your blood speaks peace louder than trauma speaks pain.

We dwell under the shadow of Your peace-bearing cross. It is well—within and around us.

In Jesus' name, Amen.

PROSPERITY

Standing on Better Promises

> "But now he has obtained a more excellent ministry, by so much as he is also the mediator of a better covenant, which has been enacted on better promises."
> — Hebrews 8:6 WEB

Almighty Covenant-Keeper, I honor the One who mediates for me by His own blood. I stand today, not on the shaky ground of earthly hope, but on the solid rock of a better covenant. This blood-sealed covenant carries better promises—promises of prosperity, peace, preservation, and purpose for me and my entire household.

I reject the inheritance of the old man and the curses of the past. I embrace the better—better blessings, better access, better supply. The blood of Jesus enforces every promise and guarantees its delivery. I declare that my family walks under the blessing of Abraham, the provision of Isaac, and the favor of Joseph, because Christ is the fulfillment of all covenant promises.

Let every word You've spoken over us come to pass swiftly. Let our lives be living proof that the new covenant is not only spiritual but practical. Every promise You made, sealed with blood, we receive with faith and thanksgiving. No devil can annul it, and no demon can reverse it.

In Jesus' name, Amen.

PEACE

Peace in Full Redemption

> "In whom we have our redemption through his blood, the forgiveness of our trespasses, according to the riches of his grace."
> — Ephesians 1:7 WEB

Redeeming Lord, I rejoice that the blood of Jesus has purchased my full release from sin and its torment. No shadow of guilt can stand before the light of Your grace. I declare over my life and my family that our peace is untouchable, for it rests on the unshakable foundation of redemption.

In this holy covenant, You have erased every accusation and made us whole. Your grace floods our hearts with quiet strength, teaching us to rest in the certainty that we are forgiven and free. The storms of the past have no voice in our present, for the blood has spoken "It is finished."

I decree that my household will live in the richness of Your grace, walking in rest, joy, and security. The peace of full redemption will guard our hearts, heal our wounds, and bless our days. In Jesus' name, Amen.

DAY 15

PARDON

FAITH IN THE BLOOD ALONE

> "Whom God sent to be an atoning sacrifice, through faith in his blood..."
> — Romans 3:25 WEB

Righteous Judge and Gracious Redeemer, my faith today is not in my own goodness but in the blood of Jesus. You presented Him as the atoning sacrifice—not hidden, but publicly displayed—so that I could place my trust in His blood alone. That blood justifies me, covers me, and grants me peace with You.

Let faith rise in my spirit and saturate my household. Let my children, my spouse, and generations after me walk in bold trust, not in works but in the power of the blood. I reject guilt and religion, and I embrace the finished work of Christ. The blood has settled the case, and I believe it fully.

I decree that we will not waver in our standing. Our righteousness is not fragile—it is founded on blood that speaks forever. We have access, acceptance, and assurance through faith. Let our lives reflect the confidence of those who trust in the blood of the Lamb.

In Jesus' name, Amen.

PROTECTION

COVENANT BLOOD BREAKS ALL PRISONS

> "...because of the blood of your covenant, I have set your prisoners free..."
> — Zechariah 9:11 WEB

Mighty Deliverer, I thank You for the blood covenant that has the power to open prison doors and tear down demonic strongholds. Today, by the blood, I break every invisible chain holding me and my family captive—whether emotional, spiritual, financial, or generational.

I invoke the terms of Your covenant, sealed by the precious blood of Jesus. Let every confinement placed by fear, limitation, or trauma be shattered. Where the enemy thought he had locked us in, the covenant blood now speaks release and freedom.

I decree freedom from mental torment, from cycles of delay, from family bondage, and from the grip of sin. By this blood covenant, my household walks in liberty. No trap of the enemy can hold us, for we have been set free by a superior and eternal agreement.

Let the blood covenant shout over our lives: "Free!" Let every chain break, every door swing open, and every captive walk out into destiny.

In Jesus' name, Amen.

PREVAIL

Warfare by the Blood, Not Flesh

> "The weapons of our warfare are not of the flesh…"
> —2 Corinthians 10:4 WEB

O Mighty God of Battle, I step into the arena of warfare not with carnal weapons, but with the blood-drenched sword of the Spirit. I refuse to fight by the flesh—my victory is not in arguments, manipulation, or fear. My victory is by the blood, the Word, and the anointing that breaks yokes.

By the blood of Jesus, I pull down every stronghold operating in my mind, my home, and my environment. I silence mental torment, cast down imaginations, and destroy lofty arguments that exalt themselves against the knowledge of Christ. I fight with purity, with worship, with prophetic decrees soaked in blood-born authority.

Lord, empower me and my family to war like priests and kings. Let us not be drawn into the enemy's battleground. Let us ascend in praise, descend in power, and execute vengeance through divine strategies. Victory is ours because the blood is our weapon, and Your name is our banner.

In Jesus' name, Amen.

PRESERVATION

Washed from Sin's Decay

"...washed us from our sins by his blood..."
— Revelation 1:5 WEB

Lamb of God, I thank You that Your blood does not just forgive—it washes. Every stain, every mark, every sin-induced affliction is washed away. I am no longer corroded by iniquity or decaying under the weight of old guilt. I am clean. I am healed.

Where sin once invited disease, I now receive deliverance. Where shame bred cycles of defeat, I now walk in resurrection power. I renounce every physical symptom rooted in past rebellion. Your blood breaks the curse, restores my health, and renews my spirit.

Lord, I speak over my household—let every hidden sin be exposed and removed. Let no foothold of darkness remain to invite affliction. May the blood of Jesus wash us wholly—body, mind, and soul. Let healing spring up where sin had decayed.

We are not victims of our past. We are the washed and redeemed—whole in You.

In Jesus' name, Amen.

PROSPERITY

No Lack in My Life

> "Yahweh is my shepherd: I shall lack nothing."
> — Psalm 23:1 WEB

Shepherd of my soul, I declare today under the blood of Jesus that lack has no place in my life. You lead me, feed me, and cover me. Because I am in covenant with You through the blood of the Lamb, I declare with boldness: I shall not lack—spiritually, emotionally, relationally, or financially.

You are my Source, not my job, not people, not circumstances. The blood has purchased my sufficiency. Every area of insufficiency bows to Your shepherding grace. Let overflow be my portion, and divine provision be my reality. My table is spread, even in the presence of opposition, because the covenant speaks for me.

My family is not forsaken. Our needs are supplied in abundance. I cancel the voice of scarcity and command every resource we need to locate us swiftly. The Shepherd who shed His blood for us is watching over every detail of our provision.

In Jesus' name, Amen.

PEACE

A Renewed Mind for Peace

> "For the mind of the flesh is death, but the mind of the Spirit is life and peace."
> — Romans 8:6 WEB

Spirit of Truth, I yield my thoughts to You, for the blood of Jesus has broken the chains of carnal thinking. I receive the mind of Christ—a mind filled with life and peace. Over my family and me, I declare that we will think in harmony with Heaven, guided by Your Word and not by fear.

Through the covenant blood, every toxic thought pattern is uprooted, and every lie is replaced with the truth of God's promises. Our minds are renewed, our emotions settled, and our hearts aligned with Your purposes. Life and peace flow like a river through our home.

I decree that we will not be moved by the chaos of the world, but will dwell in the stillness that comes from being spiritually minded. The blood of the Lamb has secured for us this priceless gift, and we will guard it faithfully. In Jesus' name, Amen.

DAY 16

PARDON

PRECIOUS BLOOD, PRICELESS RANSOM

> "Redeemed… with precious blood, as of a lamb without blemish…"
> — 1 Peter 1:18–19 WEB

Holy and Worthy Lord, I lift my heart in reverence for the precious blood that redeemed me—not with silver or gold, but with the priceless blood of Jesus, the spotless Lamb. I was ransomed from an empty, cursed way of living and brought into the richness of divine inheritance.

Lord, help me never treat this blood as common. Let awe flood my soul every time I think of what it cost You to redeem me. Over my family, I release the revelation of value and worth. We are not cheap. We are not forgotten. We were purchased with the highest price ever paid.

Let this truth establish our identity and silence every lie of worthlessness or rejection. I declare that the precious blood of Jesus has made us royalty, and we will live as sons and daughters of the King. Because of the blood, we are redeemed, restored, and revered in Your eyes.

In Jesus' name, Amen.

PROTECTION

ANCHORED IN AN ETERNAL COVENANT

"...the blood of the eternal covenant..."
— Hebrews 13:20 WEB

Eternal Father, I anchor my life and my family in the unshakable covenant sealed by the blood of Jesus. This is not a fragile agreement—this is an everlasting bond that secures us through every storm, trial, and attack of the enemy.

By this eternal covenant, I speak divine preservation over my lineage. We are not exposed to chaos or casualties. We are held in covenant safety, a safety that is not dependent on human ability but on the faithfulness of a God who cannot lie.

Let the eternal blood covering insulate us from crisis and wrap our journey in peace. I declare that no matter what shifts in the world, we are anchored by the unchanging promise of divine protection through the blood.

Because of this covenant, my children are safe, my marriage is guarded, and our destiny is preserved. We dwell in security that never expires.

In Jesus' name, Amen.

PREVAIL

WASHED AND EMPOWERED TO PREVAIL

> "...to him who loves us, and washed us from our sins by his blood..."
> —Revelation 1:5 WEB

Lover of My Soul, I thank You for loving me with a love that did not flinch at the cross. You didn't just forgive me—you washed me. I am no longer stained, no longer chained. By Your blood, my family and I are washed clean and empowered to walk in purity and dominion.

Sin has lost its grip. Guilt has lost its voice. The stains of yesterday are no longer written in our story. I declare that shame, regret, and compromise shall no longer define our steps. We are blood-washed warriors—cleansed to conquer, purified to prevail. No sin cycle shall enslave us. No secret bondage shall return.

Preserve us in holiness, Lord. Let the power of the blood not only cleanse but continue to sanctify. Let my home be a sanctuary where righteousness reigns and darkness flees. We have been washed—now we rise to win.

In Jesus' name, Amen.

PRESERVATION

HEALING THE BROKENHEARTED

"He heals the broken in heart…"
— Psalm 147:3 WEB

Tender Shepherd, I lift my eyes to You, the only One who binds up what no surgeon can see. You see the tears that never fall. You hear the cries buried in silence. And You respond with healing—deep, blood-born healing for the broken heart.

I yield the places in me that ache—the betrayals, the losses, the disappointments. Let Your healing virtue flood every emotional wound. I refuse to live fractured. I receive the fullness of heart You purchased with Your own. You are near to the broken, and today, I am near to You.

I declare over my family: every heartbreak is being restored. Let the wounds of children, spouses, parents, and siblings be healed by Your love. Let reconciliation arise. Let trust be rebuilt. Let mourning be turned to joy by the hand that bled.

You don't just patch us up—you make us whole again. We are healed by love, and sealed by blood.

In Jesus' name, Amen.

PROSPERITY

Generational Blessing by the Blood

> "I will establish my covenant between me and you and your offspring after you throughout their generations for an everlasting covenant, to be a God to you and to your offspring after you."
> — Genesis 17:7 WEB

Eternal God of covenant, I rise today to declare: the blood of Jesus has grafted me into an everlasting lineage of blessing. What You promised to Abraham, You fulfilled in Christ, and now that promise rests on me and my seed. My family is marked for generational prosperity and purpose, not by works but by blood.

I invoke the everlasting covenant over every child, every grandchild, and all those who carry my name and legacy. I declare that cycles of poverty, sickness, and failure are broken. We are not cursed—we are covenant people! The blood of Jesus speaks into the future, calling forth destiny, protection, provision, and honor for my descendants.

Let every generational gate swing open for the purposes of God. I speak prosperity that multiplies and righteousness that endures. The blood has signed it, and heaven enforces it. This covenant is not fragile—it is forever.

In Jesus' name, Amen.

PEACE

Peace as My Inheritance

> "Peace I leave with you. My peace I give to you; not as the world gives, I give to you. Don't let your heart be troubled, neither let it be fearful."
> — John 14:27 WEB

Jesus, my Covenant King, I embrace the peace You have left for me—a peace sealed and secured by Your blood. This is no fragile calm that shatters under pressure, but a heavenly stillness that steadies my soul. I declare that my family and I will live in this inheritance daily, unmoved by fear, untouched by turmoil.

Your peace is a treasure the world cannot give or take away. It guards my heart, settles my mind, and establishes our home in divine rest. I choose to release every burden into Your hands, for the blood testifies that our victory is complete.

I decree that our hearts will remain untroubled and fearless, for we are anchored in the covenant of peace. No storm can shake what the cross has secured. In Jesus' name, Amen.

DAY 17

PARDON

SET APART BY HIS BLOOD

"That he might sanctify the people through his own blood..."
— Hebrews 13:12 WEB

Sanctifying Savior, I praise You for the blood that not only saves but separates. You did not just redeem me to rescue me—you redeemed me to set me apart for Yourself. The blood has marked my life, and I will never be the same. I belong to You, and my household belongs to You.

Let this sanctifying power touch every area of my life. Purge our minds from compromise, our habits from corruption, our homes from every unclean thing. Set a boundary of holiness around my family, that we may live consecrated lives in a generation of confusion. The blood has drawn the line—we are set apart.

Let our actions reflect this calling. Let our words, decisions, and relationships be drenched in purity. May Your name be honored in our home. The blood has sanctified us, and we receive the grace to walk worthy of the calling we've received.

In Jesus' name, Amen.

PROTECTION

WASHED AND KEPT BY THE BLOOD

"...washed us from our sins by his blood..."
— Revelation 1:5 WEB

Lamb of God, I exalt You for the cleansing power of Your blood. Not only have You washed me, but You continue to keep me. Your blood didn't just remove my past—it actively shields me from the accuser's reach and condemnation's grip.

I declare over my life and family that we are not under guilt, shame, or threat. The blood has erased our failures and sealed our future. The voice of self-condemnation is silenced, and the stain of sin is removed from our history.

By the blood, we stand accepted, defended, and protected. I plead this blood over our hearts and minds—that we remain free from fear, free from sin's power, and free from every chain that tries to reattach.

Let the blood that washed me keep me. Let it be a river that never runs dry, flowing daily over my household with grace and power.

In Jesus' name, Amen.

PREVAIL

Victory in My Redeemed Identity

> "Let the redeemed of Yahweh say so…"
> —Psalm 107:2 WEB

I am the redeemed of the Lord, and I declare it with boldness! Let the heavens hear it, let hell tremble before it, and let my atmosphere shift because of it. I do not whisper my freedom—I decree it. I am blood-bought, Spirit-filled, and warfare-ready. My family walks in covenant covering and unshakeable deliverance.

By Your redemption, I have a voice. By the blood, I have authority. I declare that every victory we possess shall be enforced and preserved by the power of redemption. No more silence. No more passive suffering. I say so, and I say it loud: we are redeemed from poverty, bondage, sickness, and shame.

Let this confession ring in my home. Let my children say so. Let generations yet unborn carry this declaration. We are not defeated. We are not forgotten. We are the redeemed—and victory is our heritage.

In Jesus' name, Amen.

PRESERVATION

IDENTITY JUSTIFIED BY THE BLOOD

> "...justified by his blood..."
> — Romans 5:9 WEB

Righteous Judge, I rejoice that my identity is no longer defined by sin, failure, or rejection—I have been justified by the blood of Jesus. No longer accused, I stand acquitted. No longer shamed, I walk in sonship. You call me righteous, and that truth heals me.

Let every lie that said I'm unworthy be drowned in the crimson flow. I reject the voice of condemnation and receive the testimony of the blood—it says I am accepted, valued, and healed. Where rejection once shaped my life, I now rise in royal identity.

Over my family, I proclaim healing of identity. Let every person under my roof know who they are in Christ—cleansed, called, and covered. Let no label from man or wound from childhood distort the truth that we are justified and beloved.

We are no longer broken by judgment. We are made whole by justification.

In Jesus' name, Amen.

PROSPERITY

Let the Blood Speak Increase

> "...to Jesus, the mediator of a new covenant, and to the sprinkled blood that speaks better than that of Abel."
> — Hebrews 12:24 WEB

O Jesus, Mediator of my prosperity, I thank You for the blood that still speaks. It does not speak vengeance—it speaks increase, access, and advancement. Every time the enemy accuses, the blood intercedes. Every time lack tries to speak, the blood speaks louder.

Let the voice of Your blood silence every voice of limitation in my life. Let it echo through the courts of heaven and the circumstances of earth: I am redeemed, I am blessed, I am multiplied. The blood declares increase over my home, my business, my finances, and my future.

I align myself with what the blood is saying. I reject every report of decrease, delay, or denial. My family is under the divine proclamation of abundance. Better things are our portion—better doors, better outcomes, better supply.

In Jesus' name, Amen.

PEACE

Perfect Peace in Trust

> "You will keep whoever's mind is steadfast in perfect peace, because he trusts in you."
> — Isaiah 26:3 WEB

Faithful Keeper, I set my trust fully upon You. The blood of Jesus has made me Your own, and You have pledged to keep me in perfect peace. I declare that my mind is steadfast, unshaken by shifting circumstances, for my hope rests in the covenant.

Over my household, I speak stability. We will not be tossed about by fear or uncertainty, for our trust is in the unchanging God of peace. Your Spirit steadies our hearts, and Your blood speaks a continual assurance that we are safe in Your hands.

I decree that our thoughts will remain fixed on You, our words filled with faith, and our atmosphere saturated with peace. We walk in this promise as our inheritance. In Jesus' name, Amen.

DAY 18

PARDON

COMPLETELY WASHED AND RESTORED

> "You were washed, you were sanctified, you were justified…"
> — 1 Corinthians 6:11 WEB

Cleansing Fountain, I rejoice in the finished work of redemption. I am not what I used to be. I have been washed clean by Your blood, sanctified by Your Spirit, and justified in Your sight. Every accusation has been overturned, every stain removed. I walk in complete restoration.

Thank You, Lord, for the totality of what You've done. This is no halfway salvation—it's full and final. My family is not partly clean—we are fully restored. Let every generational shame fall away. Let every voice of the enemy be silenced. The blood declares us clean.

We will live like those who are free—no longer chained by sin, but empowered by grace. We are washed vessels, holy instruments, and justified sons and daughters. Let this be the song of our lives: "We are clean. We are changed. We are Yours."

In Jesus' name, Amen.

PROTECTION

WASHED AND GUARDED IN SPIRIT

> "...hearts sprinkled... bodies washed with pure water."
> — Hebrews 10:22 WEB

Precious Redeemer, I receive the sanctifying touch of Your blood this day. Wash my heart, sprinkle my spirit, and let purity surround every aspect of my being. I declare that I, and my family, are vessels made holy and protected by the cleansing stream of heaven.

Let no spiritual defilement gain access to us. Let no dark imagination take root. May the water of the Word and the blood of the Lamb create a fortress around our souls. We are cleansed from the inside out and guarded against the temptations and attacks of the enemy.

Our thoughts are washed, our desires are purified, and our actions are sanctified. Let this continual cleansing set us apart, make us strong, and keep us from slipping into compromise.

We walk in spiritual cleanliness and divine defense. We live washed, sprinkled, and protected by the unrelenting love of God.

In Jesus' name, Amen.

PREVAIL

JUSTIFIED AND SAVED FROM WRATH

> "...justified by his blood... saved from God's wrath..."
> —Romans 5:9 WEB

Righteous Judge, I bless You for the blood that justifies. I stand before You blameless, not because of my deeds, but because of the blood that has silenced every accusation. My record is clean, my status is righteous, and my sentence is freedom. I will not live under condemnation—I've been acquitted by the blood.

Your wrath has passed over me. I am no longer under judgment, but under grace. I refuse to rehearse guilt, relive shame, or entertain the devil's charges. My family is justified. Our name is cleared. Our future is secure. Let every voice of the accuser be silenced by the blood-soaked verdict of Heaven.

Preserve us in this truth, Lord. Let the assurance of righteousness give us boldness to stand, faith to pray, and power to resist. We are justified, not just forgiven. We are seated, not striving. And we are preserved, not perishing.

In Jesus' name, Amen.

PRESERVATION

Restored Like a Child Again

> "...his flesh came again... like the flesh of a little child..."
> — 2 Kings 5:14 WEB

Miracle-Working God, just as You restored Naaman's flesh when he obeyed, I surrender to Your healing instruction. I yield in faith, believing that what was diseased will be made new. I speak divine restoration over every cell, joint, and bone in my body.

Let my youth be renewed. Let my skin, organs, and strength return to childlike vitality. Your covenant does not leave me patched up—it makes me new. Where aging accelerated and sickness stole, I claim the restoration of my original design.

I decree over my family full bodily renewal. Let the aged regain strength. Let the weak rise strong. Let chronic symptoms reverse. As Naaman dipped and came up healed, we too submit to the process that leads to wholeness.

We are being restored—body, soul, and strength—through covenant obedience and blood-bought mercy.

In Jesus' name, Amen.

PROSPERITY

POWER TO PRODUCE WEALTH

"But you shall remember Yahweh your God, for it is he who gives you power to get wealth…"
— Deuteronomy 8:18 WEB

Yahweh my God, I remember You today as the One who gives power—not just promises. Your blood-bought covenant empowers me to create, multiply, and steward wealth. I do not wait for handouts; I activate divine capacity. Because of the blood, my hands are blessed, my ideas are inspired, and my labor is fruitful.

I declare that I and my family are wealth creators, kingdom financiers, and stewards of abundance. Let the anointing to innovate and increase rest mightily upon us. I cancel every generational curse of financial failure and unlock the ability to prosper in every season.

Father, let contracts be awarded, let clients be drawn, let streams multiply. Give me strength to build, wisdom to manage, and heart to give. I prosper by covenant, not by chance.

In Jesus' name, Amen.

PEACE

Peace Guarding My Emotions

> "The peace of God, which surpasses all understanding, will guard your hearts and your thoughts in Christ Jesus."
> — Philippians 4:7 WEB

Lord of Glory, I welcome the peace that comes from Your throne—a peace that surpasses understanding and shields my heart like a fortress. By the blood of Jesus, this peace is mine and my family's to dwell in forever.

Your peace guards our emotions from the attacks of anxiety, anger, or fear. It stands like sentinels around our minds, ensuring that we think and feel according to Your truth. Through the covenant blood, I declare that every troubling thought is cast down, and every wave of unrest is calmed.

I decree that our hearts are fortified in Christ Jesus, immune to the enemy's disruptions. The peace of God will remain our constant companion, a blood-bought shield for every season. In Jesus' name, Amen.

DAY 19

PARDON

ROBES WASHED IN THE BLOOD

"They washed their robes and made them white in the Lamb's blood."
— Revelation 7:14 WEB

Lamb of God, I thank You for the blood that purifies like nothing else. The saints in glory are clothed in radiant white—not because of what they did, but because they washed their robes in Your blood. So I come, Lord, and wash again. I bring my heart, my soul, my household—we soak our garments in Your cleansing flow.

Let every spot be removed. Let every residue of compromise be scrubbed away. I decree that we shall wear garments of praise, not shame—robes of righteousness, not regret. I declare over my family that we will not walk stained or disqualified. We are clothed in what heaven calls holy.

Purity is our inheritance. Righteousness is our portion. Because of the blood, we are prepared for Your presence, dressed for glory, and ready for eternal purpose. Let the world see the evidence of the blood in how we walk, speak, and shine.

In Jesus' name, Amen.

PROTECTION

BLOOD-CLEANSED AND ENEMY-PROOFED

> "...cleanse your conscience... to serve the living God?"
> — Hebrews 9:14 WEB

Righteous God, I thank You for the power of the blood to cleanse not only my sins, but my conscience. I declare that no guilt, torment, or false accusation shall live rent-free in my mind. The blood has gone deeper than behavior—it has cleansed my internal world.

Let every voice of shame, regret, or fear be silenced by the blood. I decree that my household shall not serve You from a place of fear, but from a place of holy boldness, joy, and love. Let the blood purge every hidden accusation and break the influence of enemy lies.

My conscience is clear. My inner world is at peace. My spirit is free to worship, to serve, and to obey. Let this cleansing guard our minds and protect our future.

We are shielded within and without—washed in truth and protected by love.

In Jesus' name, Amen.

PREVAIL

PERFECTED TO WALK IN AUTHORITY

"...he has perfected forever those who are being sanctified."
—Hebrews 10:14 WEB

Perfecting Savior, I rise today not in my strength, but in the finished work of the cross. You have made me complete, lacking nothing. I am being sanctified daily, but in the eyes of Heaven, I am already perfected by the blood. I carry no shame—I carry authority.

This blood-born perfection gives me boldness in battle. I do not fight as one trying to earn acceptance—I war as one already approved. Let this perfection echo through my thoughts, my home, and my decisions. I am not the enemy's plaything. I am God's perfected warrior, refined for dominion.

Let the blood preserve my household from every identity crisis, every lie of inadequacy, every weight of performance. We walk in grace-fueled power, covered and carried by the perfection of the Lamb. Where others see flaws, You see fulfillment. Let this truth set us ablaze for You.

In Jesus' name, Amen.

PRESERVATION

Freedom from Pain and Limits

> "...set your prisoners free..."
> — Zechariah 9:11 WEB

Covenant Deliverer, I cry out under the authority of blood. Where affliction imprisoned my body and pain held me captive, I now command release. Because of the blood covenant, I am no longer a prisoner to chronic pain, immobility, or invisible torment.

Let every cell respond to the decree of liberty. Let my nervous system realign, inflammation dissolve, and strength arise. I am not called to suffer endlessly—I am called to walk free. Your blood speaks louder than my symptoms.

I declare over my household: every limitation is broken. Let chains of infirmity, fatigue, and inherited restrictions be shattered. We are blood-marked and blood-liberated. No diagnosis will define our future. No recurring affliction will dominate our days.

We are out of the prison. We are walking in divine release.

In Jesus' name, Amen.

PROSPERITY

Abundant Life Over My Finances

> "For the life of the flesh is in the blood..."
> — Leviticus 17:11 WEB

Holy God, I release the life-flow of the blood of Jesus into every financial area of my life. I decree: no more dead ends, no more barren accounts, no more lifeless business endeavors. Where the blood flows, life reigns—and I declare abundant life in my finances and family resources.

Every dying dream, every withering investment, every paralyzed opportunity—I speak resurrection power by the blood. Let the same life that raised Christ flow into my economic reality. I curse stagnation and command the blessing of divine circulation.

Let financial life surge—unexpected income, supernatural debt cancellations, multiplied seed, and preserved harvests. The blood secures vitality and vigor, not just for my body but for my financial house.

In Jesus' name, Amen.

PEACE

SANCTIFIED IN THE PEACE OF THE BLOOD

> "...in sanctification of the Spirit, that you may obey Jesus Christ and be sprinkled with his blood..."
> — 1 Peter 1:2 WEB

Holy and Righteous God, I thank You that the blood of Jesus has been sprinkled over my life, setting me apart for Your purposes. This blood speaks peace into my soul and consecrates my family to live in the beauty of holiness.

In this sanctifying peace, we are empowered to obey You without fear. The turmoil of sin is broken, the chaos of rebellion is silenced, and the tranquility of Your Spirit fills our home. By the blood, we are not only forgiven—we are transformed.

I decree that my household will walk in this holy peace daily, manifesting the joy and rest that comes from living set apart for You. We are kept in the covenant by the sprinkled blood, and nothing shall disturb our harmony. In Jesus' name, Amen.

DAY 20

PARDON

FORGIVEN AND FOREVER FREE

> "As far as the east is from the west, so far has he removed our transgressions from us."
> — Psalm 103:12 WEB

Faithful Father, I praise You for the blood that has not just forgiven, but completely removed my sins. You didn't sweep them under the rug or keep a record to remind me later. You've cast them far away—so far that they will never return. This is the power of redemption.

I declare that my family will no longer live under the shadow of past mistakes. What was done has been undone by the cross. What was broken has been restored. Let the blood remove every guilt-laced memory, every generational iniquity, every trace of condemnation. We are free—truly free.

Let this freedom bring joy to our household. Let laughter return. Let peace dwell here. We are not bound by what was—we are driven by who You've made us to be. As far as the east is from the west, so far have You removed it all. Hallelujah!

In Jesus' name, Amen.

PROTECTION

Renewed in Covenant Safety

> "...this is the blood of the covenant..."
> — Exodus 24:8 WEB

Covenant-Keeping God, I renew my alignment today with the blood of the covenant. I do not live uncovered—I live bound to a promise sealed by sacrifice. I declare that this covenant is active over me and my family, preserving our lives and marking us for protection.

Let every danger that seeks to approach us see the sign of the covenant and turn back. Let the terms of divine safety and favor override every threat and cancel every evil expectation. This is not a human agreement—it is a heavenly bond written in blood.

I claim covenant rights of peace, defense, and divine intervention. I declare that sickness, strife, and sudden destruction are rebuked by covenant terms. My home is a blood-covered territory, and every door is marked with divine preservation.

Thank You for this covenant that cannot fail. I walk in its confidence and live in its shelter.

In Jesus' name, Amen.

PREVAIL

Pushing Back Every Adversary

> "Through you, will we push down our adversaries…"
> —Psalm 44:5 WEB

God of Vengeance and Victory, I rise in Your strength, ready to push back every adversary that has risen against me and my family. I do not retreat. I do not fear. Through You, I trample every force of resistance. By Your name and Your blood, we advance with power.

I declare that territorial spirits, generational giants, and stubborn enemies are no match for the God I serve. Let every adversary be scattered. Let every blockade be broken. Let every gate be lifted. My feet are anointed for conquest, and my mouth for triumph. Through You, we do valiantly.

Preserve our progress, Lord. Let every victory be sealed. Let no backlash arise. Let the shout of the King be heard among us as we press through resistance into supernatural preservation. The battle is fierce—but the blood prevails.

In Jesus' name, Amen.

PRESERVATION

Healing from Gethsemane's Blood

> "...his sweat became like great drops of blood..."
> — Luke 22:44 WEB

Man of Sorrows, acquainted with grief, I worship You for the anguish You bore in Gethsemane. Even Your sweat turned to blood as You carried the weight of human sorrow. And now, that blood speaks healing for my stress, my trauma, and my mental agony.

I lay down every heavy burden—emotional exhaustion, relentless pressure, and unspoken anxiety. Where trauma etched itself into my nervous system, I now receive peace. Let the blood that fell in the garden cleanse my memory, heal my nervous system, and still my soul.

Lord, over my family, I declare healing from every traumatic event, every mental breakdown, every emotional overload. Let Your peace infiltrate our nights, calm our storms, and regulate our responses. The weight You carried means we no longer have to break under pressure.

From the garden of sorrow came my healing. From Your agony flows our peace.

In Jesus' name, Amen.

PROSPERITY

Justified to Receive God's Best

> "Much more then, being now justified by his blood, we will be saved from God's wrath through him."
> — Romans 5:9 WEB

Merciful Justifier, I praise You for the verdict spoken over my life: not guilty! By the blood of Jesus, I am justified and qualified to receive every good and perfect gift. I do not stand in condemnation, and I do not live under guilt. I am an heir, not a beggar.

Every blessing You've stored up for me is now released without hindrance. The blood has silenced every accuser. Shame has no hold, and unworthiness is not my portion. I receive Your best—not by merit, but by mercy secured in blood.

Let abundance come swiftly. Let provision be unstopped. Let prosperity flow freely. I am justified to receive divine supply, favor, promotion, and overflow.

In Jesus' name, Amen.

PEACE

Peace in God's Holy Presence

> "Having therefore, brothers, boldness to enter into the holy place by the blood of Jesus…"
> — Hebrews 10:19 WEB

Majestic King, I rejoice that the blood of Jesus has opened the way into Your holy presence. With boldness, I enter today—not as a stranger, but as a beloved child. Here in Your presence, peace flows like a river and fills every part of my being.

This peace is not fleeting; it is born from the assurance that I belong to You. I declare that my family will live with this same holy boldness, drawing near daily to the throne of grace. The closer we are to You, the deeper our peace becomes.

By the covenant blood, fear is banished, guilt is erased, and rest is restored. We will remain in this place of communion, letting Your presence be the source and sustainer of our peace. In Jesus' name, Amen.

DAY 21

PARDON

SINS CAST INTO THE SEA

> "You will cast all their sins into the depths of the sea."
> — Micah 7:19 WEB

Gracious Redeemer, I thank You for Your incomprehensible mercy. You do not deal with us according to our sins, nor remember them forever. You don't just forgive; You cast them into the deepest sea, never to be retrieved. What You have removed cannot return. I rest in the assurance that the blood of Jesus has caused You to forget what once separated me from You.

Lord, I lift up every lingering sense of guilt in my heart and home. Let Your mercy wash over my family. Where we have replayed mistakes and carried shame like baggage, help us release it fully into the ocean of Your forgiveness. Let this truth saturate our hearts: when You forgive, You forget. We don't need to perform, strive, or rehearse our failures again.

Let the memory of sin be replaced with the memory of grace. May we live boldly as those completely pardoned, not because we deserved it, but because Jesus paid for it in full. Our sins are not hidden—they're gone. Buried. Sunk forever in mercy's sea. In Jesus' name, Amen.

PROTECTION

PROTECTED FROM SICKNESS AND AFFLICTION

> "But he was pierced for our transgressions. He was crushed for our iniquities. The punishment that brought our peace was on him; and by his wounds we are healed."
> — Isaiah 53:5 WEB

O healing Redeemer, by the power of the blood of Jesus, I decree divine protection over my body and the bodies of my loved ones. Every infirmity, disease, or affliction lurking in darkness must bow to the finished work of the cross. The blood that flowed from Your wounds secures our health, and I stand in that covenant today declaring that no plague shall claim us, no diagnosis shall define us, and no symptom shall persist.

Let the healing virtue of the Lamb flow through every cell, every organ, and every system in my household. I declare supernatural immunity for my children, divine strength for my spouse, and restoration for every area of our health. We reject the grip of sickness and command its grip broken now by the blood. Let Your healing wings overshadow us daily.

Where affliction has lingered, I command the reversal now. The blood testifies louder than symptoms. It declares healing, wholeness, and divine alignment with heaven's will. I cover my family in that testimony today. No terminal word will prevail, and no generational affliction will continue. By His wounds, we are healed and preserved. In Jesus' name, Amen.

PREVAIL

STANDING IN BLOOD-BOUGHT AUTHORITY

> "I give you authority... over all the power of the enemy..."
> —Luke 10:19 WEB

King Jesus, the Sovereign One who rules with justice and fire, I rise today clothed in the authority You have given me. This authority is not self-earned—it was purchased by Your blood. I am not powerless. I am not under siege. I carry divine jurisdiction to crush every enemy underfoot, and by that authority, I establish dominion over darkness concerning me and my household.

Every power of the enemy—witchcraft, torment, affliction, manipulation, accusation—bows to the voice of blood-backed authority. I release that authority now into my home, my relationships, my finances, and every battle zone of my life. Let serpents and scorpions be trampled. Let confusion be scattered. Let demonic resistance break by the weight of covenant.

Father, I thank You for this unshakable empowerment. Let my children know it, walk in it, and grow in it. Let every lie that tells us we are weak be silenced by this truth: the blood has given us power to tread, to triumph, and to reign. We do not shrink back—we stand and overcome by Your decree.

In Jesus' name, Amen.

PRESERVATION

MERCY FOR EVERY WEAK MOMENT

> "...find mercy and grace for help in time of need."
> — Hebrews 4:16 WEB

Merciful Father, I come boldly before Your throne today—not in my own strength, but by the blood of Jesus. In this hour of need, I call upon the blood-bought mercy that never fails. Though my body may grow weary and my strength may falter, Your grace is my anchor and Your mercy, my healer.

I release every weakness—emotional, mental, and physical—into the hands of the High Priest who sympathizes with my frailty. Your mercy is not delayed, and Your grace does not expire. Even when I feel unworthy, Your blood declares me worthy of restoration and healing.

I speak this over my family now: when we are at our lowest, Your mercy meets us there. When we are too tired to pray, grace upholds us. Let healing come to our bones, our hearts, and our emotions. Let divine help spring forth in every hidden battle.

We are not without help. We are not abandoned. Mercy covers us, and grace restores us.

In Jesus' name, Amen.

PROSPERITY

HEIR, NOT A BEGGAR

> "Therefore you are no longer a bondservant, but a son; and if a son, then an heir of God through Christ."
> — Galatians 4:7 WEB

Father, I thank You for the blood of Jesus that has changed my identity forever. I am no longer a slave to lack, limitation, or the lies of the enemy. I stand today not as a servant begging for scraps, but as a rightful heir to the abundance of Your house. The blood has purchased my sonship, and I boldly take my place as one who walks in the full rights and benefits of covenant inheritance.

Lord, I renounce every mindset of poverty, every whisper of unworthiness, and every generational curse of insufficiency. I am not cursed—I am covered. I do not grovel—I govern. I am seated with Christ in heavenly places, and all that the Father has is mine through Him. I operate from the riches of grace, not the rags of self-effort.

Let this blood-bought revelation saturate my family. May we walk with the dignity of heirs, not with the fear of orphans.

May doors open to us, not by manipulation, but by divine inheritance. We declare that favor is our portion, wealth is our responsibility, and prosperity is our rightful station—because we are sons, not slaves.

In Jesus' name, Amen.

PEACE

Peace As My Warfare Weapon

> "They overcame him because of the Lamb's blood, and because of the word of their testimony. They didn't love their life, even to death."
> — Revelation 12:11 WEB

Almighty God, Captain of my salvation, I lift my voice today in the authority of the blood of Jesus. The enemy's schemes are silenced, his accusations shattered, and his strategies overthrown, for the blood has already secured my victory. Through this holy blood, I receive Your peace as a weapon—a divine force that crushes confusion, disarms fear, and drives back the darkness from me and my family.

I declare that every storm sent to disrupt our minds, our emotions, or our relationships is met with the stillness of Heaven's shalom. The peace purchased by the blood is not passive; it is a militant calm, a ruling force that breaks the back of chaos. This peace shields our home, surrounds our hearts, and keeps us unshaken in the face of battle.

By the testimony of Christ in my life, I announce that my family walks in triumph. No evil can prevail against the sound of the blood that covers us, and no fear can withstand the peace that floods us. We stand victorious, resting in the covenant that will never fail.

In Jesus' name, Amen.

DAY 22

PARDON

BLOTTED OUT AND MADE NEW

> "Repent... so that your sins may be blotted out..."
> — Acts 3:19 WEB

Father of Compassion, I come with a heart willing to turn. You call me not just to confess but to repent, to turn from sin and step into newness. And when I do, You blot out my sins—not smudge, not edit—You erase them completely. Thank You for such restoration and the invitation to return to You wholeheartedly.

Let the grace of repentance flood my household. May we not see it as punishment but as a door back to joy. Let our hearts be quick to yield, quick to respond, and quick to return. Where hardness has crept in, soften us. Where cycles of sin remain, break them with holy sorrow that leads to life.

I declare that times of refreshing are coming. Our sins are being blotted out—removed from the record, washed from our conscience, and replaced with righteousness. We are not defined by what we've done, but by the mercy that met us when we turned. We choose the path of repentance that leads to restoration.

In Jesus' name, Amen.

PROTECTION

Purity That Disarms the Accuser

> "But if we walk in the light as he is in the light, we have fellowship with one another, and the blood of Jesus Christ, his Son, cleanses us from all sin."
> — 1 John 1:7 WEB

Righteous Father, I run under the cleansing flow of Jesus' blood and declare that every stain of guilt, shame, or sin is washed away. Let the light of Your presence shine upon me and my family, purging every hidden defilement. We are no longer vulnerable to the accuser because the blood speaks on our behalf—it silences every claim and breaks every condemnation.

I declare our conscience is clear, our hearts purified, and our spirits renewed. We will not walk under false guilt or the manipulation of past mistakes. The enemy's access is revoked, his evidence dismissed, and his voice muted. We belong to the blood-washed, and we will not be bound again.

Every member of my household is covered. Our thoughts, our behaviors, and our decisions come under divine cleansing. May we walk in unity, accountability, and holy joy. Let the purity purchased for us manifest practically, that we live blameless and bold.

In Jesus' name, Amen.

PREVAIL

EQUIPPED BY COVENANT BLOOD

> "...the blood of the eternal covenant... equip you..."
> —Hebrews 13:20-21 WEB

God of the Eternal Covenant, I thank You that Your blood not only redeems—it equips. By this everlasting covenant, I declare that I lack nothing for the battles I must face. I am thoroughly furnished, divinely supplied, and fully empowered by the One who shed His blood for my preservation.

I rise today knowing that heaven's provision has already been released to fulfill every assignment on my life. My mind is equipped with wisdom. My hands are trained for war. My heart is fortified with courage. Let every spiritual weapon secured by the covenant be activated in my life. I will not fight in my own strength—I move with the power of what has been eternally sealed in blood.

Lord, let my family move in this equipping grace. Let the covenant speak over my children. Let supernatural insight, angelic protection, divine strategies, and enduring strength flood our lives. We are not merely saved—we are sent, strengthened, and sustained by the eternal blood covenant.

In Jesus' name, Amen.

PRESERVATION

Healing by Atonement's Power

> "...make atonement... once in the year..."
> — Exodus 30:10 WEB

Holy Atoner, I bless You for the eternal power of the blood that speaks beyond the veil. Though atonement was once made annually under the law, Your blood has secured continual covering. The altar of my healing is now eternally active, because You have poured out life for my restoration.

I do not need another ritual or offering—Your blood has made complete provision for my body, soul, and spirit. I step into the overflow of atonement. Let every affliction rooted in sin, shame, or guilt be dissolved by this eternal transaction. Let blood-soaked mercy silence every legal claim of sickness against me.

Over my family, I apply this covering. I plead the atonement over our minds, our bloodlines, our medical history, and our future health. No curse of affliction can stand under the cleansing flood. We are marked by the once-and-for-all offering of Christ.

Atonement still speaks. Healing still flows. The price has been paid in full.

In Jesus' name, Amen.

PROSPERITY

Drinking from the Covenant Cup

> "He took the cup after supper, saying, 'This cup is the new covenant in my blood, which is poured out for you.'"
> — Luke 22:20 WEB

O Covenant-Keeping God, I lift the cup of Your blood and drink deeply of all You have provided. This is not a mere symbol—it is a living agreement sealed in the blood of Jesus. I receive into myself the riches of divine provision, favor, and fullness that this covenant guarantees.

As I drink from this cup by faith, I ingest supernatural supply. Let every lack in my life be filled with Your fullness. Let every dry well spring up again. Let divine wisdom come, divine opportunities arise, and divine connections manifest. I drink into wealth, not just for myself, but for generations to come. This cup breaks the curse of not enough and establishes the blessing of more than enough.

Let my household be saturated with covenant favor. Let every child of mine be clothed in glory and supplied with heaven's best. We will not live by the sweat of our brow, but by the Word of covenant sealed in blood. As for me and my family, we drink of Your abundance until our cup overflows.

In Jesus' name, Amen.

PEACE

Anchored in Christ's Finished Peace

> "I have told you these things, that in me you may have peace. In the world you have oppression; but cheer up! I have overcome the world."
> — John 16:33 WEB

Lord Jesus, Prince of Peace, I anchor my soul in the harbor of Your victory. You have spoken, and Your word is unshakable: in You I have peace, not as the world gives, but as Heaven supplies. This peace is anchored in the unchangeable truth that You have already overcome every trial, temptation, and torment that could rise against me and my household.

Though the waves of life roar and the winds howl, I refuse to drift into fear or despair. Your finished work is my mooring; the blood of the cross is my proof. You have subdued every enemy, conquered every threat, and disarmed every weapon of the wicked.

Therefore, I lay my family's hearts, minds, and futures in Your steady hands. We choose cheer in the face of pressure, because the Victor Himself dwells within us. Peace flows like a river through our home, silencing anxiety, calming our thoughts, and keeping us steadfast. We are hidden in You, and in You, we are unmovable.

In Jesus' name, Amen.

DAY 23

PARDON

No More Condemnation

> "There is therefore now no condemnation…"
> — Romans 8:1 WEB

Lord Jesus, thank You for breaking the voice of condemnation in my life. Because of Your blood, I no longer live under the weight of judgment or guilt. I am not condemned—I am forgiven, accepted, and free. You have declared me not guilty, and Your word is final.

I silence every voice that says otherwise. Whether it's my past, my feelings, or the enemy himself, they no longer get to define me. There is now—right now—no condemnation. The blood has made peace between me and God. Let this truth saturate my soul and renew my mind.

Over my family, I declare freedom from shame. No more hiding. No more beating ourselves up. We will live as children of the light, bold and secure. The cross settled it, and the blood speaks mercy, not accusation. We are covered, clean, and confident.

In Jesus' name, Amen.

PROTECTION

COVERED BY PSALM 91 PROTECTION

> "No evil shall happen to you, neither shall any plague come near your dwelling."
> — Psalm 91:10 WEB

Mighty Deliverer, I stand in the security of Your covenant, declaring that because of the blood, Psalm 91 is not just a promise but our daily reality. I decree that no evil will come near our family—no harm will touch our dwelling, no plague will overtake our health, and no terror will pierce our peace.

I activate divine protection over every room, every vehicle, and every location we set foot on. The blood of Jesus marks our entrances, saturates our atmosphere, and surrounds us like fire. Angels are dispatched because the blood speaks. Destruction must pass over.

Every evil plot, seen or unseen, collapses before it even begins. Every arrow sent against our lives returns to the sender. The blood is our insurance policy—unbreakable, unstoppable, and forever effective. Under this covering, we walk confidently, we sleep peacefully, and we live boldly.

In Jesus' name, Amen.

PREVAIL

Warring From Peace, Not Panic

> "...made peace through the blood of his cross..."
> —Colossians 1:20 WEB

Prince of Peace, I bless You for the stillness Your blood has established over my soul. In the midst of spiritual warfare, I do not war in panic—I war from peace. The peace You purchased is not fragile. It is a force. It silences storms and stills chaos. By that peace, I enter every battle with the confidence of one already victorious.

Let anxiety be driven out. Let fear dissolve. Let nervous striving cease. I declare that panic has no place in my prayers and no voice in my atmosphere. Because Your blood made peace between Heaven and earth, I stand anchored even as war rages around me. The conflict may be loud, but the peace is louder.

Father, blanket my family in this divine calm. Let our decisions be birthed in stillness. Let our prayers rise from assurance. Let our hearts be guarded by the peace that guards all who dwell under the shadow of the cross. Our warfare is fierce, but our foundation is unshakable.

In Jesus' name, Amen.

PRESERVATION

Healing from Heaven's Tree

"...leaves of the tree were for healing..."
— Revelation 22:2 WEB

Eternal Source, I drink deeply from the river of life and stretch out my heart to the Tree that never withers. From the veins of the Lamb flows life, and from that Tree, leaves of healing fall into every part of my being. I receive healing from the roots of Heaven, from the place where blood and grace flow freely.

Let every part of me—seen and unseen—be nourished by the supernatural provisions of Calvary. The cross is my Tree of Life, and its fruit is health to my marrow, strength to my mind, and power to my soul. I do not look to earthly sources alone. I pull healing from the river of God.

Let my family flourish like trees planted by those healing waters. Let our skin be radiant, our organs whole, our immunity strong. Let healing be our daily bread—flowing not only from doctors, but from Heaven's throne through blood-sealed covenant.

Everything connected to Jesus carries healing. We receive from His wounds, His word, and His tree.

In Jesus' name, Amen.

PROSPERITY

The Blood on Our Door

> "The blood shall be to you for a token on the houses where you are. When I see the blood, I will pass over you, and no plague will be on you to destroy you..."
> — Exodus 12:13 WEB

Mighty Deliverer, I apply the blood of Jesus to the doors of my finances, my business, my household, and my legacy. Just as in Egypt, when the destroyer saw the blood and passed over, so today, every spirit of financial ruin, every unexpected loss, and every economic plague must pass over me.

By the authority of the blood, I declare that my family is immune from cycles of debt, sudden disasters, and generational poverty. Our lives are marked by divine exemption. Let insurance failures, market crashes, and business disruptions see the blood and retreat in fear. We are covered by covenant.

Let the blood of Jesus be seen in our stewardship, our giving, and our declarations. We sow in faith and reap in peace. No weapon formed against our provision shall prosper. The destroyer may roam, but he cannot touch what the blood has sealed. Our finances are guarded by the same power that broke Pharaoh's grip.

In Jesus' name, Amen.

PEACE

Resting in the Unshakable Covenant

> "For the mountains may depart, and the hills be removed; but my loving kindness will not depart from you, and my covenant of peace will not be removed," says Yahweh who has mercy on you.
> — Isaiah 54:10 WEB

Faithful Covenant Keeper, my heart bows in awe of Your unbreakable promise. The mountains may tremble, the very ground may shift, but the covenant of peace sealed in the blood of Jesus will never fail. It stands eternal, unshaken by time, trial, or the threats of the enemy.

I rest my life and my family in the stronghold of this peace. When the world shakes with instability, we stand on the foundation of Your mercy. Your covenant does not shift with circumstances; it is rooted in the blood that forever speaks on our behalf.

Lord, we refuse to be moved by the instability around us. We dwell in the shelter of Your covenant love, confident that no power can remove the peace You have decreed over us. Let this divine calm guard our hearts, saturate our relationships, and steady our emotions every day of our lives.

In Jesus' name, Amen.

DAY 24

PARDON

Righteous By His Blood

> For him who knew no sin he made to be sin on our behalf; so that in him we might become the righteousness of God.
> —2 Corinthians 5:21 WEB

Holy God, how can it be that You would make me righteous? Jesus, You took on my sin, my shame, and my punishment so that I could be made right with God. This is not a borrowed righteousness—it's a divine exchange. You wore my sin so I could wear Your purity.

Help me walk in this reality every day. Let me stop striving for approval and start standing in the identity You've given. I am the righteousness of God—not because of my performance, but because of the blood that covers me. Let that truth shape how I think, speak, and live.

Over my family, I release this identity. We are not bound by guilt or defined by past failures. We are clothed in righteousness, royal in standing, and beloved in Your eyes. Let the boldness of that truth propel us into purpose.

In Jesus' name, Amen.

PROTECTION

Secured As God's Protected Property

> "They sang a new song, saying, 'You are worthy to take the book and to open its seals, for you were killed, and bought us for God with your blood...'"
> — Revelation 5:9 WEB

Worthy Lamb, I lift my voice in agreement with heaven's chorus—I am purchased, redeemed, and secured by Your blood. My life and the lives of my family members are not up for negotiation. We are God's property, sealed and protected from every trespassing spirit, force, or fear.

Because You paid the ultimate price, no demon can claim legal ground. I decree every attempt of the enemy to access our lives is denied. We are not abandoned; we are under divine ownership. Your mark is upon our hearts, our names are inscribed on Your hands, and our destiny is wrapped in Your covenant.

We belong to the Most High. I declare this over my spouse, my children, and every generation to come. Our lives are guarded, our purposes preserved, and our steps ordered by Your Spirit. The blood speaks redemption, and that redemption includes divine protection.

In Jesus' name, Amen.

PREVAIL

CLEANSED TO SERVE IN POWER

> "...cleanse your conscience... to serve the living God..."
> —Hebrews 9:14 WEB

O Consuming Fire, I stand before You, a servant washed clean by the blood of Jesus. My conscience no longer drips with shame, fear, or accusation. I am free from dead works, and I am alive to serve with boldness. Let every guilt-stained memory be erased, and let the blood speak freedom over my heart and mind.

I am not disqualified—I am cleansed. I am not discarded—I am chosen. By the blood, I rise as a vessel ready for service. Let the fire of purpose ignite within me. Let holy passion return. Let every area of hesitation and compromise be purified so I may serve You fully in this warfare of faith.

Father, equip my household to be fearless servants of the Most High. Let clean hands and pure hearts mark our legacy. Let our worship be undistracted, and our obedience uncompromised. We are no longer hindered by past sins—we are loosed by the blood to war in righteousness.

In Jesus' name, Amen.

PRESERVATION

Speedy Healing by Covenant Blood

> "...your healing will spring forth speedily..."
> — Isaiah 58:8 WEB

Covenant Healer, I decree today that delay is broken. Your blood has authorized not only healing—but speedy healing. I stand in alignment with Heaven's timeline and declare that affliction must go now. Let my recovery break forth like the dawn. Let the light of Your redemption flood every shadow of sickness.

What took years to develop, You can reverse in days. I reject prolonged suffering and receive sudden restoration. I declare that the blood of Jesus overrides time, age, and natural barriers. Where my health has been stagnant, I call forth acceleration by divine intervention.

I speak over my family: swift turnarounds, rapid recoveries, and accelerated miracles. May every diagnosis bow quickly. May healing break forth in our bones, our minds, and our atmosphere. The blood seals this promise and rushes restoration into every room of our home.

We move from prolonged waiting to sudden miracles. Our healing springs forth speedily.

In Jesus' name, Amen.

PROSPERITY

God Delights in My Prosperity

> "Let those who favor my righteous cause shout for joy and be glad. Yes, let them say continually, 'Yahweh be magnified, who has pleasure in the prosperity of his servant!'"
> — Psalm 35:27 WEB

Jehovah, my Rewarder, I declare that You are pleased when I prosper—not by greed, but by covenant. You take delight in blessing the work of my hands because I honor You with my life and my substance. I am not ashamed to prosper, for it brings You glory.

Let my life become a testimony of divine provision. Let every bill paid, every debt canceled, and every increase received be an echo of Your goodness. My prosperity is not for show—it is for service. I steward wealth to expand Your kingdom, bless the poor, and raise altars to Your name.

Lord, magnify Yourself in my family's finances. Break the ceiling of survival and release us into the realm of overflow. Let our children see what it means to walk with God and lack nothing. Let joy fill our homes as we walk in favor and fulfillment. You are pleased when we flourish, so we boldly receive the fullness of our inheritance.

In Jesus' name, Amen.

PEACE

THE PEACE OF HIS LIFTED FACE

> "Yahweh lift up his face toward you, and give you peace."
> — Numbers 6:26 WEB

Abba Father, when Your face shines upon me, every shadow flees. Through the blood of Jesus, I stand in the light of Your countenance, embraced by Your gaze of love. In that holy presence, my fears dissolve, my heart stills, and my mind finds perfect rest.

I invite the fullness of this peace over my family today. Let the light of Your lifted face break through every cloud of heaviness, driving away oppression and weariness. Where there has been tension, release harmony; where there has been confusion, release clarity; where there has been unrest, release stillness.

Lord, we live beneath Your blessing. Your peace is not a passing moment—it is our continual covering. As You look upon us with favor, may the fragrance of Your presence linger in our home, drawing us ever deeper into Your embrace.

In Jesus' name, Amen.

DAY 25

PARDON

WASHED AND RENEWED

"...he saved us... by the washing of regeneration..."
— Titus 3:5 WEB

Father of Renewal, I thank You for the spiritual washing that made me new. It wasn't by works or religion, but by Your mercy. You poured out Your Spirit and washed away everything old. You gave me new birth, new identity, and a new heart. The blood of Jesus didn't just forgive me—it transformed me.

Let this renewing flow over every part of me. Cleanse my thoughts, purify my desires, and restore what sin has damaged. Let Your Spirit regenerate areas I thought were beyond hope. Over my family, bring renewal—revive what's been weary, refresh what's been dry, and make all things new.

I declare we are not who we used to be. The old has passed, the new has come. We've been washed in mercy's fountain, and we are being daily renewed by Your Spirit. Let that freshness mark our home, our faith, and our walk with You.

In Jesus' name, Amen.

PROTECTION

Hidden In Christ Through Communion

> "He who eats my flesh and drinks my blood lives in me, and I in him."
> — John 6:56 WEB

Living Bread from Heaven, I enter the sacred mystery of communion and declare that I and my household are hidden in Christ. Your blood is not just symbolic—it is active, it is powerful, and it brings union with divine life. We drink of that covenant and declare that every work of darkness is cut off from us.

By the blood, we are no longer exposed. By the blood, we live in You, and You in us. Our dwelling place is not just our home but Your presence. Every enemy that seeks to find us finds You first, and they flee. We live from the inside out, carried by Your Spirit, covered by Your life.

Let communion be our daily shield. I bless every meal as holy ground, and every remembrance of You as a wall of fire around us. My family shall not be shaken. We are saturated in divine presence, consumed by covenant, and fortified in fellowship.

In Jesus' name, Amen.

PREVAIL

VICTORY BY DAILY SPRINKLING

"...sprinkling of the blood of Jesus..."
—1 Peter 1:2 WEB

Precious Lamb of God, I call upon the daily sprinkling of Your blood over my life, my family, and every dimension of our dwelling. Let the fresh application of Your blood cleanse, cover, and consecrate us anew. I do not rely on yesterday's covering—I receive today's provision of supernatural preservation.

I declare that the blood speaks over our doorposts today. It shields us from the enemy's plots, protects us from unseen snares, and sanctifies every step we take. As priests under this new covenant, we apply the blood in faith, believing for divine immunity and angelic assistance. Our sleep, our travel, our work, and our warfare are covered.

Let Your blood be on our minds for soundness, on our hands for purity, and on our paths for protection. May my children rise clothed in this holy armor, untouched by the defilements of the world. We walk clean, we walk bold, and we walk victorious—because the blood is ever fresh.

In Jesus' name, Amen.

PRESERVATION

Deliverance from Demonic Oppression

> "...healing all who were oppressed by the devil..."
> — Acts 10:38 WEB

Anointed Deliverer, I thank You that healing is not just a physical miracle—it is deliverance from oppression. Every sickness rooted in torment, every affliction tied to demonic activity must flee. I enforce the blood of Jesus over my body, breaking the grip of darkness.

Let every oppressive weight lift now—mental pressure, emotional heaviness, unexplainable fatigue, cycles of affliction. The same anointing that rested on Jesus rests on me, and it destroys the works of the devil. I refuse to be a prisoner to any form of demonic sickness.

I cover my family under this healing power. Let spiritual atmospheres shift. Let torment cease. Let fear and fatigue give way to joy and freedom. Every hidden spirit behind affliction is now cast out by the blood.

We are healed and delivered. The devil is defeated, and the blood has the final word.

In Jesus' name, Amen.

PROSPERITY

Double for My Shame

> "Instead of your shame you will have double; and instead of dishonor, they will rejoice in their portion. Therefore in their land they will possess double. Everlasting joy will be to them."
> — Isaiah 61:7 WEB

O God of restoration, I stand on the power of the blood and decree: every financial shame, every moment of begging, every embarrassment of insufficiency is now being swallowed up in double honor. The blood cries louder than my past. It declares a future of restoration and abundance.

Where I once walked in silence and scarcity, now I shall shout with rejoicing in my portion. You are replacing lack with laughter. No more will I hide my bank statements or fear the knock of collectors. You are crowning me with honor, giving me land, legacy, and laughter. The days of scraping by are over.

Let my family possess the double. Let our name no longer be associated with struggle, but with strength. Our children will inherit not just wealth but wisdom. Where dishonor once lingered, everlasting joy shall now reside. Thank You, Lord, for the blood that qualifies us for more than we deserve.

In Jesus' name, Amen.

PEACE

Peace as My Divine Blessing

> "Yahweh will give strength to his people. Yahweh will bless his people with peace."
> — Psalm 29:11 WEB

Mighty God, You are my Strength and my Shield. Today I lift my hands in thanksgiving for the blessing of peace that flows from Your throne, secured for me through the blood of the Lamb. This is not the peace the world offers—it is Heaven's own substance, breathed into my spirit and my home.

Lord, let this blessing saturate my family's hearts. May it be strength to the weary, calm to the troubled, and courage to the faint. Let Your peace guard the doors of our minds and the gates of our relationships, driving out every intruder of fear, strife, and unrest.

We stand in the full assurance that this peace is a gift from You—unchangeable, irrevocable, and unending. It is the climate of Heaven made manifest in our lives. We walk in it, we rest in it, and we war with it, knowing that peace is our heritage.

In Jesus' name, Amen.

DAY 26

PARDON

LIVING BY FAITH IN THE BLOOD

> "I live... by faith in the Son of God, who loved me
> and gave himself for me."
> — Galatians 2:20 WEB

Jesus, I thank You for the life I now live—it's not mine alone, but Yours living through me. You loved me and gave Yourself for me, and because of that, I no longer live by sight or effort but by faith in Your blood. This is a daily walk of dependence and trust.

Let faith rise in me afresh today. Let it not be faith in circumstances, emotions, or my own strength, but faith in the unshakable sacrifice of Jesus. Your blood didn't just save me—it sustains me. Let that faith fuel my prayers, my decisions, and my vision.

Over my family, I release grace to live by this same faith. Let the truth of the cross be our foundation and the love of God be our lens. Because You gave Yourself for us, we will live fully for You—one step, one day, one act of faith at a time.

In Jesus' name, Amen.

PROTECTION

Mercy Prevails Over Judgment

> "He shall take some of the blood of the bull, and sprinkle it with his finger on the mercy seat…"
> — Leviticus 16:14 WEB

Merciful Father, I thank You that the blood of Jesus now speaks from the true mercy seat in heaven. Every judgment, every curse, every deserved consequence has been overruled by mercy. I declare that mercy speaks louder than the enemy's accusations. Mercy covers my family. Mercy defends our destiny.

Let the sprinkled blood silence cycles of judgment and condemnation. Where we've fallen short, mercy intervenes. Where we've missed the mark, mercy restores. I call upon mercy to invade my bloodline, break generational yokes, and cleanse patterns of defeat.

I release mercy over our finances, our health, our decisions. I plead the blood over every legal matter, every medical diagnosis, every family dispute. The mercy seat is not far—it is active now. Let its voice reverberate through every room of our home.

In Jesus' name, Amen.

PREVAIL

Maintaining Victory Through Purity

> "...washed their robes and made them white in the Lamb's blood."
> —Revelation 7:14 WEB

Holy One enthroned in purity, I thank You that the blood not only washes once but empowers me to remain clean. I declare that the garments of my life—my thoughts, decisions, and lifestyle—are daily washed and made white by the blood of the Lamb. I do not walk defiled. I walk in the beauty of holiness.

Sin will not stain my steps. Secret compromise will not shadow my light. The blood maintains what it cleanses. I reject every invitation to impurity, rebellion, and spiritual pollution. I speak over my family: we are marked by purity, we are mantled in righteousness, and we reflect the glory of our King.

Father, let Your grace to walk upright rest heavily on our home. Let temptation lose its grip and deception be exposed. Let Your Spirit remind us daily of our robe's worth. We have been washed, and we will remain white. This is our preservation, our testimony, and our inheritance.

In Jesus' name, Amen.

PRESERVATION

WHOLENESS IN EAR, HAND, AND FOOT

> "...put some of the blood... on the right ear, thumb, and toe..."
> — Leviticus 14:14 WEB

Consecrating Savior, I thank You for the power of blood to sanctify every part of me. Today, I apply the blood to my ear—heal my hearing. I apply it to my hand—heal my actions. I apply it to my foot—heal my walk. Let my entire body come under the order of divine health.

Sanctify my senses, my service, and my steps. Let my hearing be free of lies and affliction. Let my hands be strong, clean, and skillful. Let my walk be steady and unbroken. I offer every extremity and every function to You for consecration through the blood.

Over my family, I declare complete alignment—ears that hear You, hands that do Your will, and feet that walk in peace. Let there be no area untouched by the covenant. Where there was limping, let us run. Where there was shaking, let us stand.

We are healed to hear, work, and walk in Your ways. Fully covered. Fully whole.

In Jesus' name, Amen.

PROSPERITY

Calling Provision into Being

> "...calls the things that are not, as though they were."
> — Romans 4:17 WEB

El Shaddai, the All-Sufficient One, I step into my blood-bought authority and call forth the provision that is mine in Christ. I do not wait for evidence—I declare the invisible into visibility. I call resources from the north, south, east, and west. I speak to empty accounts, barren fields, and dormant dreams, and I command them to arise!

By the power of the blood, I do not speak as a victim—I decree as a vessel of divine authority. I command provision to align with Your promise. I speak clients into my business, favor into my workplace, solutions into my challenges, and wealth into my hands. Heaven backs my words because they are rooted in covenant.

Let my family speak likewise. Let our mouths be filled with faith, not fear. Let our language shift from limitation to expectation. The blood has opened the gates of supply, and now we walk through with confident declarations. Provision is not just coming—it is here, because You have said so.

In Jesus' name, Amen.

PEACE

THE BLOOD SPEAKS PEACE

> "...and to Jesus, the mediator of a new covenant, and to the blood of sprinkling that speaks better than that of Abel."
> — Hebrews 12:24 WEB

Lord Jesus, Mediator of my covenant, I thank You for the blood that speaks louder than accusation, louder than fear, and louder than the storms that rage around me. Your blood speaks peace—a peace so deep it subdues every force of darkness.

Today, I bring my family under the sound of that voice. Let the declaration of Your blood silence every shout of confusion, cancel every whisper of anxiety, and break every echo of past pain. Let its proclamation be heard in every corner of our lives: "Peace, be still."

We yield to this holy announcement. We live under the constant proclamation of mercy, restoration, and calm. Your blood does not merely speak in the heavens; it speaks here, now, in our hearts and in our home. We agree with its testimony, and we walk in its unshakable peace.

In Jesus' name, Amen.

DAY 27

PARDON

HEARTS SPRINKLED CLEAN

> "...having our hearts sprinkled from an evil conscience..."
> — Hebrews 10:22 WEB

Lord, I come close—not with fear or shame, but with full assurance because of the blood. You've sprinkled my heart clean. Where guilt once ruled, peace now reigns. My conscience is no longer plagued by sin; it is purified by the sacrifice of Christ.

Let this cleansing go deep. Heal the inner places where memories torment and regrets linger. Let the blood speak louder than accusation. I declare peace of mind and clarity of heart over myself and my household. We will not be ruled by an evil conscience, but by the righteousness You've secured.

Thank You for giving us access to Your presence. We come boldly, not as strangers but as children washed and welcomed. Let the peace of a clean conscience anchor our days and stabilize our souls.

In Jesus' name, Amen.

PROTECTION

BLOOD DISARMS DEATH AND HELL

> "...that through death he might bring to nothing him who had the power of death..."
> — Hebrews 2:14 WEB

Conquering Savior, I declare that death has lost its sting and hell its power because of Your shed blood. You did not just die—you disarmed. You did not just suffer—you shattered every force that enslaved us. I proclaim that over my life and my family: we are not captives to fear, torment, or death.

Let the authority of the blood break every agreement with the grave. I renounce premature death. I cast off fear of disaster. My home is a fortress surrounded by resurrection power. You brought the enemy to nothing, and I declare his tactics are powerless against us.

Let my family walk in the confidence of divine life. Let joy, strength, and peace flow through our days. We are blood-protected, not accident-prone. We are life-carriers, not victims of death's shadow. What You conquered, we now overcome.

In Jesus' name, Amen.

PREVAIL

Gratitude for Constant Victory

> "Thanks be to God, who gives us the victory..."
> —1 Corinthians 15:57 WEB

God of Triumph, I overflow with thanks! You give me victory—not occasionally, not randomly—but constantly and continually through Christ. Every battle I win is a gift. Every enemy that falls is a sign of Your covenant love. I will not complain in warfare—I will give thanks, for Your blood ensures I never fight in vain.

Let the atmosphere of my home shift with gratitude. Let my heart burst with thanksgiving. Even in the tension, I give thanks for triumph. Even in the waiting, I bless Your name for the victory already sealed by the cross. Let complaining die and worship arise.

May my family be a grateful people. Let our gratitude be our weapon. Let praise go before us like a banner. We are not losing—we are learning, we are winning, and we are preserved in every season by the God who never loses.

In Jesus' name, Amen.

PRESERVATION

HEALTH THROUGH THE SANCTIFIED SACRIFICE

> "...sanctified through the offering of the body..."
> — Hebrews 10:10 WEB

Holy Sacrifice, I worship You as the Lamb who gave His body to make mine whole. You offered Yourself once for all, and that offering sanctifies me. I receive the blessing of a sanctified body—cleansed from affliction, preserved in divine strength.

I reject every defilement that tries to enter my flesh—through fear, through food, through fatigue. I present my body as holy because it has been redeemed by the blood. What You sanctified, no sickness can claim. I walk in the inheritance of consecrated health.

Over my household, I declare our bodies are set apart. No plague shall defile. No disease shall remain. Let the power of Your once-for-all sacrifice purify our diets, protect our sleep, and sustain our energy. We are not common—we are covenant.

Our health is holy. Our lives are preserved.

In Jesus' name, Amen.

PROSPERITY

CLEANSED FOR COVENANT ACCESS

> "These are those who came out of the great suffering. They washed their robes, and made them white in the Lamb's blood."
> — Revelation 7:14 WEB

Holy Redeemer, I praise You for the blood that washes me clean—not just for salvation but for supernatural access. Because of the Lamb's blood, I approach the throne not with guilt, but with grace. I am cleansed, clothed, and qualified to walk in divine prosperity.

Let every stain of financial failure be removed. Let every memory of shame be erased. I am no longer marked by my mistakes—I am marked by mercy. I stand robed in white, ready to receive every blessing written in my name from before time began. Nothing disqualifies me when the blood has justified me.

My family walks in the same cleansing. We are a household of favor, dignity, and wealth—not because of works, but because of the finished work. We do not disqualify ourselves—we step into our access. Let the clean robe of covenant favor shine on our lives and attract every divine connection we need.

In Jesus' name, Amen.

PEACE

GRACE AND PEACE THROUGH THE CROSS

> "Now about the things which I write to you, behold, before God, I'm not lying."
> — Galatians 1:20 WEB

God of all grace, I receive the flow of Your grace and peace made mine through the crucified Christ. This peace is not earned; it is gifted, purchased with holy blood and secured in an everlasting covenant.

Let this grace lift every weight from my shoulders and dissolve every tension in my spirit. Let this peace, born from the cross, anchor my emotions and safeguard my thoughts. Lord, may my family walk in the rhythm of grace, free from the push and pull of fear.

We stand in the reality that grace has brought us near, and peace has made us whole. Through the power of the blood, we reject the turbulence of this world and embrace the stillness of Your presence.

In Jesus' name, Amen.

DAY 28

PARDON

CRUCIFIED WITH CHRIST

"...our old man was crucified with him..."
— Romans 6:6 WEB

Jesus, I declare today that the old me has died with You. The part of me ruled by sin, fear, and shame was nailed to the cross with Christ. It no longer controls me. Through Your death and resurrection, I am free from the power of sin.

Let this truth become my reality. Remind me daily that I am not a slave to old habits or defeated by temptation. The cross broke sin's grip, and I walk in resurrection life. Let this freedom flow into my home—breaking cycles, healing wounds, and releasing liberty.

Over my family, I declare: the old has passed away. We are new creations. What bound us before no longer defines us. We've been crucified with Christ, and now we live by His power and for His glory.

In Jesus' name, Amen.

PROTECTION

Victory Over Every Demonic Force

> "Having stripped the principalities and the powers, he made a show of them openly, triumphing over them in it."
> — Colossians 2:15 WEB

Triumphant King, I lift high the banner of Your victory. By the blood, You disarmed every principality and made a public spectacle of their defeat. Today, I align my family with that triumph. No demon, hex, or power of hell can stand against the blood-stained banner of Christ.

We are not afraid of the enemy's plots. We expose them, dismantle them, and reverse them by Your authority. I declare over my household: we are not harassed, we are not tormented, we are not afflicted. We are seated with Christ in heavenly places, covered by blood, empowered by the Spirit.

Let angels be dispatched. Let darkness be scattered. Let demonic resistance break and bow. My home is a victory zone. My children carry Your authority. My spouse walks in Your dominion. Together, we enforce the cross's victory in every room, every day.

In Jesus' name, Amen.

PREVAIL

BLOOD POWER TO TRAMPLE DARKNESS

> "You will tread on the lion and cobra..."
> —Psalm 91:13 WEB

Mighty One who trains my feet for battle, I take my rightful stance as one who tramples over the forces of darkness. Every lion that roars and every cobra that slithers—be it intimidation, deception, or demonic intimidation—must fall under the authority of the blood. I do not run from darkness—I crush it beneath covenant feet.

I declare that I will not be bitten by betrayal or devoured by fear. I trample on torment, I walk over witchcraft, and I tread through trials without being scorched. My household walks in this same dominion. Let every lurking enemy be exposed and every hidden serpent be rendered powerless.

Father, empower us to tread boldly. Let every step we take be ordered, anointed, and guarded. The power of the blood beneath us, the Spirit within us, and angels beside us—this is our security. We are not prey—we are pursuers of the kingdom.

In Jesus' name, Amen.

PRESERVATION

QUICKENED BY THE SPIRIT OF LIFE

"...will also give life to your mortal bodies..."
— Romans 8:11 WEB

Spirit of Resurrection, breathe on me now. Let the same Spirit that raised Jesus from the dead invade my mortal body and release life. I declare that my body is not a graveyard—it is a dwelling place for the Living God. Therefore, vitality must rise, and death must go.

Every system in my body responds to resurrection power. Lethargy is replaced with energy. Weakness with strength. Pain with praise. I am not declining—I am rising. The Spirit quickens me daily because I belong to the blood-sealed covenant.

I speak over my family the breath of life. Let aging be reversed. Let fatigue give way to divine energy. Let every child, parent, and spouse feel the quickening within. No more dragging through days—we rise in supernatural strength.

We are energized by the Spirit. We are restored by resurrection. We are healed through the Blood.

In Jesus' name, Amen.

PROSPERITY

Eternal Redemption, Eternal Provision

> "...but through his own blood, entered in once for all into the Holy Place, having obtained eternal redemption."
> — Hebrews 9:12 WEB

Lord Jesus, Eternal Lamb of God, You didn't just redeem me for a moment—you obtained eternal redemption. And with that eternal redemption comes eternal provision. I am not subject to the ups and downs of the world system. I live under the unchanging flow of Your finished work.

Let the power of this eternal covenant secure my household. Our provision is not seasonal—it is secured. Our prosperity is not circumstantial—it is covenantal. Because You entered once for all, I receive once for all. My needs are met not just for today, but for every tomorrow. My family will never beg bread because we are eternally redeemed.

May our lives reflect the security of Your blood. We do not hoard—we honor. We do not panic—we praise. You have obtained redemption that cannot be revoked, and from that redemption flows prosperity that cannot be blocked. Thank You for securing our future in blood.

In Jesus' name, Amen.

PEACE

THE LIFE OF PEACE IN THE BLOOD

> "For the life of the flesh is in the blood; and I have given it to you on the altar to make atonement for your souls: for it is the blood that makes atonement by reason of the life."
> — Leviticus 17:11 WEB

Eternal God, I thank You for the life that flows through the blood of Jesus—a life brimming with peace. This life has replaced the unrest of my soul, healed the fractures in my mind, and restored harmony to my relationships.

Today, I receive that life afresh for myself and my household. Let it course through every weary place, revitalizing our faith, our hope, and our love. Let it drive out the poison of anxiety, the sickness of fear, and the strain of division.

Lord, this life is indestructible, unstoppable, and eternal. It is our inheritance, purchased at the altar of the cross. As we abide in this life, peace flows without ceasing, saturating every word we speak, every step we take, and every connection we share.

In Jesus' name, Amen.

DAY 29

PARDON

LIFE THROUGH COMMUNION

> "Whoever eats my flesh and drinks my blood has eternal life..."
> — John 6:54 WEB

Jesus, I thank You for the mystery and power of communion with You. You are the Bread of Life, and Your blood is my eternal covenant. When I partake of You—through faith, worship, and daily surrender—I receive life, real life, everlasting life.

Let this truth transform how I approach Your table. It's not a ritual—it's relationship. You offered Your body and poured out Your blood so that I could have unbroken communion with You. Fill my spirit with hunger for more of You. Satisfy my soul with Your presence.

Let my family live in constant connection with the Living Christ. We receive Your life flowing through us—strength for our bodies, joy for our spirits, and grace for every step. Eternal life is not far away—it begins now through fellowship with You.

In Jesus' name, Amen.

PROTECTION

God Is On Our Side

> "What then shall we say about these things? If God is for us, who can be against us?"
> — Romans 8:31 WEB

Father of Glory, I declare that the blood of Jesus is the eternal proof that You are for us. You did not spare Your Son, and by His blood, we are marked as Yours. Who can challenge our standing? What force can oppose our peace?

I decree that no plan against my family shall prosper. We are not abandoned, we are backed by heaven. Let every fear dissolve in the revelation of Your favor. The blood says, "God is with you." I speak that over my household, our business, our future.

Every opposition must fail. Every tongue that rises in judgment is silenced. Every shadow of resistance is overcome. You are our defender, our fortress, our Father. And because of the blood, we are forever safe in Your will.

In Jesus' name, Amen.

PREVAIL

Trusting the Lamb to Win

"...the Lamb will overcome them..."
—Revelation 17:14 WEB

O Victorious Lamb, I rest my confidence in You. You are the Lion and the Lamb, and every enemy that rises is already outmatched by Your glory. I do not fear what surrounds me—I trust in who fights for me. The Lamb has never lost, and He never will. My battles belong to You, and my victory is sure.

Let every threat against me and my family be laid before Your throne. Let every demonic agenda meet Your overcoming power. I trust not in my strength, nor in human systems—I trust the blood-stained Lamb who reigns forever. You are overcoming even now, in ways I cannot see.

Preserve our peace as we trust You. Let our posture be worship. Let our eyes stay fixed on You. No matter how fierce the fight, we win because the Lamb goes before us and prevails with nail-pierced hands.

In Jesus' name, Amen.

PRESERVATION

Washed from Sickness Residue

"...made them white in the Lamb's blood."
— Revelation 7:14 WEB

Pure and Spotless Lamb, I come under the cleansing flow of Your blood. I thank You that not only does it remove sin—it purges every residue of sickness. I declare my spirit is pure, my soul is clean, and my body is free from every lingering trace of disease.

I am not just forgiven—I am transformed. Let the blood wash away fear of recurrence, trauma from diagnosis, and hidden toxins from past battles. What the Lamb has cleansed, nothing can defile again. I am white-robed and whole.

I plead this purity over my household. Let our immune systems be reset. Let past illnesses leave no scar. Let spiritual toxins be purged and emotional damage healed. We are not marked by what we've been through—we are marked by the Lamb.

The blood makes us white. The blood makes us whole.

In Jesus' name, Amen.

PROSPERITY

Abundance by Covenant Right

> "The Lord will grant you abundant prosperity—in the fruit of your womb, the young of your livestock and the crops of your ground—in the land he swore to your ancestors to give you."
> — Deuteronomy 28:11 WEB

O Faithful Covenant God, You swore by Yourself to bless us, and through the blood of Jesus, we are now partakers of that oath. I declare that abundance is my covenant right—not a wish, not a dream, but a guaranteed inheritance ratified in blood.

Let my household be fruitful. Let our work multiply. Let our ground yield increase. I thank You that every area of my life is touched by the abundance You promised: our children are thriving, our income is growing, our legacy is increasing. We prosper in every season because we are planted in promise.

Let my family carry the evidence of this truth. Let our lives provoke the world to ask, "What God do you serve?" We are not self-made—we are covenant-kept. We do not trust in the systems of man—we trust in the blood-sealed promise of a God who never fails.

In Jesus' name, Amen.

PEACE

Living in Kingdom Peace

"For God's Kingdom is not eating and drinking, but righteousness, peace, and joy in the Holy Spirit."
— Romans 14:17 WEB

Righteous King, I step into the reality of Your Kingdom—one where peace reigns, joy overflows, and righteousness stands immovable. This is the inheritance purchased for me through the blood of Jesus, and I claim it for myself and my family today.

Let kingdom peace govern our home, making it a sanctuary where Your Spirit is welcome and Your will is done. Let kingdom joy strengthen our hearts and keep our relationships full of life.

We refuse to live by the lesser systems of this world. Our atmosphere is the atmosphere of Heaven, our security is the blood, and our peace is unshakable. In this Kingdom, fear has no throne, chaos has no crown, and the enemy has no say.

In Jesus' name, Amen.

DAY 30

PARDON

CLEANSED BY LIVING WATER

"I will sprinkle clean water on you..."
— Ezekiel 36:25 WEB

Holy God, I praise You for Your promise to cleanse me. You said You would sprinkle clean water on me and wash away all my filth and idols. You are not content with surface change—you desire deep transformation. Thank You for cleansing me by Your Spirit and the blood of Jesus.

Let that water flow freely over my heart. Wash away every compromise, every secret sin, every residue of rebellion. Let Your cleansing not only remove what is wrong but also make room for what is holy. Over my household, I release the purifying presence of the Lord.

We are not defiled—we are clean. We are not distant—we are restored. Let our thoughts, our words, and our actions reflect hearts made pure by God. Clean hands and pure hearts shall be our legacy, by the power of Your Word and Spirit.

In Jesus' name, Amen.

PROTECTION

Angelic Protection Activated by Blood

> "The angel of Yahweh encamps around those who fear him, and delivers them."
> — Psalm 34:7 WEB

Commander of the Lord's Armies, I invoke the power of Your blood to activate angelic encampments around my life and my family. We stand under Your fear and reverence, and because of the blood, divine escorts surround us night and day.

Let Your angels guard our children as they sleep, go to school, and walk in this world. Let them shield us from accidents, ambushes, and sudden calamity. I declare that no demonic tracking, no wicked plan, no hidden danger can penetrate the covering of angelic fire.

Let dreams be guarded, peace be preserved, and journeys be protected. My household is not vulnerable—we are divinely defended. Where danger lurks, let angels war. Where evil plots, let angels frustrate. The blood has summoned heaven's guard, and we walk in holy safety.

In Jesus' name, Amen.

PREVAIL

Freedom from Sin's Dominion

> "Sin will not have dominion over you…"
> —Romans 6:14 WEB

Holy Redeemer, I declare this day that sin shall not rule me or my family. The reign of darkness is broken, the grip of compromise is loosed, and the power of transgression is crushed under the weight of the blood. We are not bound—we are free. The blood has changed our nature and shifted our authority.

I reject every lie that says I must live in cycles of failure. I declare that holiness is possible, purity is attainable, and victory is sustainable. The blood does not just forgive—it empowers. My family walks in this freedom. We live by grace, not by guilt. We war in righteousness, not by striving.

Lord, let this freedom be guarded daily. Let no door be opened to sin's voice. Let no foothold be granted to its lies. We are under grace, ruled by the Spirit, and covered in blood. Sin will not reign where the Lamb has risen.

In Jesus' name, Amen.

PRESERVATION

THE BLOOD-COVERED WORD HEALS

> "He sent his word and healed them…"
> — Psalm 107:20 WEB

Faithful Sender, I declare that every word You send carries healing, and Your Word does not return void. I receive the Word today, covered in the blood of Jesus, flowing with supernatural power to heal. It is not mere text—it is living, active, and wrapped in redemptive fire.

Let the Word target every affliction in me—bone, tissue, mind, memory. Let it sever lies, mend what's torn, and reverse what's broken. Your Word heals in places medicine cannot reach. I open my spirit to its full work.

I speak this over my family: may the Word dwell in us richly and work deeply. Let every verse we read become medicine. Let every promise be blood-sealed and manifested in our health. We send the Word over our children, our homes, and our future.

Your Word is sent. Your blood backs it. Healing is happening now.

In Jesus' name, Amen.

PROSPERITY

Bound by the Blood to Provide

> "Moses took the blood, and sprinkled it on the people, and said, 'Behold, the blood of the covenant, which Yahweh has made with you concerning all these words.'"
> — Exodus 24:8 WEB

Father of the Covenant, I stand sprinkled by the blood that binds You to Your word. You have sworn by the blood that You will provide, protect, and promote. I hold You to Your Word—not with arrogance, but with honor. Your Word is Your bond, and the blood is the seal.

Let the provisions written in Scripture be manifested in my life. Let every "you shall be the head and not the tail" become flesh in my family. Let every "you shall lend and not borrow" be lived out in my finances. The blood has made these words unbreakable.

I bind my household to the Word through the blood. We shall not be moved. We shall not be shaken. We are people of the covenant, and therefore, provision is our portion. Thank You, Lord, for swearing Yourself to our supply. We live in the blessing that cannot be revoked.

In Jesus' name, Amen.

PEACE

SANCTIFIED BY THE GOD OF PEACE

> "May the God of peace himself sanctify you completely. May your whole spirit, soul, and body be preserved blameless at the coming of our Lord Jesus Christ."
> — 1 Thessalonians 5:23 WEB

God of Peace, I welcome Your sanctifying work in every part of me. Through the blood of Jesus, cleanse my spirit, steady my soul, and strengthen my body. Leave no anxious thought, no fearful feeling, and no restless place untouched by Your peace.

Lord, let this same sanctifying power cover my family. May we be wholly set apart—our minds guarded, our emotions healed, our bodies strengthened. Let peace be the seal upon us, a divine mark that we are Yours.

We choose to live preserved, protected, and perfected by Your peace until the day of Your appearing. Nothing missing, nothing broken, nothing stolen—only the fullness of shalom reigning in us.

In Jesus' name, Amen.

DAY 31

PARDON

BOUGHT AND PAID FOR BY HIS BLOOD

> "...church of God, which he purchased with his own blood."
> — Acts 20:28 WEB

Lord Jesus, I thank You for the ultimate price You paid for me. Your blood was not spilled by accident—it was poured out with purpose. You didn't just redeem a people; You bought us individually, personally, and completely. I am not my own. I am blood-bought and heaven-owned.

Let this truth calm every anxious place in me. I don't belong to fear, guilt, or confusion. I belong to You. You purchased me with blood that cannot be refunded or revoked. Let that reality secure my identity and settle my heart. I was worth dying for—and now I live to glorify the One who gave everything for me.

May my family also rest in this blood-bought peace. We are not abandoned or forgotten. We are the church You died to purchase. Let the weight of our value in Your eyes silence every lie of the enemy. We are precious, chosen, and fully paid for. In Jesus' name, Amen.

PROTECTION

MARKED FOR DIVINE PURPOSE

> "You shall take some of its blood and put it on the tip of the right ear of Aaron, and on the tip of the right ear of his sons, and on the thumb of their right hand, and on the big toe of their right foot."
> —Exodus 29:20 WEB

Mighty God, I stand today under the covenant power of the blood of Jesus. As one marked for divine purpose, I receive the sanctifying touch of the blood upon every part of my being. Let the blood touch my ears—consecrate my hearing. Let my ears be sensitive only to Your voice. May every other sound be silenced—the noise of fear, distraction, and the world's deception.

Let the blood sanctify my hands. All that I touch shall prosper in righteousness. My hands shall not be instruments of harm but healing. My labor is covered. My work is redeemed. My family's efforts are washed in the blood of protection and purpose. No curse shall cling to our hands.

Let the blood be upon our feet. We will not wander into destruction. Our steps are ordered in righteousness. We tread over serpents and scorpions. As for me and my house, we walk in paths of peace, authority, and protection. We are sealed in the covenant of purpose and power.

Father, we are wholly Yours—ear, hand, and foot. No part of us is left uncovered. Let this divine marking distinguish our family in the spirit realm. We are consecrated and kept for Your glory. In Jesus' name, Amen.

PREVAIL

Flood-Resistant Standard Raised

> "...when the enemy comes in like a flood..."
> —Isaiah 59:19 WEB

Mighty Redeemer, I declare that though the waters of the enemy may rise like a flood, Your crimson standard stands immovable over me and my family. The torrent of adversity may roar—deception, calamity, spiritual strongholds—but the blood of Jesus forms a barrier no flood can breach. I refuse fear. I raise the blood banner high.

By that standard, I divide the water—what was meant to overwhelm now becomes the pathways of triumph. Every assault, every flood-tide of adversity is halted at the line of Your covenant. I stand in faith, anchored by the blood that sealed our preservation. My home, my finances, my children, my mind—all sheltered behind the blood-signed rampart.

Father God, let Your deliverance roar over us like a mighty wave that drowns all threats. Let angels stand guard at every river bank. Let the floods become our springboard, not our drowners. We are preserved, upheld, and secured by the blood line You set. Let this declaration echo in every flood zone. We are not submerged—we are delivered. In Jesus' name, Amen.

PRESERVATION

HEALING THAT TOUCHES GENERATIONS

> "Abraham prayed to God, and God healed Abimelech…"
> — Genesis 20:17 WEB

Righteous Father, I thank You for being the God who heals not just individuals, but entire households. Today, I lift up my life and the lives of my family members before Your holy altar. Let Your healing power flow like a river from the cross of Christ into our bloodlines. Let the blood of Jesus undo every generational affliction, disease, or disorder assigned to our lineage.

Lord, as You healed Abimelech at Abraham's intercession, I stand in my priestly authority, declaring total healing for every member of my family. Let the power of covenant prayer, backed by the blood, silence every sickness. I apply the blood of Jesus over our immune systems, organs, minds, emotions, and environments. Whatever has afflicted our health — known or hidden — is now arrested by the authority of Christ's sacrifice.

I declare that my household shall not be plagued. We are covered, cleansed, and healed by the same blood that reversed

Abimelech's barrenness and restored his house. Even unspoken illnesses and silent sufferings are uprooted by faith. Because the blood still speaks, I decree healing shall not be delayed but released swiftly, fully, and lastingly.

In Jesus' name, Amen.

PROSPERITY

Multiplied Through Covenant Obedience

> "I will bless you greatly, and I will multiply your offspring greatly like the stars of the heavens, and like the sand which is on the seashore."
> — Genesis 22:17 WEB

Lord, Covenant-Keeping God of Abraham, I declare that the blood of Jesus has brought me into the lineage of blessing and multiplied increase. Just as You honored Abraham's obedience with unstoppable multiplication, I stand today under the same covenant, sealed by better blood, and I receive the blessing of increase over my life and my family.

Because of Christ's sacrifice, I step into exponential growth—spiritual, financial, generational. Let my obedience unlock divine strategy and provision. Let every act of faith on my part yield a harvest too numerous to count. You are not a man that You should lie; Your promise to bless and multiply is as alive now as it was on that mountain.

Father, multiply my seed sown, my opportunities, and my influence. Let my children walk in legacy and not labor. I break every ceiling of limitation and receive the Abrahamic blessing through Jesus' obedience on the Cross. My household will increase, our hands will prosper, and our name will be associated with generational wealth—because we obey and believe the covenant.

In Jesus' name, Amen.

PEACE

REST IN THE SHADOW OF THE CROSS

> "In peace I will both lay myself down and sleep, for you alone, Yahweh, make me live in safety."
> — Psalm 4:8 WEB

O Lord, my Shield and my Peace, I thank You for the blood of Jesus that speaks a better word over my nights. I declare that every restless thought, every anxiety, and every midnight terror is stilled by the power of His cross. Your covenant blood covers my household like a warm blanket of divine safety, shutting the door to every harassing spirit.

I decree over myself and my family that our beds shall be altars of rest, not battlegrounds of the mind. The blood of Jesus has silenced the accuser, and His peace now reigns in our hearts and minds. Even as we close our eyes, angels stand guard at our doors, and the Prince of Peace lays His hand upon our heads.

Lord, because of the blood, I reject insomnia, fear, and dread. I receive holy rest as a gift purchased at Calvary. We shall awaken refreshed, strengthened, and filled with joy, knowing that our lives are hidden in Christ. No disturbance, no noise, no invisible storm can steal this rest. We lie down in peace, and we rise in peace. In Jesus' name, Amen.

DAY 32

PARDON

GRATITUDE FOR CHRIST'S MERCY SEAT WORK

> Therefore he was obligated in all things to be made like his brothers, that he might become a merciful and faithful high priest in things pertaining to God, to make atonement for the sins of the people.
> —Hebrews 2:17 WEB

Jesus, my High Priest and Sacrifice, I honor You for becoming the mercy seat on my behalf. You didn't just cover sin—you satisfied justice. You bore the wrath I deserved and turned it into favor. Your blood has forever changed my standing with God.

Thank You for stepping into my place. You didn't plead for mercy from a distance; You became the very offering mercy required. Let gratitude flood my soul for the compassion You showed when You stood in my place. The cross became my mercy seat, and Your blood became my covering.

Let this revelation bring peace into my emotional storms. I am no longer judged, I am justified. I am no longer condemned, I am counted righteous. And my family is under that same mercy. Let us walk humbly, worship deeply, and rejoice fully in Your propitiating love. In Jesus' name, Amen.

PROTECTION

BLOOD-COVERED SENSES FOR DISCERNMENT

> "The priest shall take some of the blood of the trespass offering, and the priest shall put it on the tip of the right ear of him who is to be cleansed..."
> —Leviticus 14:14 WEB

O Most Holy One, by the blood of the Lamb, I bring my family under the divine touch of consecration. Just as the priest anointed the ear, thumb, and toe with blood, I declare today that our spiritual senses are blood-covered for divine discernment. No longer shall our ears be polluted by the voices of deception.

I speak over my family's ears—may we hear heaven clearly. Let every lie be muted, every manipulation shattered. Let the whisper of the Holy Spirit become unmistakably clear. I declare the blood covers our eyes to see as You see, our minds to perceive by Your Spirit, and our hearts to respond in holiness.

Father, let this blood application go beyond symbol and become our daily reality. We shall not touch what is unclean, nor walk where You have not sent us. The blood is our filter—safeguarding us from defilement and guiding us into purity.

May our children grow in discernment. May we move with holy wisdom. Let every part of our family be consecrated through this sprinkling of Christ's blood. In Jesus' name, Amen.

PREVAIL

VICTORY OVER THE WORLD'S STORMS

> "...take heart! I have overcome the world."
> —John 16:33 WEB

Prince of Peace, I lift my family in the truth that You have overcome the world. We face storms—economic uncertainty, cultural pressure, relational conflicts—but because the One who shed His blood lives, we walk above every shaking ground. We take heart, we stand unafraid, and we move in triumph.

I refuse to be robbed by discouragement or shaken by worldly trials. The world's pain, darkness, and chaos cannot claim what the blood has secured. Our hearts rest in the assurance of victory. We are heirs of resurrection power. We march through trials, never as victims but as overcomers, knowing the final score is settled in Heaven.

Holy Father, preserve this peace in our souls. Let our confidence not rest in circumstances, but in the One who conquered. Let our family echo songs of victory even when the world grows silent. We walk in supernatural preservation through the blood-bought triumph of Christ.

In Jesus' name, Amen.

PRESERVATION

RISING INTO BLOOD-RIGHTEOUS HEALING

> "But to you who fear my name shall the sun of righteousness arise with healing in its wings."
> — Malachi 4:2 WEB

O Glorious King, You are the Sun of Righteousness, rising over my life with healing in Your wings. Let the radiance of Your righteousness pierce through every shadow of sickness and pain in my life and in the lives of my family members. I receive the warmth of Your healing light, flowing directly from the finished work of the cross.

Today, I position myself and my household beneath Your wings of divine preservation. Because of the righteousness imputed to me by the blood of Jesus, I rise above affliction, inflammation, and fatigue. I rise into wholeness, vigor, and vitality. I call for every cell in our bodies to respond to the rising light of Your righteousness.

Let the wings of Your healing presence fan away every chronic condition. Whether emotional burdens, spiritual wounds, or physical ailments, I declare they are dissolved by the fire of Your rising. We are not forsaken; we are covered by covenant. Our health is not seasonal — it is established by blood.

In Jesus' name, Amen.

PROSPERITY

Overcoming Financial Warfare

> "They overcame him because of the Lamb's blood, and because of the word of their testimony."
> — Revelation 12:11 WEB

Victorious Lord, I declare that every financial battle waged against my life and household is now subdued under the blood of the Lamb. By the authority of the blood and the power of my testimony, I overcome every demonic resistance, every devourer, and every sabotage assigned to my increase.

The blood of Jesus testifies louder than debt, louder than scarcity, louder than generational curses. I silence the voice of lack and rise in the triumph of covenant victory. I am not a victim—I am a blood-covered overcomer. Let the roar of the redeemed echo through my finances and household, causing every enemy to flee.

Father, let every attack on our harvest be reversed. Let angels of provision war on our behalf. My family walks in victory—we do not retreat. Our wealth is not fragile, our blessing is not vulnerable. The enemy may come in one way, but by the blood, he flees in seven.

In Jesus' name, Amen.

PEACE

Covered in Peaceful Protection

> "The blood shall be to you for a token on the houses where you are; and when I see the blood, I will pass over you, and no plague will be on you to destroy you..."
> — Exodus 12:13 WEB

Mighty Deliverer, I lift my voice in gratitude for the blood of the Lamb that speaks mercy over my home. By this blood, every plague, sickness, and calamity is forbidden to cross our threshold. I declare that my family is sealed in covenant protection, hidden in the cleft of the Rock.

Father, Your Word assures me that peace is my portion because protection is my inheritance. No disease, no sudden disaster, and no work of darkness shall overtake us. The blood of Jesus is the mark that Heaven recognizes and Hell fears. I rest in the truth that the destroyer cannot pass through the door where the blood is applied.

I declare peace within our walls and safety in our dwelling places. Every assignment of harm is canceled, every snare is broken, and every demonic entry point is closed. The blood has spoken, and its voice thunders: "Peace!" Over my children, my spouse, my household, and all that concerns us, divine peace reigns like a fortress. In Jesus' name, Amen.

DAY 33

PARDON

Deep Cleansing And Restoration

"Purge me with hyssop, and I will be clean…"
— Psalm 51:7 WEB

Father, I echo David's cry—purge me. Wash me deeply, not just on the surface. Use the hyssop of Your mercy and the power of the blood to reach into the places I've tried to hide. I long not just for forgiveness but for wholeness. Make me truly clean.

Sometimes the stains feel stubborn, the regrets replay too often—but Your cleansing is stronger. What the blood touches, it transforms. Let the cleansing of Jesus reach my thoughts, emotions, and memories. Let shame be uprooted, and let joy be restored. I don't want to be partially healed—I want to be made whole.

Over my family, I declare a fresh washing. Cleanse us from every sin, every habit, every lie we've believed. Let the hyssop of Your Spirit reach our deepest places. You promise we shall be whiter than snow—so let it be. Let peace come through restoration.

In Jesus' name, Amen.

PROTECTION

Sealed from Harm and Judgment

> "Don't harm the earth, neither the sea, nor the trees, until we have sealed the bondservants of our God on their foreheads!"
> —Revelation 7:3 WEB

Righteous Judge and Covenant Keeper, I declare today that my household is sealed by the blood of Jesus! We are not left to chance, uncovered in the chaos of this world. Your seal is upon our heads, our lives, our destinies. The destroying winds of judgment will not come near because we bear the mark of the blood.

Father, just as You delayed harm until Your servants were sealed, delay destruction and devastation from reaching my family. The seal of Christ's blood is upon our doors, minds, and hearts. We are hidden under the crimson mark. We are counted among the preserved.

I prophesy that calamity will pass over us. No weapon formed will prosper. We are distinguished by the eternal covenant. The same Spirit that sealed the saints of old now affirms our divine exemption. My children, my spouse, and I stand secure.

Thank You for the seal that cannot be removed, for the protection that is unshakable. We are engraved in You. Let this mark testify continually in the courts of heaven that we belong to the Lamb. In Jesus' name, Amen.

PREVAIL

Let the Blood Fight

"Yahweh will fight for you..."
—Exodus 14:14 WEB

Warrior God, You declared that You will fight for me—my unseen battles, those hidden assignments against my peace, health, and family. I rest in that promise. I step back from striving. I submit to the finished work of the cross. Your blood fights, not human effort. Let angels marshal, demonic agendas scatter, and justice fall.

I don't wrestle in my own power. I stand covered. Every unseen opposition assigned to my family is routed by Your sovereign blood. You wage war on my behalf. I refuse to align with fear-driven tactics. I refuse to rely on fleshly schemes. I trust wholly in the One whose blood reigns victorious in the unseen.

Father, breathe peace. Let Your divine intervention show up where natural help fades. Let Your name advance when intimidation looms. I rest under Your blood-borne justice. My family is shielded, preserved, delivered. The battle is Yours.

In Jesus' name, Amen.

PRESERVATION

BLOOD-ANOINTED FOR PRESERVATION

> "...you shall sprinkle them with blood..."
> — Exodus 29:21 WEB

Holy God, I stand under the covenant of sprinkled blood — not of bulls or goats, but of the spotless Lamb. I thank You that this blood sanctifies, consecrates, and preserves. I now anoint my body, my family, and every room in my dwelling with the power of the blood of Jesus.

Let the blood mark every doorpost and every threshold of my life. Let it cover our minds, ears, and hands. Where sickness has entered, let the sprinkled blood evict and cleanse. Where threats loom, let the blood defend. I release divine preservation over our health, our spaces, and our futures through this blood-soaked consecration.

I call for holy fire to be kindled wherever the blood is sprinkled. Let it be a barrier against disease and disaster. Let it guard our going out and our coming in. As priests under a better covenant, I sprinkle my environment with expectation — expecting healing, restoration, and divine interruption to anything that would steal health or peace.

In Jesus' name, Amen.

PROSPERITY

No Sorrow in My Blessing

> "The Lord's blessing brings wealth, and he adds no trouble to it."
> — Proverbs 10:22 WEB

Faithful Provider, I praise You for the blessing that enriches without anxiety. I reject toil without fruit and embrace wealth that comes from Your hand alone. The blessing of the Lord is upon me through the blood of Jesus, and I declare that sorrow and striving shall have no place in my prosperity.

Every heavy yoke of financial stress is broken. I step into rest-driven results, not hustle-induced hardship. You give me power to get wealth without it draining my peace. Your blessing is complete—it brings joy, not burdens; honor, not shame.

Lord, let my family walk in this blessing. Let laughter fill our home instead of worry. May our financial story glorify You, not our efforts. I declare a divine distinction: we prosper without compromise, without corners cut, without sleepless striving. The blood has opened the door, and we walk through it joyfully.

In Jesus' name, Amen.

PEACE

Pardon That Calms the Soul

> "...for this is my blood of the new covenant, which is poured out for many for the remission of sins."
> — Matthew 26:28 WEB

Loving Redeemer, I lift my hands in awe of the blood poured out for my complete pardon. Because of this covenant, shame is silenced, guilt is erased, and peace flows like a river into my heart. Every failure, every regret, and every dark memory bows to the authority of the cross.

Lord, I declare over myself and my family that we are forgiven, fully and forever. The record of wrongs has been washed away, and the accusing voices are muted. We will not live under the shadow of condemnation, for the blood of Jesus has brought us into the light of Your love.

Let emotional storms be calmed right now. Let troubled consciences be soothed. Let strained hearts exhale the breath of relief. By the blood, I choose to embrace peace—not as a distant hope, but as a present reality. Our home will be a sanctuary where forgiveness reigns, joy flourishes, and love is restored. In Jesus' name, Amen.

DAY 34

PARDON

Rejoicing In Erased Records

"I have blotted out... your sins."
— Isaiah 44:22 WEB

Lord, I rejoice today because the record of my sins is gone. Not covered, not overlooked—blotted out. Like ink washed from a page, the evidence of my failure has vanished beneath the blood of Jesus. There is no longer a case against me in heaven's courtroom.

Let my soul rest in this assurance. I don't have to relive what You've erased. I don't have to rehearse what You've forgotten. You have blotted out my sins like a mist blown away by the morning wind. Teach me to rejoice not in perfection, but in redemption.

For my family, I declare the same joy. No matter how deep the sin or long the history, You've blotted it out. We will not walk around with the weight of old guilt. We will dance in the freedom of clean records and open arms. Let this joy be our strength.

In Jesus' name, Amen.

PROTECTION

Exempt by the Mark of Blood

> "Kill utterly the old man, the young man and the virgin, and little children and women; but don't come near any man on whom is the mark."
> —Ezekiel 9:6 WEB

God of Justice and Mercy, I stand as one covered by the mark of the blood. In the day of judgment and shaking, let this divine mark be evident upon my household. As destruction moves through the land, let the seal of Jesus' blood scream "EXEMPTED!" over my family.

Father, not by our righteousness but by the righteousness of Christ, we are set apart. The destroyer shall not draw near. We are not subject to the judgment of the wicked. Your mercy speaks louder than wrath. We wear the crimson mark upon our foreheads—visible in the spirit realm, unremovable, eternal.

Let every demonic force that scans for vulnerability bypass us. Let every spirit of death and violence skip our homes. We are marked for life, safety, and divine preservation. My children shall live and not die. My spouse is covered. Our household is hidden in the secret place.

This mark is covenantal. It speaks louder than accusations and protects stronger than earthly guards. We remain within Your boundaries of mercy and grace. In Jesus' name, Amen.

PREVAIL

Trust in Blood, Not Strength

> "Some trust in chariots… but we trust in Yahweh…"
> —Psalm 20:7 WEB

Lord Almighty, though nations arm themselves, and flesh has its strategies, I refuse to lean on human strength. My trust stands in the blood that fashioned my salvation and established covenant peace. We do not depend on prestige, position, or power—we depend on Your blood-bought authority.

Let the enemy's boasts crumble. Let financial moves, human connections, and personal plans bow to the blood's supremacy. My family stands in covenant trust—not in worldly solutions but in divine preserve. When human armor fails, the blood remains unshaken. We are held by the reliable, not the fickle.

Father, embed this trust deep in our hearts. Let our children refuse to fear scarcity or bypass Your covering. Let our decisions rise from covenant assurance, not hype. Blood reigns. Flesh subsides. We walk in confidence that the One who shed His life holds all our days.

In Jesus' name, Amen.

PRESERVATION

Healing from Sin's Root

> "For this is my blood… for the remission of sins."
> — Matthew 26:28 WEB

Precious Redeemer, I honor the power of Your blood — blood that was poured not just to cover sins but to completely erase them. Today, I receive that same blood as healing balm for every sickness rooted in sin, guilt, or condemnation in my life or in the lives of my family members.

Where we opened doors through disobedience, I plead the blood. Where our bodies suffer because of unrepented patterns or past transgressions, I apply the remission power of Your cross. Let the blood run deep into our bloodstream, organs, and cellular memory, removing disease and reversing decay.

No longer shall we carry shame-induced afflictions. We are not defined by our mistakes but by Your mercy. And the blood that forgives also heals. I decree that diseases born of trauma, bitterness, and brokenness are now being uprooted. We are cleansed, restored, and made whole — not just in spirit, but in body.

In Jesus' name, Amen.

PROSPERITY

Supernatural Provision Without Currency

> "Come, everyone who thirsts, to the waters! Come, he who has no money, buy, and eat!"
> — Isaiah 55:1 WEB

Holy Source of All, I lift my hands to receive the supply that does not require natural currency. I come to the well of grace, to the marketplace of mercy, where Your blood has already paid my price. I buy without money and eat without debt. I receive supernatural provision by faith.

Let divine resources flow into my life and family. Let doors open that no man can explain. You are not limited by economy, by account balance, or by human systems. I live in the reality of grace economics—where You supply all my needs according to the riches of glory, not the poverty of circumstance.

Lord, let my household be marked by miracles. Provide what we didn't earn. Deliver what we didn't pay for. Let us testify of how we received more than we asked, simply because we believed. We feast where others famine, we rise where others fall—because we live by grace, not gold.

In Jesus' name, Amen.

PEACE

BREAKING THE CURSE'S GRIP

> "Christ redeemed us from the curse of the law, having become a curse for us..."
> — Galatians 3:13 WEB

Chain-Breaking Savior, I stand in the victory of the cross and declare that every generational curse is shattered by the blood of Jesus. Mental torment, cycles of fear, depression, and confusion have no legal right to remain in me or my family.

By the authority of the blood, I uproot every inherited bondage and declare that the blessing of Abraham rests on our minds. I renounce every lie that says we are bound to repeat the failures of the past. The curse has been removed, and in its place, peace like a river floods our hearts and thoughts.

Lord, I receive the renewing of the mind for myself and my household. Every dark cloud is dispersed, every tormenting thought is silenced, and clarity comes. We shall walk in soundness of mind, strength of heart, and wholeness of soul. The blood of Jesus has spoken freedom, and we will not return to chains. In Jesus' name, Amen.

DAY 35

PARDON

WALKING IN THE POWER OF THE COVENANT

"...This cup is the new covenant in my blood..."
— Luke 22:20 WEB

Jesus, thank You for inviting me into a better covenant—a new and living way sealed with Your blood. When You lifted the cup at the Last Supper, You weren't offering religion, You were offering relationship. You established an unbreakable bond between heaven and earth, sealed not with ink but with blood.

Help me walk in the power of this covenant daily. Let it affect how I pray, how I think, and how I see myself. I am not just saved—I am in covenant with the King. You are committed to me, and I am committed to You. Let covenant peace reign in my heart.

Over my home, I speak covenant security. We are not orphans; we are blood-bound to God. This covenant provides peace, provision, and protection. We claim all that Jesus paid for—because this blood speaks better things.

In Jesus' name, Amen.

PROTECTION

COVENANT BLOOD ESTABLISHES MY SHIELD

> "He said to him, "Bring me a heifer three years old, a female goat three years old, a ram three years old, a turtledove, and a young pigeon." He brought him all these, and divided them in the middle, and laid each half opposite the other..."
> —Genesis 15:9-10 WEB

O Covenant-Making God, You initiated a blood covenant with Abraham that speaks even today through Christ. As the pieces were laid in the ancient path of promise, so the blood of Jesus has laid down a shield around my household. We are encompassed by covenant.

This covenant is not of man, but of God. It cannot be broken, voided, or erased. Because of it, we are shielded from destruction, defended in battle, and surrounded by divine fire. The sacrifice has already been made. The blood has already spoken.

Lord, I step into the pathway of promise, just as Abraham did. I bring my family into this ancient, unbreakable bond. We walk between the pieces—between judgment and mercy—and we come out sealed by love and protection.

Let this covenant answer every attack. Let it defend us in the unseen realm. Let the God who cut covenant with blood rise to defend our home. In Jesus' name, Amen.

PREVAIL

Boldness Granted by Blood Access

> "Having therefore boldness to enter... by the blood..."
> —Hebrews 10:19 WEB

Bold Savior, Your blood has given me entrance into the Holy Place with confidence. I approach with boldness, unafraid of threats, intimidation, or condemnation. My prayers, my petitions, my declarations come before You with unmoved faith. We stand fearless, clothed in covenant access.

I refuse to shrink back. I refuse to hedge my prayers. I hold high the blood banner and step into supernatural space. My family and I speak boldly against darkness. Our posture in prayer disarms fear, dismantles legal charges, and repositions us in dominion. Blood gives entry. Boldness flows.

Father, infuse that boldness through every generation in my household. Let us walk in fearless prayer, fearless decree, fearless obedience. When the enemy taunts or the atmosphere thickens, we push forward. The blood opens heavenly courts and releases heavenly power.

In Jesus' name, Amen.

PRESERVATION

No Plague Near Our Dwelling

> "No evil shall happen to you, neither shall any plague come near your dwelling."
> — Psalm 91:10 WEB

Covenant-Keeping God, I declare today that my family and I dwell in the shelter of the Most High. Because of the blood of Jesus, no plague, pestilence, virus, or outbreak shall invade our dwelling. The blood is our boundary. The blood is our defense.

I paint our doorposts afresh with faith. I speak divine immunity over our lungs, skin, minds, and bones. Every attempt of the enemy to introduce affliction is halted by the bloodline of Christ. No weapon formed against our bodies shall prosper. No sudden sickness or stealthy attack shall find legal ground here.

Let angelic sentries patrol our home. Let the atmosphere be saturated with heaven's health. Let the covenant of Psalm 91 be sealed by the crimson mark of the Lamb. We are surrounded, safeguarded, and sanctified.

In Jesus' name, Amen.

PROSPERITY

SATISFACTION IN EVERY FAMINE

> "They shall not be disappointed in the time of evil.
> In the days of famine they shall be satisfied."
> — Psalm 37:19 WEB

God of Unfailing Supply, I declare that no season can rob me of provision. Though the world may fear famine, I walk in blood-backed satisfaction. You are my Source, and in You, my family is never forsaken. Even in scarcity, we thrive. Even in drought, we drink.

I break the grip of recession over my household. I cancel every agreement with fear and speak abundance into every barren place. In times of shaking, You establish me. While others store up in fear, I sow in faith and reap in peace.

Let satisfaction reign in our home. Let our children never know lack. May our pantry, our accounts, and our joy remain full—proof that we are the Lord's. Thank You for being our Shepherd in the storm and our Table-setter in the wilderness.

In Jesus' name, Amen.

PEACE

Freedom from the Inner Prison

> "As for you also, because of the blood of your covenant, I have set free your prisoners from the pit in which there is no water."
> — Zechariah 9:11 WEB

Delivering King, I worship You for the power of the blood that breaks the locks of inner captivity. I declare that every prison of fear, grief, and despair in my life and in my family is opened now.

Lord, You have called us out of dry, barren places into the well-watered gardens of Your peace. By the blood, I speak freedom over every heart weighed down by heaviness, over every soul trapped in memories of pain. The prison doors swing wide, and we step into the light of Your joy.

No longer shall we be bound by silent tears or unspoken sorrow. The chains have fallen, and the pit has lost its hold. We receive the liberty of the children of God, walking in the freedom purchased at Calvary. The blood has made us free indeed. In Jesus' name, Amen.

DAY 36

PARDON

EMBRACING THE BLOOD FOUNTAIN

> "...a fountain opened... for sin and for uncleanness."
> — Zechariah 13:1 WEB

Lord, I thank You for the fountain that flows from Calvary. It is always open, always enough, and always cleansing. This fountain wasn't opened once and then closed—it continues to wash all who come. No sin is too deep, no stain too dark for the flow of Your blood.

Let me run to that fountain every day. Let me not try to clean myself before coming—because it is the fountain that makes me clean. I embrace its power to purify my mind, heal my emotions, and calm my inner storms. This blood is my peace.

I bring my family to the fountain. Let Your cleansing stream flow over our relationships, our words, our choices. Let what was unclean become holy. Let the power of that blood wash over every generation. We stand beneath the fountain—and we are whole.

In Jesus' name, Amen.

PROTECTION

Engraved in God's Hands

> "Behold, I have engraved you on the palms of my hands…"
> —Isaiah 49:16 WEB

Father, how precious and powerful is Your promise! I declare today that I and my household are not forgotten, not forsaken, but engraved upon the very palms of Your hands. The blood of Jesus has written our names where no man or devil can erase them.

This engraving is not symbolic—it is covenantal. It means we are permanently remembered, perpetually protected, and eternally seen. Every time You stretch forth Your hand, You see us. Every move of Your power carries our names within it.

I rest in the knowledge that Your hands are mighty to save. My family is within Your grasp. No matter what arrows fly, what storms arise, or what chaos surrounds, Your engraved palm preserves us. You carry us close, shield us strong, and lead us sure.

Because of the blood, we are not among the forgotten. We are family to the Almighty. We are not drifting—we are held. In Jesus' name, Amen.

PREVAIL

LIFE DECLARED OVER DEATH THREATS

"The life... is in the blood..."
—Leviticus 17:11 WEB

Life-Giver, Your Word declares that life resides in the blood, and by that life, we overcome the threat of death. I speak life—abundant, healing, relational, generational—into every corner of my family. We will not be overtaken by sickness, accident, despair, or hopelessness. The life in the blood courses through us.

No terminal report shall define our legacy. No fear of death shall overshadow our steps. Heart disease, anxiety, spiritual depression, ancestral infirmity—they all submit to the life force in the blood that flows through veins of redemption. Our habitation is charged with vitality.

Father, pour that life into our home. Let physical revival, emotional health, and spiritual vitality arise. Let future generations live out the fullness of that blood-life. Where death threatened, life triumphs. Where darkness lurked, light enters. Blood sustains us.

In Jesus' name, Amen.

PRESERVATION

Let the Blood Speak Healing

> "...the blood that speaks better than that of Abel."
> — Hebrews 12:24 WEB

Almighty Advocate, I come to the courts of heaven and present the blood of Jesus. Let it speak louder than every diagnosis, louder than pain, louder than fear. Let it cry out for healing, restoration, and supernatural intervention over my family and me.

This blood does not accuse; it intercedes. It pleads mercy. It declares healing, not harm. Where the voice of sickness has roared, I now tune my ear to the voice of the blood. It speaks better things — better than medicine, better than generational reports, better than statistics.

I silence the voice of infirmity, chronic illness, and medical confusion. I decree that the only verdict over our health is life and life more abundantly. The blood says, "You shall live and not die." The blood says, "You are made whole." I agree with heaven's final word — the blood!

In Jesus' name, Amen.

PROSPERITY

OVERFLOW IN ALL THINGS

> "God is able to make all grace abound to you, that you, always having all sufficiency in everything, may abound to every good work."
> — 2 Corinthians 9:8 WEB

All-Sufficient King, I lift my voice in gratitude for the overflow secured by the blood. You are able—and I believe. I declare over my life and family: we will never lack for anything necessary to do Your will. Grace abounds, and sufficiency is our standard.

Every area of insufficiency is now flooded with grace. You've equipped me to be a vessel of generosity, not just survival. We abound to every good work. We give, sow, build, bless—because You keep filling and refilling us. The more we pour, the more You provide.

Father, let this grace touch my entire household. Let us become a well that never runs dry. We operate in overflow—not just for ourselves but for the mission You've assigned us. The blood has guaranteed access, and we walk in the abundance of Your ability, not our own.

In Jesus' name, Amen.

PEACE

HEALING FOR THE BROKEN HEART

> "He heals the broken in heart, and binds up their wounds."
> — Psalm 147:3 WEB

Compassionate Healer, I lift my heart before You, trusting in the power of the blood to bind up every wound. Lord, where there has been betrayal, loss, or rejection, let the soothing balm of Calvary's love flow freely.

I declare over my family that every shattered heart is being mended stitch by stitch with cords of divine love. The blood of Jesus wipes away the stains of sorrow, closing the breaches left by pain. No wound is too deep for the Great Physician, and no scar is beyond His touch.

Lord, replace the ache with assurance, the grief with gladness, and the turmoil with tranquility. Let peace reign where pain once dwelled, and let joy overflow where mourning had a seat. In the blood, there is healing, and today we embrace it fully. In Jesus' name, Amen.

DAY 37

PARDON

Thanksgiving for Blessed Pardon

> "Blessed are those whose iniquities are forgiven…"
> — Romans 4:7 WEB

Father, how blessed I am to be forgiven. You didn't just overlook my iniquity—you removed it. You called me blessed not because I've done everything right, but because You made everything right through the blood of Jesus. My sins were many, but Your mercy was more.

Thank You for this incredible pardon. Let gratitude never grow cold in me. Every day I live, every prayer I pray, every blessing I enjoy—it's all because of forgiveness. Let me walk humbly in the awareness of what I've been set free from.

Over my family, I release this same blessedness. We are not cursed—we are forgiven. The enemy has no legal ground because the blood has settled the debt. Let joy replace regret and celebration replace shame. We are the forgiven—and we are free.

In Jesus' name, Amen.

PROTECTION

UNTOUCHABLE UNDER BLOOD PROTECTION

> "I give eternal life to them. They will never perish, and no one will snatch them out of my hand."
> —John 10:28 WEB

Great Shepherd, I rejoice in the eternal security found in Your hand. I speak boldly today that my family is untouchable, for we are kept in the hand of the One who never fails. The blood has sealed us in, and no force can snatch us out.

The enemy may try, but he cannot penetrate the grip of God. Death may threaten, but it cannot overrule the covenant. Because of the blood, we are covered by the hand that holds galaxies and commands angels. This hand is our home, our shield, our hiding place.

I decree that no snare, accusation, or attack will remove us from the grip of divine safety. The hand that holds us is pierced with love. The hand that saved us is strong with power. My children are in that hand. My marriage is in that hand. We rest secure.

Thank You, Jesus, for holding us. No fear shall prevail. No enemy shall succeed. We are covered in Your grasp, and we shall never be lost. In Jesus' name, Amen.

PREVAIL

BLOOD-CRIES FOR VENGEANCE

> "...avenge our blood on those who dwell on the earth..."
> —Revelation 6:10 WEB

Justice-Seeking Lord, I hear the cry of blood calling for vengeance—not for vengeance of hate, but for divine justice. For every attack against my life, every defilement of my family, every injustice assigned by spiritual wickedness—I ask You to avenge by Your covenant power. Let Your blood-signed justice move swiftly, decisively, and eternally.

No conspiracy goes unnoticed. No assignment against my destiny remains unpunished. The blood demands reckoning, and I trust You to act righteously. Let Your vengeance cleanse our name, secure our honor, and terrify the enemy. Let the cry of the blood no longer echo unanswered.

Father, uphold us. Let the enemy quake at the voice of vengeance mixed with mercy. Let my family walk in vindication, not defeat. You are our Judge and our Avenger, and under Your blood-wrought justice, we stand vindicated.

In Jesus' name, Amen.

PRESERVATION

Sustained on the Sickbed

"Yahweh will sustain him on his sickbed..."
— Psalm 41:3 WEB

Merciful Healer, You are the God who sits by the bed of the afflicted. When others flee in fear, You draw near with comfort and power. I thank You that Your presence is my family's hospital room, and Your blood is the medicine of miracles.

Even when strength fails, You lift. Even when breath is weak, You breathe. I decree that anyone in my household fighting illness — be it physical, emotional, or mental — is now sustained by divine power. You are raising them up from the sickbed. You are turning the tide of affliction into recovery.

Lord, let Your healing hand lay upon every part of our bodies that need Your touch. Where doctors see no improvement, You release restoration. Where we've grown weary, You infuse hope. We are not forsaken; we are sustained — because Your blood never loses its power.

In Jesus' name, Amen.

PROSPERITY

No More Guilt, Only Grace

> "For this is my blood of the new covenant, which is poured out for many for the remission of sins."
> — Matthew 26:28 WEB

Redeeming Savior, I rejoice in the blood that has forever erased my guilt. Every trace of sin, shame, and unworthiness has been washed away. I am no longer disqualified. I am righteous by the blood, and therefore, prosperity can no longer be hindered.

I break agreement with every lie that says I don't deserve abundance. The blood says I'm clean. The Cross says I'm worthy. I reject condemnation and walk in holy confidence. My financial increase is not based on perfection—it's rooted in the remission of sin.

Let my family live free—free from the shame of past mistakes, free from the fear of judgment, free to prosper with joy. We walk boldly into the inheritance Jesus died to give us. The stain is gone. The door is open. The blessing flows freely.

In Jesus' name, Amen.

PEACE

Peace in Reconciliation

> "But all things are of God, who reconciled us to himself through Jesus Christ, and gave to us the ministry of reconciliation."
> — 2 Corinthians 5:18 WEB

Father of Mercy, I thank You for reconciling me to Yourself through the blood of Jesus. Because I have peace with You, I declare peace in every relationship connected to my life and my family.

Lord, by this covenant, I break the power of offense, bitterness, and division. Let every wall that separates hearts be torn down. Where misunderstandings have grown roots, let truth and love uproot them. The blood of reconciliation speaks unity, and I declare that we shall walk in its power.

Make our home a dwelling of harmony, where the love of Christ is our language and peace is our atmosphere. Restore the bridges that have burned, and mend the ties that have frayed. We embrace the ministry of reconciliation and walk in the joy of restored fellowship. In Jesus' name, Amen.

DAY 38

PARDON

Receiving God's Full Forgiveness

> "I will remember their sins no more."
> — Hebrews 8:12 WEB

Gracious God, Your memory is perfect—yet You choose to forget. You don't just forgive my sins, You refuse to remember them. You don't hold them over my head or revisit them later. Your forgiveness is full, final, and freeing.

Let this truth break every chain of regret. If You don't remember it, I won't relive it. I release every self-accusing thought. I walk away from the prison of my past and into the peace of divine forgetfulness. Your blood has erased the record, and my heart is free.

For my family, I declare this same release. Let no member of our household carry guilt You've already removed. Let the power of forgiveness flow like a river—washing over every relationship, healing every wound, and silencing every accuser.

In Jesus' name, Amen.

PROTECTION

THE BLOOD SILENCES EVERY ACCUSER

> "Who could bring a charge against God's chosen ones? It is God who justifies."
> —Romans 8:33 WEB

Justifier and Redeemer, I lift my voice today in the courtroom of heaven. I stand covered in the blood that silences every accusation. My family is not at the mercy of hell's opinions—we are justified by the blood!

Every charge the enemy has formed, every curse spoken, every lie released, is now rendered null and void. I decree: Let the blood answer! Let the accuser be silenced! Let every generational curse be broken, every legal ground dissolved.

We are chosen and covered. The blood testifies louder than any voice of guilt or shame. My household is shielded from condemnation. We are the righteousness of God in Christ. No tongue that rises against us shall prosper.

Father, thank You that Your verdict over us is "JUSTIFIED." The Judge of all the earth has ruled in our favor, and the blood is our defense. In Jesus' name, Amen.

PREVAIL

COVENANT RIGHTS DEPLOYED

"Behold, the blood of the covenant…"
—Exodus 24:8 WEB

Creator God, I see Your covenant signed in blood and declare that its rights are active in every realm of our life. I claim every covenant provision—protection, presence, promise—against spiritual attack. We step into warfare with heavenly rights: healing, deliverance, peace, destiny. The blood is not silent—it speaks covenant.

I enforce those rights now. I walk under the cover of promise. I invoke the blood that sealed our presence before You, the blood that built altars and released angels. My family and I enact that covenant in daily battle. Every threat that rises meets covenant authority, and every scheme against our joy dissolves under the weight of Your rights.

Father, activate that covenant in our bloodline. Let children, generations, and unseen realms know: we are sealed, safeguarded, and sovereign through the covenant. The enemy may wage war—but covenant wins.

In Jesus' name, Amen.

PRESERVATION

Flesh Like a Child's

> "...his flesh came again as the flesh of a little child..."
> — Job 33:25 WEB

God of miracles and marvels, I praise You for the promise of full restoration. I receive that promise for myself and for every member of my family. Where sickness has left scars, let Your healing restore. Where disease has aged us prematurely, let Your blood rejuvenate.

Let our flesh be renewed like the flesh of a child — soft, whole, untouched by trauma or decay. I speak to aging joints, failing organs, thinning skin, and weary bones: Be restored. I call for divine regeneration — not only healing from pain, but a reversal of its effects.

Let youthfulness spring up again by the power of the blood. Let vitality, strength, and energy return. We will not grow old in affliction, but strong in the Lord. By covenant, our days shall be long, fruitful, and full of health. Our flesh shall bear witness to the blood that makes all things new.

In Jesus' name, Amen.

PROSPERITY

Abrahamic Wealth Flows to Me

> "Abram was very rich in livestock, in silver, and in gold."
> — Genesis 13:2 WEB

God of Abraham, Isaac, and Jacob, I declare that I am a child of the covenant. What flowed to Abraham now flows to me through the blood of Jesus. I step into covenant wealth—not by lineage of the flesh, but by the lineage of faith.

Make my household rich—not just in possessions, but in purpose. Let silver and gold serve the mission. Let our wealth be proof of Your faithfulness. You made Abraham rich, and You've not changed. What You did then, You do now—through the better covenant sealed in Christ's blood.

I refuse to settle for less than what You promised. I receive land, legacy, and livestock in whatever form it takes today—properties, businesses, influence, and divine ideas. Let my children grow up in the atmosphere of abundance. Let our family story echo the testimony of Abraham.

In Jesus' name, Amen.

PEACE

CLEANSED FROM GUILT'S GRIP

> "According to the law, nearly everything is cleansed with blood, and apart from shedding of blood there is no remission."
> — Hebrews 9:22 WEB

Holy God, I thank You that the blood of Jesus has cleansed me and my family from every stain of sin. The heavy yoke of guilt is broken, and peace floods the places where shame once lived.

Lord, I refuse to carry burdens that the cross has already lifted. The voice of accusation is silenced, and the courtroom of Heaven has ruled us free. We are not condemned; we are cleansed. We are not stained; we are spotless by the blood.

Let this cleansing open the door for complete emotional healing. Let our hearts rest in the truth that nothing stands between us and Your presence. We walk in peace, we breathe in peace, and we live in the joy of the forgiven. In Jesus' name, Amen.

DAY 39

PARDON

JOY IN DIVINE FORGIVENESS

"Blessed is he whose disobedience is forgiven..."
— Psalm 32:1 WEB

Lord, I rejoice in Your forgiveness! You didn't wait for me to fix myself—you stepped in while I was still in disobedience and offered grace. And now, I am blessed—truly, deeply, irreversibly blessed—because You've forgiven me.

Let this joy be more than a moment. Let it fill my days and fuel my worship. I am not under wrath—I am under blessing. Not because I earned it, but because Jesus paid for it with His own blood. Let the freedom of that truth bring laughter to my heart and peace to my soul.

Over my household, I declare joy. Where shame once sat, let singing arise. Where regret lingered, let rejoicing break forth. We are a forgiven family—blessed not by what we've done, but by what Christ has done for us.

In Jesus' name, Amen.

PROTECTION

Renewed Covering by Atoning Blood

> "Aaron shall make atonement on its horns once in the year... with the blood of the sin offering."
> —Exodus 30:10 WEB

Merciful High Priest, I thank You that atonement is not a thing of the past—it is alive today through Your eternal blood. I bring my family under the yearly renewal of covering, established forever through the Lamb.

Every cycle of evil is broken. Every unrepented sin is cleansed. Every spiritual door is closed. We are not uncovered—we are atoned for! The blood on the altar has secured perpetual protection for our household.

Father, let this divine transaction be renewed upon our lives. As Aaron anointed the altar once a year, so I plead the blood afresh over every altar in my life—family, work, worship, and destiny. Let Your mercy speak louder than our faults. Let Your grace shield us again.

We are not exposed to the devourer. The blood still works, still covers, still cries out for us. Thank You for atonement that never expires. In Jesus' name, Amen.

PREVAIL

Superior Voice of Jesus' Blood

> "The voice of your brother's blood cries…"
> —Genesis 4:10 WEB

Righteous Judge, You spoke that Abel's blood called out from the ground. Yet that voice of Jesus' blood is superior—it cries life, restoration, justice, and vindication. I release the voice of that blood over every broken part of my life and my family's story. Let it speak where accusation roars, where generational shame lingers, where failure echoes.

That voice speaks louder than any foe. It demands justice, restoration, healing, deliverance, and destiny. Let every false witness be silenced. Let every crime against us be heard and repaired. Let every stolen moment be recovered. The voice of the Lamb's blood is louder than crime, death, bitterness.

Father, let that voice resonate now. Let the enemy quake. Let oppressed heartlines rise. My family shall not be defined by injustice but by the voice that demands right. We walk resurrected, redeemed, vindicated by blood.

In Jesus' name, Amen.

PRESERVATION

Look and Live

> "...and it happened that if a snake had bitten any man, when he looked at the bronze serpent, he lived."
> — Numbers 21:9 WEB

Jehovah Rapha, my eyes are fixed on the cross, the fulfillment of the bronze serpent lifted in the wilderness. I turn away from the symptoms and look upon Your sacrifice. As the Israelites lived by a single gaze, so I declare that my family and I shall live — whole and unharmed — by the power of Your blood.

Where the venom of the enemy has poisoned bodies and minds, let the cross now neutralize it. I rebuke every serpent of infirmity, chronic fatigue, and mysterious conditions. Let every sting of death be swallowed up in victory. We look upon the crucified Christ, and we live!

Not merely survive — but live abundantly. Live with joy, strength, and divine health. We are not snake-bitten victims. We are cross-covered victors. Healing is not a wish but a covenant reality, because our eyes are on the Lamb.

In Jesus' name, Amen.

PROSPERITY

Equipped for Prosperity

> "Now may the God of peace... through the blood of the eternal covenant... make you complete in every good work, to do his will..."
> — Hebrews 13:20–21 WEB

God of Peace and Purpose, I thank You for the blood of the eternal covenant that equips me with everything needed for abundance. I am not lacking—I am complete. I have everything I need to walk in divine prosperity and to fulfill my assignment.

Make me skilled in stewardship, strong in wisdom, and sharp in discernment. Equip my family to carry the weight of blessing without being crushed. Let every good work be supplied—nothing missing, nothing broken. Through the blood, You've not only redeemed me, but resourced me.

May the work of our hands prosper because Your hand is upon us. Let our lives reflect the completeness that comes from You alone. We lack no good thing, because we serve a good God. Through the eternal blood covenant, we are empowered for eternal results.

In Jesus' name, Amen.

PEACE

Peace as God's Purchased Possession

> "Take heed, therefore, to yourselves and to all the flock, in which the Holy Spirit has made you overseers, to shepherd the assembly of the Lord and God which he purchased with his own blood."
> — Acts 20:28 WEB

Righteous Father, I rejoice that I am not my own—I was bought with a price, the precious blood of Jesus. My worth is not determined by the world but by the value You placed on me.

I declare over my family that we are God's treasured possession, carried close to His heart. Because we belong to You, no evil can snatch us from Your hand, and no storm can unsettle our peace. The blood that purchased us has also sealed us, and that seal cannot be broken.

Lord, let our identity in You become the anchor of our souls. Let peace be the fruit of knowing we are wanted, chosen, and eternally loved. We will not live in fear of abandonment or rejection, for the One who bought us will keep us forever. In Jesus' name, Amen.

DAY 40

PARDON

FREEDOM FROM LEGAL ACCUSATIONS

> "…blotting out the handwriting… against us…"
> — Colossians 2:14 WEB

Jesus, thank You for canceling every legal accusation against me. Every charge the enemy wrote down—every sinful word, thought, and deed—was nailed to Your cross and blotted out by Your blood. The case is closed, and the record is gone.

I refuse to live under the voice of accusation any longer. The handwriting was real, but so was the cross. And Your blood was enough. Let peace fill my mind where torment once ruled. Let me walk freely, fully assured that no charge can stick when You've wiped the record clean.

Over my family, I break every lingering guilt, every legal hold of darkness. The handwriting has been erased. The enemy has lost his case. We walk in freedom, in peace, and in the finished work of the cross.

In Jesus' name, Amen.

PROTECTION

HEDGE OF PROTECTION BY THE BLOOD

> "Haven't you made a hedge around him and around his house and around all that he has, on every side?"
> —Job 1:10 WEB

Faithful Protector, I declare today that my household is surrounded. You have built a hedge that no enemy can breach. This is not mere favor—it is blood-wrought defense. The same hedge that covered Job now covers me, through the blood of Jesus.

Around my family, You've placed fire. Around our health, You've stationed angels. Around our property, You've drawn the line with Your crimson power. Every side is defended. No back door left open. No hidden gate exposed.

Let this hedge remain unbroken. Let no curse jump it. Let no witchcraft scale it. The blood is the boundary! The hedge is the testimony! My children play within its safety. My spouse and I labor under its shade.

Thank You for divine perimeter. Thank You for surrounding love. Thank You for the ever-working power of the blood. We dwell securely inside the hedge. In Jesus' name, Amen.

PREVAIL

Christ, Warrior in Blood

> "...their lifeblood is sprinkled on my garments..."
> —Isaiah 63:1-3 WEB

Lord Jesus, Mighty Warrior, I behold You returning from battle, garments drenched in victory blood—the very blood of enemies defeated by Your supremacy. You are soaked in triumph. I stand with You, clothed in that same victory, sealed in preserved promise. My battles are won before they begin.

Where enemy blood once marked defeat, we now walk in You. The blood on Your garments is my assurance. Every stronghold is shattered. Every tyrant's judgment crushed. My family stands with the blood-stained Warrior, not as survivors but as heirs of conquest. We are robed in triumph.

Father, let that victorious power radiate through us. Let oppressive regimes within our family tree collapse. Let the fragrance of victory uplift every corner of our home. We follow the Warrior drenched in red—into peace, into provision, and into eternal victory.

In Jesus' name, Amen.

PRESERVATION

HEALTH AND PROSPERITY BY BLOOD

> "Beloved, I pray that you may prosper in all things
> and be healthy, even as your soul prospers."
> — 3 John 1:2 WEB

Lord of the Covenant, I stand on the eternal prayer released by Your Word — that I and my family may prosper and be in health, even as our souls prosper. I receive this blessing through the power of the blood that purchased wholeness for every area of our lives.

Let our souls be sanctified, our minds renewed, and our emotions stabilized — and let that prosperity ripple through our bones, muscles, organs, and cells. No part of us shall lag behind. What You have joined in Your will — prosperity and health — I join now in prayer.

I come against anything that separates prosperity from health — stress, overwork, anxiety, compromise. Let the blood be our balance. Let the blood be our alignment. We prosper not in spite of our health but because we are rooted in Christ's full redemption.

In Jesus' name, Amen.

PROSPERITY

My Year is Crowned

> "You crown the year with your bounty. Your carts overflow with abundance."
> — Psalm 65:11 WEB

Lord of the Harvest, I decree that this is the year of divine abundance. You have crowned it—marked it, blessed it, and filled it with Your goodness. I step into each month with faith, each day with favor, and each hour with expectancy. Your carts overflow, and I ride in the river of Your plenty.

Let every month bring fruit. Let every season produce joy. My family will not survive the year—we will thrive in it. Your blood has already purchased the blessing, and we simply walk in it. No more begging. No more barrenness. The year has been crowned.

I speak over my household: this year, we will see increase like never before. Projects will prosper, debts will dissolve, ideas will ignite. We will eat in plenty and praise the name of the Lord. The blood is speaking, and it speaks overflow.

In Jesus' name, Amen.

PEACE

Peace in the Family Circle

> "...and might reconcile them both in one body to God through the cross, having killed the hostility through it."
> — Ephesians 2:16 WEB

Prince of Peace, I thank You for the cross that ends hostility and restores harmony. I speak Your blood-bought reconciliation into every strained relationship in my family.

Lord, where there has been distance, let there be closeness. Where there has been anger, let forgiveness flow. Where coldness has settled in, let the warmth of love return. The blood of Jesus has ended the war and signed the treaty of peace over our home.

I declare that our conversations will be seasoned with grace, our disagreements clothed with understanding, and our fellowship marked by joy. Let the peace of Christ reign over our meals, our gatherings, and our everyday moments. By the power of the cross, our family stands united in love. In Jesus' name, Amen.

DAY 41

PARDON

DECLARING JESUS AS SAVIOR

> "She shall give birth to a son. You shall name him Jesus, for it is he who shall save his people from their sins."
> — Matthew 1:21 WEB

Righteous Redeemer, I boldly declare that Jesus is my Savior, the One appointed by heaven to rescue me from sin's grip. No other name carries the power to cleanse, transform, and deliver. I embrace the full authority of Your saving work. Sin no longer defines me—salvation through Your blood now shapes my destiny.

Let this salvation speak over my household. Every bondage is broken, every stain removed, every chain shattered. We are not a people of guilt—we are a people of grace. Because Jesus saves, no sin is too deep, no pattern too long-standing. We are rescued, redeemed, and released by Your mercy.

Today, I walk in the identity of the saved. I declare peace over my past, freedom in my present, and hope for my future. And my family shall walk in the same. The blood of Jesus is our legacy, our banner, and our shield. We live because the Savior has come—and His name is Jesus.

In Jesus' name, Amen.

PROTECTION

Walk in Strength and Wholeness

> "He brought them out with silver and gold. There was not one feeble person among his tribes."
> — Psalm 105:37 WEB

O Lord, my Mighty Redeemer, I stand under the protection of the same covenant that brought Your people out of bondage whole, strong, and lacking nothing. By the power of Jesus' blood, I declare that weakness, disease, and infirmity have no hold over me or my household. Let the same force that raised Israel in strength now surge through every fiber of our being.

Father, I release the blood of Jesus into every cell, every system, and every function of our bodies. Let divine vitality flood our bones, energy return to our limbs, and mental clarity be restored. We shall not grow weary, and we shall not be worn down by affliction or fatigue. We walk in supernatural stamina, preserved by the covenant of strength sealed in Jesus' blood.

I decree over my family that no one among us shall be feeble. No child shall be weak, no spouse shall be downcast, no parent shall be broken. Strength is our portion and vitality our inheritance. The blood speaks power into our physical frame and sets a divine standard of wellness.

Thank You, Jesus, for making us a tribe of the unbroken and undefeated. In Jesus' name, Amen.

PREVAIL

REBUKING THE ACCUSER THROUGH BLOOD AUTHORITY

"Yahweh said to Satan, 'Yahweh rebuke you, Satan!'"
—Zechariah 3:2 WEB

O Sovereign Judge of Heaven, I stand under the authority of the blood that speaks louder than any accusation! I come boldly before You, clothed not in my own righteousness but in the righteousness of Christ, declared clean and worthy because of His precious blood. Today, I invoke the power of Your divine rebuke against every voice of the accuser rising against me and my family.

By the blood of Jesus, I silence the tongue of every lying spirit, every whisper of guilt, shame, or condemnation that seeks to penetrate our minds and hearts. Let the same fire that fell when You rebuked Satan fall now upon every satanic interference in our lives. I declare that no accusation, no legal claim, and no curse shall stand against the covenant of grace that covers me and my household.

Because of the blood, I am no longer on trial—I am justified. My family is not under the court of condemnation, but the mercy seat of Christ's eternal redemption. We walk free and confident, knowing the Lord Himself rebukes every enemy that rises up against us.

In Jesus' name, Amen.

PRESERVATION

IMMEDIATE HEALING BY CONTACT

> "Immediately the flow of her blood was dried up, and she felt in her body that she was healed of her affliction."
> — Mark 5:29 WEB

O Lord of sudden breakthroughs, I come boldly into Your healing flow. You are the God who turns desperation into transformation, and I press into Your blood with expectancy. Let the same power that surged through the woman with the issue of blood be released into my body and my household. I declare that the same healing virtue that flowed from Your Son flows into us now.

I align myself with the hem of Christ's garment, that place where blood, righteousness, and mercy meet. By faith, I make contact. Let every chronic condition dissolve. Let inherited infirmities be uprooted. I speak immediate restoration over every organ, system, and cell in our bodies. We touch the covenant by faith and declare that healing manifests now.

My family and I are no longer spectators—we are recipients. That same tangible healing, that undeniable shift in the physical realm, invades our lives. As Your healing power surged through that woman's frame, so let Your blood surge through every area of pain, lack, or affliction in my household.

In Jesus' name, Amen.

PROSPERITY

Days in Prosperity, Years in Pleasure

> "If they listen and serve him, they shall spend their days in prosperity, and their years in pleasures."
> — Job 36:11 WEB

Majestic Father, I step into the promise of covenant prosperity through the obedience You empower. I don't labor under obligation, I walk in joyful surrender. My ears are tuned to Your voice, and my heart is ready to follow. Because I listen and serve You, I lay claim to days filled with abundance and years filled with joy.

Let every area of my life—my health, my home, my business, my finances, and my family—come into alignment with the decree of this Word. May our household be a testimony that obedience is not a burden but a blessed pathway to overflow. As I serve You with integrity, You crown my life with satisfaction.

Let my children live in the fruit of my yieldedness. Let their days be long and their paths be straight. We are not trapped in toil—we are tethered to Your goodness. I reject every lie that says prosperity is for others. I declare: our family will spend our days in prosperity, and our years in pleasures, because we walk in covenant obedience.

In Jesus' name, Amen.

PEACE

Peaceful Life Through Righteous Blood

> The work of righteousness will be peace, and the effect of righteousness, quietness and confidence forever.
> — Isaiah 32:17 WEB

Righteous King, I thank You for clothing me and my household in the robe of righteousness purchased by the blood of Your Son. Because of that holy blood, the verdict over my life is no longer condemnation but divine acquittal. I decree that the righteousness of Christ works in us today, producing a peace that cannot be shattered and a quietness that storms cannot disturb.

By the power of the cross, I silence every voice of accusation, fear, and unrest that would war against our minds. The righteousness imputed to us becomes a shield, and the peace it produces becomes a river flowing through our home, our relationships, and our inner thoughts. Every hidden anxiety must bow to the Prince of Peace who reigns in our midst.

Lord, let this confidence in Your finished work be unshakable. Cause our lives to radiate the calm authority of those who know they stand blameless before You. May our very atmosphere testify that righteousness bears fruit in peace, and that our home is a sanctuary under the crimson covering of Christ's sacrifice. In Jesus' name, Amen.

DAY 42

PARDON

Christ Our Ransom

> "Then he is gracious to him, and says, 'Deliver him from going down to the pit. I have found a ransom.'"
> — Job 33:24 WEB

Holy Deliverer, I praise You for the ransom that was found—Jesus Christ, the Lamb who took my place. I was destined for the pit, condemned by guilt, and unworthy of redemption, but You spoke mercy and provided blood. The cross became my rescue, and the grave lost its grip.

You didn't delay or debate my worth; You declared it by offering Christ. My soul rejoices in this divine exchange. The sentence over me and my family has been revoked. The curse has no claim, and death has no power. The ransom has been paid—and paid in full by the precious blood of Jesus.

I stand today not as one condemned, but as one delivered. I lift my voice in freedom and call my family into the same liberty. We will not return to the pit; we belong to the redeemed. The ransom speaks louder than accusation. The ransom speaks peace.

In Jesus' name, Amen.

PROTECTION

Cancel Every Weapon Formed

> "No weapon that is formed against you will prevail..."
> — Isaiah 54:17 WEB

Almighty Defender, by the authority of the blood of Jesus, I dismantle every weapon that has been fashioned against me and my household. No arrow, curse, hex, or strategy of the wicked shall penetrate the covering You have placed around us. Let every plan of darkness crumble before it takes form.

I invoke the blood of Jesus as our impenetrable shield. Every spoken curse is reversed. Every spiritual attack is rendered powerless. Every demonic plot is exposed and neutralized. We stand untouched because the blood renders every weapon ineffective and every accusation void.

Let the blood nullify generational curses, break ancestral pacts, and terminate lingering assaults in the spirit. My family walks in an atmosphere where weapons disappear before impact. The blood of Jesus renders every strategy of hell null and void.

Father, You have declared our vindication comes from You, and the blood ensures our victory. Therefore, I decree: no weapon formed shall prosper today, tomorrow, or ever again. In Jesus' name, Amen.

PREVAIL

Refusing the Thief Access Through the Blood Wall

> "The thief comes only to steal, kill, and destroy. I came that they may have life, and may have it abundantly."
> —John 10:10 WEB

Blood of Jesus, build a wall around my home! Eternal God, I lift my voice as a watchman over my household. I stand in the covenant of life and abundance, purchased with blood. I decree that the thief has no right, no access, and no claim over anything that belongs to me or my family.

We are not prey to destruction; we are protected by the covenant of Christ. I shut every spiritual door left open through ignorance, generational patterns, or fear. Let the blood of the Lamb mark the thresholds of our lives, and may every work of the destroyer be stopped in its tracks.

Let angelic warriors be stationed at every gate. Let abundance flow, and death be halted. By the blood of Jesus, I reverse every plan of the enemy—stolen peace, stolen dreams, stolen time must now be restored sevenfold. We are kept by the Blood Wall, surrounded by the life of God.

In Jesus' name, Amen.

PRESERVATION

Healing Answer to My Prayer

> "...I have heard your prayer. I have seen your tears. Behold, I will add fifteen years to your life."
> — Isaiah 38:5 WEB

Faithful Father, Healer of the broken, I thank You that You hear and respond. Just as You answered Hezekiah's cry, I believe You are answering mine. You have seen my tears and the silent pain in the night. You have not ignored the afflictions that have touched my body or the bodies of my loved ones.

With confidence, I receive the divine reversal of disease. Where death once loomed, life now flows. I call forth divine extensions, miraculous recoveries, and redemptive healing in the name of Jesus. Lord, add years to our lives—not just in quantity, but in vitality. Let my household testify of restored strength, renewed youth, and supernatural turnaround.

I decree that every diagnosis is subject to divine interruption. You are the God who overrules doctor's reports and lengthens days by Your mercy. Thank You for healing flowing through time, bloodlines, and generations. May we arise as living testimonies of answered prayer and extended purpose.

In Jesus' name, Amen.

PROSPERITY

Prosper in All You Do

> "Keep therefore the words of this covenant and do them, that you may prosper in all that you do."
> — Deuteronomy 29:9 WEB

Faithful Covenant-Keeper, I declare that my life is built on the blood-bought promises of Your Word. I choose today to honor and keep the covenant not by my strength, but by the Spirit's power. I receive the grace to walk in Your ways so that I may prosper in all that I do.

Let nothing in my life be untouched by this promise. Let my decisions prosper, my relationships prosper, my parenting prosper, my career prosper, and my household flourish. Because of the covenant, prosperity is not just a possibility—it is my portion. I reject smallness and failure, and I embrace Your grace for total life prosperity.

Let my family be known as a people who do well because they live well with You. Let the fruit of this covenant show up in our finances, our dreams, and the works of our hands. Prosperity is not a random occurrence—it is the inevitable result of covenant alignment. I walk in this promise with confidence.

In Jesus' name, Amen.

PEACE

Hope and Peace

> Now may the God of hope fill you with all joy and peace in believing, that you may abound in hope, in the power of the Holy Spirit.
> — Romans 15:13 WEB

God of all hope, I lift my heart before You, cleansed and opened by the blood of Jesus. You are the source of every pure joy and the fountain of unshakable peace. Through the covenant of the cross, You have made room in my spirit for the overflow of divine expectation.

Today, I declare that my family and I are vessels for Your peace. Every trace of despair, discouragement, and heaviness is expelled by the life-giving power of Your Spirit. The blood that was shed on Calvary dismantles hopelessness and makes way for a supernatural confidence in Your promises. Joy rises like the morning sun in our hearts, breaking the grip of night.

Lord, let Your peace settle deep in our minds, not as a fleeting feeling but as a governing force. May hope overflow in us until it touches every relationship, every decision, and every season of life. We are rooted in the unchanging truth that the God of hope has filled us and will keep filling us. In Jesus' name, Amen.

DAY 43

PARDON

God's Mercy Not Based on Merit

> "I, even I, am he who blots out your transgressions for my own sake; and I will not remember your sins."
> — Isaiah 43:25 WEB

Compassionate Father, I worship You for the mystery of Your mercy. You chose to blot out my sins not because I earned it, but because You desired it. Your mercy flows from Your heart—not from my merit. You remember my failures no more, and that brings rest to my soul.

You delight in pardoning Your children. You silence the voice of the accuser with Your own declaration: forgiven. I do not strive for acceptance—I stand in it. Because of Your covenant, my family and I are shielded from judgment. We are covered by the blood that speaks peace and pardon.

Today, I lean into this mercy. I do not try to repay it, only to receive it. I declare over my life and my family that we are no longer defined by transgressions but by grace. Your mercy rewrites our story. We walk boldly, because the blood has made a way.

In Jesus' name, Amen.

PROTECTION

God's Army, Fearless and Ready

> "With us is Yahweh our God to help us and to fight our battles."
> — 2 Chronicles 32:8 WEB

Lord of Hosts, I rise today in the assurance that You, O Mighty Warrior, are with me. The blood of Jesus has enlisted my family into a divine battalion that cannot be outnumbered or outmatched. You help us. You fight for us. And because of that, we shall not fear.

We take our stand under the covenant of blood, fearless and fortified. I decree over my home that fear shall not paralyze, worry shall not consume, and doubt shall not reign. The sound of divine warfare echoes in our atmosphere—Yahweh is near!

Let every demonic intimidation melt before the presence of the blood. Let terror be silenced, and torment broken. I call forth holy confidence in my children, boldness in my spouse, and unwavering trust in my soul. We do not fight alone; the Lord our God is our shield and strength.

So today we march forward, not in our own strength but under the banner of divine blood protection. No enemy can stand when God is with us. In Jesus' name, Amen.

PREVAIL

Canceling Guilt and Shame in Spiritual Warfare

> "For this is my blood of the new covenant, which is poured out for many for the remission of sins."
> —Matthew 26:28 WEB

Merciful Redeemer, thank You for the blood poured out to cancel my sins. I lift my hands in holy gratitude that I am no longer bound by guilt or chained by shame. In the courtroom of heaven, I plead the blood over every accusation from my past that still seeks a voice.

Let every reminder of failure be silenced. I declare my conscience purified and my spirit restored. My family and I are not defined by what we've done but by what Christ has done for us. The accuser's evidence is now inadmissible—the blood has covered it all.

With hearts cleansed, we rise into warfare not as defeated sinners but as washed warriors. Shame will not rob us of confidence. Guilt will not paralyze our prayers. We fight boldly, serve joyfully, and stand firm in righteousness. The blood has cleared our name and secured our place.

In Jesus' name, Amen.

PRESERVATION

PROTECTION FOR BONES AND CORE

> "He protects all of his bones. Not one of them is broken."
> — Psalm 34:20 WEB

O Yahweh my Protector, I decree that my body and the bodies of my loved ones are hidden within the covenant of unbreakable preservation. As Christ's bones were guarded from fracture, so let our skeletal systems, inner structures, and marrow receive supernatural protection through the blood of the Lamb.

I declare divine shielding over our bones, spines, joints, and vital systems. Let calcium levels, cellular structures, ligaments, and cartilage align with the life of God. No breaks, no fractures, no degeneration. Every weakness is reversed by the power of the cross. I speak strength and alignment into our entire skeletal framework.

Let our very structure testify to the faithfulness of the covenant. May no condition that targets the bones—like osteoporosis, arthritis, or fractures—find a place to land in our household. By the blood that preserves, I decree full-body integrity, flexibility, and divine mobility over every member of my family.

In Jesus' name, Amen.

PROSPERITY

Open the Windows of Heaven

> "Bring the whole tithe into the storehouse... I will open the windows of heaven for you, and pour you out a blessing..."
> — Malachi 3:10 WEB

God of Overflow, I lift my eyes to the heavens and declare: my obedience unlocks the storehouses of abundance. I bring my tithe not out of duty but out of devotion, because the blood has already secured every promise for me. I do not operate under a curse—I live under an open heaven.

Open the windows of heaven over my life and family. Let what You pour out be so rich, so vast, so undeniable that there is not room enough to contain it. Let resources come from expected and unexpected places. Let favor locate us. Let our barns overflow and our jars never run dry.

I reject the famine mindset. I walk in the economy of heaven, which is fueled by faith and activated by covenant. I am not surviving—I'm thriving. My family will never lack. Our needs are met. Our dreams are funded. Our legacy is secure because we honor You with what is Yours.

In Jesus' name, Amen.

PEACE

CHANNEL OF PEACE

> The fruit of righteousness is sown in peace by those who make peace.
> — James 3:18 WEB

Lord of the Harvest, I thank You that the blood of Jesus has made me a sower of peace in a world of conflict. Because I am redeemed, I will plant seeds of righteousness in the soil of peace, knowing that what is sown in the Spirit will bear eternal fruit.

Let my words, my actions, and my very presence release the fragrance of Christ wherever I go. The cross has reconciled me to God and to others; therefore, I will not allow strife, bitterness, or division to take root in my home or in my heart. The peace of the covenant flows through me like a living river, nurturing every relationship and calming every storm.

Holy Spirit, make my family a living testimony that the work of the blood produces harmony. Let our lives become fertile ground where peace multiplies, influencing generations yet to come. May we walk as peacemakers who carry the authority of the cross, turning hearts toward righteousness. In Jesus' name, Amen.

DAY 44

PARDON

RETURNING TO THE FATHER THROUGH GRACE

> "He arose, and came to his father. But while he was still far off, his father saw him, and was moved with compassion, and ran, and fell on his neck, and kissed him."
> — Luke 15:20 WEB

Abba Father, I arise and return to You today. Even while I was far off, You saw me. Your eyes never left me, and Your arms never closed. The kiss of Your acceptance is my peace, and the embrace of Your grace is my restoration. I come home—not to judgment, but to joy.

You ran to me with mercy. You clothed me, fed me, and restored me. And You've done the same for my household. Though we strayed, Your love never did. Though we wandered, Your covenant remained. Your blood has made the way back, and we walk it boldly.

I declare that no shame shall keep us from Your embrace. No failure shall disqualify us from Your table. We are sons and daughters, not servants of shame. You've run to us, and now we run in freedom, wrapped in robes of righteousness. In Jesus' name, Amen.

PROTECTION

BLOOD ROUTES EVERY ATTACK

> "Yahweh will cause your enemies who rise up against you to be struck before you."
> — Deuteronomy 28:7 WEB

Victorious God, I rise and call on the blood of Jesus to route every enemy before they reach our gates. Let the enemy that rises up against me and my family meet a force far greater than their own. Let Your blood go ahead of us as a blazing defense.

Father, any attack planned in secret, launched in darkness, or whispered by the wicked—let it be reversed. Let confusion fall upon the enemy's camp. As the blood speaks, may every ambush be exposed, every plot be shattered, and every advance be turned to retreat.

I release this same protection over my children, spouse, loved ones, and spiritual community. Let every attack—physical, emotional, or spiritual—be deflected by the covenant blood. We shall not fear what rises against us because what rises against us shall fall.

Thank You, Lord, for securing our every step and striking down those who would do us harm before they ever reach us. In Jesus' name, Amen.

PREVAIL

Letting the Blood Speak Over Conflict and Accusation

> "…to Jesus, the mediator of a new covenant, and to the blood of sprinkling that speaks better things than that of Abel."
> —Hebrews 12:24 WEB

Lord Jesus, Mediator of my covenant, I thank You that Your blood still speaks! I call upon its voice now to speak over every place of conflict, warfare, and accusation surrounding me and my family. Let the blood be louder than the words of men, louder than curses, louder than slander.

Where the enemy seeks to divide, I release the voice of peace. Where offense seeks a foothold, I release the voice of forgiveness. Let the testimony of Your blood override bitterness, rejection, and every strife sent to scatter what You have joined.

I declare that my household is governed by the verdict of heaven—"Redeemed, Restored, Justified." Let the blood speak healing over our hearts, restoration over relationships, and vindication in every place of spiritual contention.

In Jesus' name, Amen.

PRESERVATION

Total Removal of All Sickness

"Yahweh will take away from you all sickness…"
— Deuteronomy 7:15 WEB

Mighty Deliverer, You are not a partial healer, You are the God of full cleansing. I stand in agreement with Your word and declare that every trace of sickness is being removed from my life and my family. Let the purifying power of Jesus' blood flush out every hidden affliction, lingering virus, and generational condition.

You are the God who takes away—not who tolerates. Remove every diagnosis, every label, every internal imbalance. Let Your fire sweep through our bloodstream, immune systems, and nervous systems. I declare that autoimmune disorders are overturned, and inflammation is consumed by the fire of the covenant.

Father, let this be the generation that walks in divine wholeness. Let my household be a sign and wonder of complete healing. As we obey You, we walk into divine health. Not one disease will return, and no new one will find place. We are blood-covered, fully preserved, and perpetually whole.

In Jesus' name, Amen.

PROSPERITY

Freedom from Financial Captivity

> "As for you also, because of the blood of your covenant, I have set free your prisoners from the pit in which is no water."
> — Zechariah 9:11 WEB

Blood-Sealing Deliverer, I declare that every chain of financial captivity over my life and family is broken by the blood of the covenant. You have seen our prison, You have heard our cry, and You have moved with power to set us free from every cycle of lack and limitation.

I speak freedom over every debt, every lingering financial bondage, and every generational curse of poverty. The pit is dry, but the blood is living! We are not stuck—we are released! I prophesy that we are coming out of financial struggle and stepping into surplus. The blood has spoken, and the pit must let go.

My family will no longer be imprisoned by scarcity, fear, or survival. We will walk in the liberty of those whose needs are met and whose futures are secure. Because of the blood, we are not only free—we are fruitful. What once held us will now serve as a platform for praise.

In Jesus' name, Amen.

PEACE

Peace with Enemies

> When a man's ways please Yahweh, he makes even his enemies to be at peace with him.
> — Proverbs 16:7 WEB

Faithful God, I stand under the cleansing stream of Jesus' blood and align my ways with Your will. Because of this covenant, my life is pleasing in Your sight—not by my merit, but by the righteousness of Christ. You have promised that such a life causes even enemies to live in peace with us.

I declare that every source of contention, hostility, and hidden attack is silenced in the presence of the Lord. The blood of the Lamb speaks a better word over my relationships, canceling the power of vengeance and hostility. Every demonic agenda to stir conflict is dismantled by the authority of the cross.

Lord, surround my family with Your shield of favor. Cause even those who once opposed us to walk in civility, respect, and peace. Let Your presence in our lives disarm hostility and establish us in supernatural rest. May our ways continually please You, drawing even adversaries into the sphere of Your reconciling power. In Jesus' name, Amen.

DAY 45

PARDON

BOLD DECLARATION OF FORGIVENESS

> "Be it known to you therefore, brothers, that through this man is proclaimed to you remission of sins."
> — Acts 13:38 WEB

Living Word, I proclaim it boldly and without apology—through Jesus Christ, my sins are forgiven. Not delayed, not pending, but fully remitted. I will not whisper this truth in shame; I will declare it in victory. The blood of Jesus has finished the work.

Let this truth echo in my home. I declare forgiveness over every member of my family. We do not carry guilt passed down through generations. We do not wear labels of failure. We are a forgiven people, called righteous by the blood of the Lamb. His forgiveness rewrites our name.

I embrace this proclamation as my daily confession. Sin's power is broken, its voice silenced, its grip destroyed. The man Christ Jesus has spoken—and I believe it. Forgiveness reigns in this house. Mercy lives in our hearts. And peace is our portion.

In Jesus' name, Amen.

PROTECTION

The Blood Fights My Battles

> "Yahweh will fight for you, and you shall be still."
> — Exodus 14:14 WEB

Warrior God, I lift my eyes and declare that the battle is not mine, but Yours. The blood of Jesus is my signal to the heavens that I am under divine defense. Where I have no strength to fight, Your blood speaks and wins.

Father, arise and contend with those who contend with my family. Let every force of resistance melt in the presence of Your justice. I silence the urge to strive in my own might and instead anchor myself in the blood that never fails.

Every demonic onslaught launched against our progress—be arrested now. Every war against our health, finances, and peace—be overturned by divine intervention. Let the blood of the Lamb stand between us and the fury of the enemy.

I rest in the stillness of victory already won. I shall not be moved, because the Lord Himself fights for me and my house. In Jesus' name, Amen.

PREVAIL

Letting God Fight Your Spiritual Battles

> "...I will contend with him who contends with you,
> and I will save your children."
> —Isaiah 49:25 WEB

Almighty God, my Defender and Contender, rise up and fight on my behalf! I call on the blood covenant that makes You my warrior and makes me Your beloved. Every hand lifted against me and my children must now face the wrath of the Covenant-Keeper.

I step aside and let You take the battlefield. I will not strive in the flesh, for You are my strength. Blood of Jesus, go before me and dismantle every trap, overturn every evil plan, and frustrate every satanic pursuit.

Let every contention in the realm of the spirit be answered with the sword of the Lord. I decree that my family is covered in the protection of divine intervention. You will contend with every disease, accusation, and affliction—You will save our children from harm.

In Jesus' name, Amen.

PRESERVATION

Cleansed in Every Dimension

> "...atonement... to cleanse you from all your sins; you shall be clean before Yahweh."
> — Leviticus 16:30 WEB

Atoning Lamb, I lift my hands in surrender to the cleansing flood of Your blood. I receive divine therapy—body, soul, and spirit. Let the atonement made by Jesus speak over every area of defilement and disease. Cleanse me from sin-rooted illnesses. Let guilt, shame, and every spiritual toxin be washed away.

Today, I declare that my family walks in supernatural purity—not because of our goodness but because of Your atoning sacrifice. Let our minds be sanctified, our emotions purified, our behaviors aligned. We are not a people of spiritual residue; we are a people made whole through the blood that never loses its power.

Cleanse every door we've left open to sickness—through unforgiveness, bitterness, fear, or sin. Wash us until we are whole again. Purify our homes, habits, and heritage. We don't just want to be healed—we want to be clean. Clean before God. Whole before man.

In Jesus' name, Amen.

PROSPERITY

Treasures in Secret Places

> "I will give you the treasures of darkness, and hidden riches of secret places..."
> — Isaiah 45:3 WEB

O God who reveals mysteries, I stand in awe of the hidden wealth You've prepared for those who walk in covenant. You do not just give bread—you reveal buried treasure. You do not just meet needs—you unveil supernatural provision stored in secret places.

I receive revelation today to see what others overlook. Open my eyes to opportunities, strategies, partnerships, and ideas that unlock prosperity for my life and household. Let every secret treasure assigned to my name come into my possession. I declare that nothing hidden shall stay hidden from the righteous.

Let my family walk in the wisdom of divine discovery. Let us possess what was stored for us. We will not live off crumbs when You've prepared treasure. What was hidden is now revealed. What was buried is now released. Because I am blood-covered, I walk with covenant insight to access what the world cannot see.

In Jesus' name, Amen.

PEACE

THE RULING PEACE OF CHRIST'S BLOOD

> And let the peace of Christ rule in your hearts, to which also you were called in one body, and be thankful.
> — Colossians 3:15 WEB

Prince of Peace, I yield the throne of my heart to You alone. By the blood of Your cross, You have purchased my peace, and I refuse to let any other ruler occupy this sacred place. Your peace is not a suggestion—it is the ruling authority over my mind, my emotions, and my household.

I decree that anxiety, fear, and agitation are dethroned in my life. Every disturbance bows to the reigning peace of Christ. My family and I walk in the calling of unity, joined together under one covenant and one Spirit. Gratitude rises in us like incense, for we know this peace is not earned but given through the sacrifice of the Lamb.

Lord, let this ruling peace govern our decisions, our conversations, and our responses. Make our hearts a sanctuary where Your calm reigns unchallenged. May the world see the evidence of Your lordship in the stability of our spirits. In Jesus' name, Amen.

DAY 46

PARDON

Worship From a Forgiven Heart

> "But there is forgiveness with you, therefore you are feared."
> — Psalm 130:4 WEB

Awesome and Holy One, I bow before You with a heart drenched in gratitude. You are not a God who delights in wrath, but One who forgives with depth and desire. Your forgiveness awakens reverence in me—deep, trembling worship birthed from mercy received.

I do not fear You because of punishment—I revere You because of pardon. You forgave me when I couldn't forgive myself. You lifted me from the depths and crowned me with compassion. My soul magnifies You, and my family joins the song. We are not forgotten—we are forgiven.

Let every room in our home be filled with the sound of praise. Let worship rise not from perfection, but from mercy. We bow before You not to earn grace, but to honor it. You are worthy of all our love because You gave all to love us.

In Jesus' name, Amen.

PROTECTION

BLOOD CRIES FOR MY JUSTICE

> "They cried with a loud voice, saying, 'How long... until you judge and avenge our blood...?'"
> — Revelation 6:10 WEB

Righteous Judge, I call upon the power of the blood that still speaks from the throne. Let the blood of Jesus answer every injustice, repay every wrong, and overturn every verdict spoken in darkness against me and my family.

Where there has been betrayal, bring restoration. Where harm was done in secret, bring divine justice in the open. Where our names have been slandered, our destinies tampered with, or our labor stolen, let the blood cry out until heaven moves in our favor.

Father, I stand under the covenant that demands righteousness. The blood of Jesus doesn't cry out for revenge—it cries out for divine justice. Let it speak against premature death, false accusation, and unrighteous loss.

Because of the blood, I declare that we shall be vindicated, recompensed, and restored. Let justice flow like a river into every area where we've been wronged. In Jesus' name, Amen.

PREVAIL

DECLARING YOUR IDENTITY AS AN OVERCOMER

> "He who has an ear, let him hear what the Spirit says... To him who overcomes..."
> —Revelation 2:7 WEB

Eternal Father, I thank You for sealing me as an overcomer through the blood of the Lamb! I don't fight to gain victory—I fight from a position of triumph. I declare that I and my household are not victims of life, but victors in Christ.

By the blood, I overcome fear, weariness, doubt, and delay. Let every identity rooted in trauma or failure be replaced with the mark of an overcomer. The same Spirit that raised Jesus is alive in us, empowering us to win every battle.

I prophesy over my family: we are not going under, we are going over. We rise in the Spirit, we conquer in the Spirit, and we walk in the dominion of those who overcome by the blood and the Word.

In Jesus' name, Amen.

PRESERVATION

Faith Unlocks Healing Power

> "...whom God sent to be an atoning sacrifice, through faith in his blood..."
> — Romans 3:25 WEB

Righteous Redeemer, today I activate my faith in the blood. I come not on the basis of how I feel, but on the authority of what You have finished. Through faith in Your blood, I receive healing, breakthrough, and preservation for myself and my household.

I stir up the covenant power of faith and release it into every weakness. Let every area of doubt be replaced with supernatural confidence. I believe in the blood's power to reverse decay, drive out affliction, and cancel inherited conditions. By faith, I declare that what was impossible is now inevitable.

My faith is not passive—it is active. I release blood-bought healing into our bones, blood, nerves, and muscles. I declare that faith activates heaven's supply and pulls future healing into the present moment. By the blood and through faith, we rise into wholeness.

In Jesus' name, Amen.

PROSPERITY

WHATEVER I DO WILL PROSPER

> "He will be like a tree planted by the streams of water... whatever he does shall prosper."
> — Psalm 1:3 WEB

Rooted and Fruitful God, I plant myself today by the waters of Your Word and covenant. I declare that I am not a wandering branch—I am a well-watered tree. My roots run deep in the truth of who You are, and because of that, everything I touch is blessed.

I decree that my efforts are not in vain. Whatever I do—every project, every meeting, every investment, every plan—shall prosper. I refuse to be moved by what I see. I stand planted in the soil of divine supply, and I draw daily from the rivers of supernatural abundance.

Let my family be trees of prosperity. Let our leaves never wither. Let our fruit never fail. We are not shaken by drought or storms—we flourish in every season. This is our covenant position: productive, prosperous, and planted by the living water of Christ's blood.

In Jesus' name, Amen.

PEACE

Peace Through Obedience by Grace

> Those who love your law have great peace. Nothing causes them to stumble.
> — Psalm 119:165 WEB

Holy Lawgiver, I bless You for the grace that enables me to love Your Word. The blood of Jesus has written Your law on my heart, turning obedience from a burden into a joy. Because I love Your commands, You promise me great peace that the world cannot steal.

I declare that stumbling is not my portion. Every trap of offense, confusion, or distraction is rendered powerless by my devotion to Your truth. My household walks in the unshakable peace that comes from aligning our lives with Your will. The Word is our anchor, and the blood is our covering.

Lord, let our love for Your law grow daily. Cause our thoughts to be shaped by Scripture, and our steps to be steady upon the path of righteousness. May our obedience draw us deeper into covenant rest, where nothing has the power to cause us to fall. In Jesus' name, Amen.

DAY 47

PARDON

CALLING ON GOD'S FORGIVING NATURE

> "To the Lord our God belong mercies and forgiveness; for we have rebelled against him."
> — Daniel 9:9 WEB

Faithful God, I lift my voice to the One in whom mercy dwells. Forgiveness is not just something You do—it is who You are. Though I have rebelled, You remain ready. Though we have strayed, Your nature has not changed. You are the God of pardon.

Today I fall upon Your mercy and call it forth for my life and my family. Where rebellion once ruled, let reconciliation reign. Let the power of Your forgiving nature flood our hearts. You are not a distant judge—you are a covenant Father, rich in compassion.

Let my home be a sanctuary of second chances. Let the legacy of forgiveness erase the record of rebellion. I trust in who You are more than in what I've done. You are merciful, and You delight to forgive.

In Jesus' name, Amen.

PROTECTION

Victory in the Garden of Agony

> "His sweat became like great drops of blood falling down on the ground."
> — Luke 22:44 WEB

Oh Jesus, Redeemer of my soul, You sweat blood so I wouldn't have to wrestle alone in the dark. You carried the agony of spiritual warfare to secure my victory before the battle even began. I plead that blood over every place in my life that feels overwhelmed and weary.

When I am pressed, Your blood empowers. When my soul is heavy, Your blood lifts the weight. Let the covering of Your bloody sweat shield my mind from collapse, my emotions from torment, and my spirit from fainting in the fight.

I release this prayer over my family. Let none of us give in to the crushing weight of warfare. The blood has already conquered it. The same blood that soaked the ground in Gethsemane now covers our ground of struggle and turns it into holy territory.

We shall not break down—we shall break through. Let the power in Your agony become the peace in our storm. In Jesus' name, Amen.

PREVAIL

SEATED IN VICTORIOUS AUTHORITY WITH CHRIST

> "He who overcomes, I will give to him to sit down with me on my throne…"
> —Revelation 3:21 WEB

Majestic King, You've raised me to reign with You! What an honor to be seated in heavenly places, covered in the blood that enthrones the redeemed. I accept my authority as one positioned in Christ, not beneath, but above every power and principality.

Let this revelation shatter the illusion of powerlessness. I do not beg—I decree. I do not retreat—I reign. My family and I take our place on the throne of spiritual governance, enforcing heaven's agenda over every area of our lives.

I bind every demonic assignment sent to rob us of identity and dominion. By the blood, we walk in wisdom, discernment, and prophetic precision. Thrones are for kings—through the blood, we rule in life by Christ.

In Jesus' name, Amen.

PRESERVATION

SIGNS AND WONDERS THROUGH BLOOD

> "...that signs and wonders may be done through the name of your holy Servant Jesus."
> — Acts 4:30 WEB

Miracle-Working God, stretch out Your hand over my family and let healing signs manifest. In the name of Jesus and by the blood of the covenant, I decree an outpouring of wonders in our bodies. Let incurable diseases disappear, and chronic pain dissolve. Let testimonies break forth like rain.

I declare this is not the age of decline but of divine demonstration. Let our lives prove the reality of the blood of Jesus. Do wonders in our bones, organs, and immune systems. Let healing break generational patterns and raise up a new lineage of divine health.

I release signs into our household: healed children, strengthened elders, restored minds, and long-standing afflictions reversed. Let neighbors marvel and doctors be confounded. The blood of Jesus is our seal, and miracles are our portion.

In Jesus' name, Amen.

PROSPERITY

Life More Abundantly

> "I came that they may have life, and may have it abundantly."
> — John 10:10 WEB

Jesus, Abundant Life-Giver, I receive what You came to give. I do not settle for mere survival. You did not shed Your blood so I could barely make it—you gave it that I might have life in overflow. Every drop of blood You shed was a declaration of abundance for me.

I embrace the full expression of life—spiritually, emotionally, financially, relationally. My life and the life of my family are marked by peace, increase, and joy. I break agreement with the thief who comes to steal, kill, and destroy. We refuse to live beneath the standard of Your blood-bought promise.

Abundance is not a dream—it is our divine reality. Our table is full, our oil is fresh, and our joy is complete. You have opened wide the gates of blessing, and we walk in boldly. The days of lack are over. We have life, and we have it more abundantly.

In Jesus' name, Amen.

PEACE

SET APART FROM EMOTIONAL CHAOS

> By which will we have been sanctified through the offering of the body of Jesus Christ once for all.
> — Hebrews 10:10 WEB

Sanctifying Lord, I thank You for the once-for-all sacrifice of Jesus' body and blood. That holy offering has set me and my family apart—not just from sin, but from the chaos, confusion, and turmoil that dominate this world.

By covenant right, I declare that our emotions are under the sanctifying power of the cross. Fear, despair, and instability have no hold on us. We are a consecrated people, chosen to live in peace even in a troubled world. Your Spirit guards our hearts, and Your blood seals our minds in stability.

Lord, keep us in this sanctified place, where Your presence defines our reality and Your peace shapes our atmosphere. Let the world see in us a calm that cannot be shaken, a joy that cannot be stolen, and a stability rooted in the blood of the covenant. In Jesus' name, Amen.

DAY 48

PARDON

CONFESSION THAT LEADS TO MERCY

> "He who conceals his sins doesn't prosper, but whoever confesses and forsakes them shall have mercy."
> — Proverbs 28:13 WEB

Righteous Judge and Loving Father, I come with open hands and an unveiled heart. I hide nothing from You. I confess what You already see—not to inform You, but to invite You. I forsake the paths that led me away from peace, and I run toward mercy.

Your Word is clear—confession is the key to mercy. So I release every hidden weight, every secret sin, every buried wound. I trade secrecy for restoration. Let mercy rise like the morning over me and my family. Let honesty break the power of darkness and usher in divine healing.

I declare this over my household: We are not a people of cover-up—we are a people of clean hands and pure hearts. Where sin once lingered, grace now rules. Because we confess and forsake, we walk in mercy that never ends.

In Jesus' name, Amen.

PROTECTION

Permanent Deliverance by the Blood

> "...through his own blood, entered in once for all into the Holy Place, having obtained eternal redemption."
> — Hebrews 9:12 WEB

Lamb of God, thank You for the once-and-for-all sacrifice that cannot be reversed. I proclaim the power of eternal redemption over my life and over every member of my household. Your blood doesn't expire—it anchors us forever in freedom.

I apply this eternal blood to every lingering chain, every oppressive pattern, and every generational curse. What the enemy says is permanent, Your blood declares undone. My deliverance isn't temporary—it's sealed by heaven's decree.

I will not revisit former bondage. My children will not repeat ancestral mistakes. My family walks in the permanence of redemption. No demon, no decision, no delay can reverse what Your blood has settled.

Thank You, Jesus, for the power of a redemption that lasts forever. We are delivered, we are secured, and we are Yours. In Jesus' name, Amen.

PREVAIL

My Victory Is Sealed

"I have been crucified with Christ... who loved me and gave himself up for me."
—Galatians 2:20 WEB

Mighty Redeemer, I declare today that I no longer live for myself, but for You who shed Your blood for me. I am a living testimony of covenant love, bought at the highest price — the blood of Your Son. That blood didn't just save me from sin; it endowed me with a heavenly inheritance of victory. The life I now live is no longer bound by fear, defeat, or ancestral yokes. I walk in the finished work of the cross, where every battle was already won.

By Your sacrificial love, I boldly claim what has been eternally secured for me: the right to rise above every bondage, the authority to trample over serpents and scorpions, and the unshakable confidence that I belong to Christ. My victory is not a wish, it is a covenant reality — blood-sealed, Spirit-breathed, and faith-activated. I declare that this victory covers my household, sanctifies our territory, and nullifies every voice of condemnation and limitation.

I silence the whispers of failure and rejection, because the One who gave Himself for me gave me more than salvation — He gave me access to rulership. I receive it with reverence. I will not cower, I will not retreat. I stand, clothed in Christ, armed by grace, and covered in blood. I declare over myself and my family — we are unstoppable in Christ, preserved in power, and destined to overcome. In Jesus' name, Amen.

PRESERVATION

Long Life Through the Blood

> "I will satisfy him with long life, and show him my salvation."
> — Psalm 91:16 WEB

Covenant-Keeping God, I lay claim to long life—not just in years, but in strength, joy, and purpose. The blood of Jesus has secured my preservation, and I declare that I and my family shall live long and live well. No assignment of premature death shall prosper.

Satisfy us with the richness of Your days. Let us enjoy generations of health, fruitfulness, and divine legacy. I cancel the expiration dates set by affliction, accident, or ancestry. Let the blood mark us as untouchable by death until our race is fully run.

I speak life into every family member. Let long life become our norm and testimony. Let us be known not by the pain of our past but by the endurance of our future. May we see our children's children and declare the faithfulness of God across the years.

In Jesus' name, Amen.

PROSPERITY

YOU ALONE ARE THE SOURCE

"Both riches and honor come from you. You rule over all..."
— 1 Chronicles 29:12 WEB

Sovereign King, I lift my hands and heart in total acknowledgment: You alone are the Source of every blessing. Riches don't come from men. Honor doesn't come from effort. They come from You—the One who sits enthroned over all the earth and rules with wisdom and mercy.

Every dollar I possess, every opportunity I receive, every platform I stand on—it all flows from Your hand. I will not worship the gift, but the Giver. I will not idolize the provision, but exalt the Provider. You are the one who elevates, promotes, and multiplies. My family will never forget that it is You who makes us wealthy.

May our home be a place of constant gratitude. Let my children grow up declaring, "God is our Source." I reject pride and self-dependence. I root myself in reverence and surrender. May our abundance point the world back to You— the One from whom all blessings flow.

In Jesus' name, Amen.

PEACE

Peace in Knowing Sin Has Been Removed

> But now once at the end of the ages, he has been revealed to put away sin by the sacrifice of himself.
> — Hebrews 9:26 WEB

Redeeming Savior, I praise You for the eternal work of the cross. Once and for all, You put away sin—not in part, but in full. This finished work brings me peace beyond measure, for I know that guilt, shame, and condemnation have no voice over my life.

I declare that my family and I walk in the freedom of complete forgiveness. The blood of Jesus has erased the record against us, silencing every whisper of the accuser. Our hearts are light, our minds are clear, and our relationships are restored because the barrier of sin has been forever removed.

Lord, let the reality of this redemption sink deeper each day. May we live as those truly forgiven, with no shadow of the past clouding our peace. Let joy and rest fill our home as we stand in the light of Your finished work. In Jesus' name, Amen.

DAY 49

PARDON

ATONEMENT FULFILLED IN CHRIST

> "For on this day shall atonement be made for you, to cleanse you. You shall be clean from all your sins before Yahweh."
> — Leviticus 16:30 WEB

High Priest of Heaven, I honor You for the once-for-all atonement You made by Your own blood. The day of atonement is no longer a yearly hope—it is a finished reality. I stand clean, not by ritual, but by redemption. The veil was torn, and the way was opened.

Let this cleansing touch every part of my being. Body, soul, and spirit—washed in the blood. Let my family stand in this same confidence. We do not await atonement—we live in it. Our sins are not postponed—they are purged. The work is complete.

I declare that no accusation can stand. No guilt can survive. The blood has spoken, and it speaks "clean." We live under the banner of atonement. And because of Jesus, we walk in peace with God forever.

In Jesus' name, Amen.

PROTECTION

THE KING IN BLOOD-SOAKED GLORY

> "He is clothed in a garment sprinkled with blood. His name is called 'The Word of God.'"
> — Revelation 19:13 WEB

King of Glory, I worship You—mighty in battle, glorious in apparel, and triumphant in blood-soaked splendor. Your victory is not stained—it is royal, righteous, and red with power. I stand under the authority of the Word made flesh and the blood You wore into battle.

Jesus, You are my banner in every war. I call upon Your kingship to reign in my home, to rule over every storm, and to silence every dark voice that would oppose us. You don't fight in theory—you fought in blood and You won in glory.

Let this same blood-drenched authority protect my household. Let it wrap around my children, my spouse, my future, and my legacy. May every plan of the enemy shatter under the force of Your victory.

We declare: our King reigns, clothed in blood, undefeated and eternal. The One who wears the Word and wields the sword is our covering. In Jesus' name, Amen.

PREVAIL

Built as an Unshakable Pillar

> "He who overcomes, I will make him a pillar in the temple of my God…"
> —Revelation 3:12 WEB

Almighty God, Fortress of my soul, I step into the victory of the overcomer. Your blood has not only saved me — it has established me. I declare that I and my household are being built into immovable pillars in Your presence. No storm can collapse what You have constructed by blood. No attack can uproot what has been anchored by grace. We are not fragile — we are fortified.

You have written Your name upon us — a mark that hell cannot erase. That name is our banner, our badge of eternal belonging. We are not wanderers in life; we are rooted in the courts of our God. The blood has made us pillars — strong, dignified, and unyielding. Every instability, every emotional and spiritual wobble, is now overridden by the permanence of divine placement. I speak that over my marriage, my children, our purpose, and every assignment You've given us.

We will not be moved by circumstances. We are not tossed by the winds of adversity. We are made for dominion, built to last, and planted in Your sanctuary. Your covenant has made us a fixture in Your kingdom, and no evil force has the power to displace us. I stand firm — not in my strength, but in Your blood's securing grace. In Jesus' name, Amen.

PRESERVATION

Health from the Blood-Soaked Word

> "...for they are life to those who find them, and health to their whole body."
> — Proverbs 4:22 WEB

Living Word, I devour Your truth today like medicine for my soul. Your Word, saturated in the blood of Jesus, is life and health to every part of my being. I declare healing over my body and my family's body as we receive the living Scripture with faith and reverence.

Let every promise become flesh in us. As we meditate on Your healing Scriptures, let diseases depart. Let our minds be renewed and our bodies be strengthened. Your Word is active, sharp, and penetrating. Let it cut away all sickness and ignite regeneration.

I decree that every organ responds to Your Word. Every hidden condition is exposed and expelled by the power of the Word and the blood. Let my household be full of Word-fed strength and blood-backed vitality.

In Jesus' name, Amen.

PROSPERITY

Expecting Every Good Thing

> "He who didn't spare his own Son, but delivered him up for us all, how would he not also with him freely give us all things?"
> — Romans 8:32 WEB

Gracious Father, if You gave Your very best—Your own Son—how could I ever doubt Your willingness to bless me with all things? I stand in awe of Your generosity and boldly expect every good thing to manifest in my life and family, not by entitlement, but by blood-bought grace.

I refuse to think small or settle for less. You have given all—so I expect all. Peace, joy, abundance, wisdom, increase—it's all included in the package of redemption. My eyes are lifted, my faith is alive, and my heart is open to receive without fear or hesitation.

Let my family live with holy expectation. Let our language shift from "maybe" to "surely." We live under the shadow of the cross, and in that shadow there is no lack. We don't have to strive for what You delight to give. We receive it all with open hands.

In Jesus' name, Amen.

PEACE

Receiving the Mind of Christ

> Have this in your mind, which was also in Christ Jesus.
> — Philippians 2:5 WEB

Lord of Glory, I thank You that through the blood of Jesus, I am not left to think as the world thinks. You have given me the mind of Christ—a mind rooted in humility, truth, and peace. This mind shapes my thoughts, my reactions, and my vision for life.

I decree that my household rejects the patterns of fear, pride, and unrest that dominate this age. The cross has renewed our minds, aligning us with the heart of the Savior. Every anxious thought is replaced with calm wisdom; every impulse toward strife is subdued by Your peace.

Lord, let this Christ-mind be evident in our speech, our choices, and our relationships. May we think Your thoughts, speak Your truth, and walk in Your ways, bearing witness to the transforming power of the covenant. In Jesus' name, Amen.

DAY 50

PARDON

SALVATION THROUGH CONFESSION AND BELIEF

> "That if you will confess with your mouth that Jesus is Lord, and believe in your heart that God raised him from the dead, you will be saved."
> — Romans 10:9 WEB

King Jesus, I confess boldly and believe deeply—You are Lord, risen and reigning. Your blood has purchased my salvation, and I declare it with joy. I am not hoping for salvation—I have received it. I am saved by grace through faith, and I will not be silent about it.

Let this confession echo through my home. Let every heart in my family confess Jesus as Lord and believe unto salvation. We are not lost—we are found. We are not bound—we are free. The blood has opened the door, and faith has brought us in.

I speak salvation into every corner of my life. My mouth will declare it, my heart will believe it, and my home will reflect it. Jesus is Lord—and because of that, we are saved.

In Jesus' name, Amen.

PROTECTION

Fire-Walled by the Blood

> "For I, says Yahweh, will be her wall of fire around her, and I will be the glory in the middle of her."
> — Zechariah 2:5 WEB

O Lord, my Consuming Fire, I stand in awe that You Yourself have become a fiery wall around my life. Let the blood of Jesus ignite this wall and make it impenetrable. I decree that every demonic arrow is burned before it can cross into our space.

Surround my family with fire. Let every window and door in the spirit be sealed by the flames of Your holiness. Let angelic sentries guard our perimeter and the glory of Your presence dwell at our center.

Inside this blood-covered firewall, no fear can thrive, no sickness can spread, and no plot can prosper. We live within divine boundaries, invisible to man but known and feared by darkness.

Thank You, Father, that the fire never fades and the blood never weakens. Our home is protected. Our destiny is preserved. You, O God, are our flaming fortress. In Jesus' name, Amen.

PREVAIL

SANCTIFIED FOR DOMINION

> "...we have been sanctified through the offering of the body of Jesus Christ once for all."
> —Hebrews 10:10 WEB

Holy and Righteous Father, I bless You for the irreversible sanctification that was secured through the precious blood of Jesus. I do not stand in shame or defeat — I stand sanctified. Set apart. Chosen for dominion. Because of Your Son's offering, my household and I are no longer common — we are consecrated vessels, fit for glory, prepared for impact.

By this blood-cleansed identity, I break free from every yoke of mediocrity and insignificance. We are not defined by past failures, generational curses, or demonic projections. We are defined by the offering that cannot be undone. The blood has marked our home as holy ground — sickness must flee, darkness must bow, and confusion must scatter. We are preserved not just for survival but for supernatural victory.

Lord, let the reality of sanctification permeate every area of our lives. Let our conversations be seasoned with heaven's purity. Let our decisions reflect divine alignment. We carry Your nature, and because of the blood, we carry it with power. I decree: no more defilement, no more compromise, no more delay. We are sanctified warriors — bold, relentless, and destined to rule in righteousness. In Jesus' name, Amen.

PRESERVATION

God's Personal Healing Vow

"...I will heal him."
— Isaiah 57:19 WEB

Faithful Father, You have made it personal. You didn't send an angel. You didn't delegate the task. You said, "I will heal him." I receive this promise with awe and assurance. This is not just a statement—it is a covenant vow. Your blood confirms it, and my spirit receives it.

You are not far off. You are present, invested, and intentional about my healing and that of my family. From the depths of our souls to the smallest cell in our bodies, we receive Your touch. Heal us in the night watches. Heal us in our emotions. Heal us in our broken places.

Because You said it, it is done. We align our mouths with Yours. We speak wholeness, peace, and health. No symptom is greater than Your Word. No pain is louder than Your promise. You will heal us, and we will testify.

In Jesus' name, Amen.

PROSPERITY

No Good Thing Withheld

> "For Yahweh God is a sun and a shield. Yahweh will give grace and glory. He withholds no good thing from those who walk blamelessly."
> — Psalm 84:11 WEB

Radiant Sun and Faithful Shield, I bless Your name for the light You shine on my path and the protection You give to my life. You are both Provider and Defender. You don't just give grace—you give glory. And because of the blood, I walk blameless before You, expecting nothing to be withheld.

You withhold no good thing. Not one. If it's good and godly, You delight to release it. I reject every thought that says You are holding back. I rebuke the lie that says I must beg for Your favor. You are my covenant Father, and You rejoice in my well-being.

Let my family walk in this truth with boldness. Every home, every career, every prayer, every plan—let it be touched by the abundance You release. We will not live beneath the blessing. We will live as those who are wrapped in grace and saturated in goodness.

In Jesus' name, Amen.

PEACE

A Calm Life Through Christ's Presence

> Now may the Lord of peace himself give you peace at all times in all ways. The Lord be with you all.
> — 2 Thessalonians 3:16 WEB

Lord of Peace, I open the doors of my life and my home to You. By Your blood, You have purchased the right to dwell with us, and Your presence is the atmosphere where peace reigns.

I declare that we receive peace at all times and in every situation. Whether the winds of change blow fiercely or the path is calm, Your presence steadies our steps. The blood of the Lamb stands between us and every storm, commanding stillness to every wave that rises against us.

Lord, walk through the rooms of our home. Fill each space with the fragrance of Your peace. Let Your nearness be the comfort that guards our hearts, the light that dispels our fears, and the strength that holds us steady. We welcome You fully, knowing that where You are, no storm can prevail. In Jesus' name, Amen.

DAY 51

PARDON

LIVING IN COVENANTAL PARDON

> "Moses took the blood and sprinkled it on the people, and said, 'Look, this is the blood of the covenant, which Yahweh has made with you concerning all these words.'"
> — Exodus 24:8 WEB

O Lord, Covenant-Keeping God, I thank You for the blood of Jesus, the Mediator of the new and better covenant. This blood was not sprinkled from bulls or goats, but from Your spotless Son—shed once and for all for the redemption of my soul. I step into the covering of that covenant today. Let the power of that blood speak on behalf of my family and me, marking us as Your own and securing our eternal pardon.

Father, I receive the benefits of this unbreakable bond—mercy instead of wrath, forgiveness instead of judgment, peace instead of fear. Your covenant stands stronger than every accusation of the enemy. Even when I fall short, Your blood reaffirms Your love and commitment to restore me. May this covenant not only cleanse but consecrate my household to You.

Seal us, Lord, by the covenantal power of the blood. Let no curse, no guilt, and no shame override what Jesus finished on the cross. Let this blood speak louder than our past and louder than the voice of condemnation. In the name of Jesus, we are forgiven, accepted, and forever Yours.

In Jesus' name, Amen.

PROTECTION

Kept From All Harm

> "Yahweh will keep you from all evil. He will keep your soul."
> —Psalm 121:7 WEB

O Mighty Keeper of Israel, I boldly declare that You who never sleep nor slumber are the Guardian of my life and the Defender of my family. By the covenant of the blood of Jesus, I claim divine immunity from all forms of evil—visible or invisible, known or unknown. Let the power in the blood serve as our barrier, our defense, our refuge. No arrow that flies by day nor pestilence that stalks at night shall come near us.

Father, keep us secure in every journey we take, in every step we make, in every room we enter, and in every relationship we engage. Let the blood of Jesus speak louder than every trap, lie, ambush, or assignment of darkness. Day and night, let Your eyes watch over us and Your angels encamp around us, enforcing the covenant that covers our household in supernatural safety.

Lord, You are our Keeper, our Shade, our Fortress, and our Shield. We are hidden in Christ, above the reach of harm and beyond the limits of natural protection. By the blood, we abide in divine preservation. No weapon formed against us shall prosper, and no evil shall befall us. We walk covered, sealed, and secured—every hour, every moment.

In Jesus' name, Amen.

PREVAIL

WEAPONS OF PRAISE AND BLOOD

> Let the high praises of God be in their mouth, and
> a two-edged sword in their hand
> — Psalm 149:6 WEB

Almighty Warrior and King of Glory, I lift my voice with the sound of high praises! I declare that the blood of Jesus and the praises of the redeemed are my undefeatable weapons. With a shout of triumph, I raise a standard in my home, over my family, and against every encroaching darkness. I decree that praise will paralyze the enemy and the blood will silence every demonic assignment against our lives.

By the finished work of the cross, the blood of Jesus has already secured our victory. So now, let the high praises rise from my lips as an incense of warfare. Let every shout shake the foundations of wickedness around us. I command strongholds to fall and atmospheres to shift as I magnify the name of the Lord. Let the enemy hear my praise and tremble before the power of the blood and the authority of my song.

Father, make my praise a weapon and my worship a sword. Let every melody be a mantle of deliverance over my household. I release the song of victory over my children, my marriage, my health, and my destiny. I declare: we shall not be moved, for our worship is rooted in covenant. The praises of the Most High are in our mouths, and the blood is on our doorposts. We are preserved, empowered, and protected by Your mighty hand.

In Jesus' name, Amen.

PRESERVATION

HEALING IN CONSECRATED SPACES

> "Moses took some of the anointing oil and some of the blood which was on the altar, and sprinkled it on Aaron, on his garments, on his sons…"
> — Leviticus 8:30 WEB

Lord Most High, I plead the consecrating blood of Jesus over every space assigned to my family—our home, our bodies, our rooms, and our resting places. As Moses sprinkled the holy anointing oil and the blood upon Aaron and his sons, I declare that our environments are now set apart, purified, and made fit for healing and restoration. No unclean spirit, affliction, or infirmity has legal access to dwell where the blood has been applied.

Father, let every room become a sanctuary of health. I speak to the atmosphere around my family—let it be filled with the breath of healing, the oil of joy, and the fire of divine health. Let no sickness dwell in our dwelling. I sprinkle the blood on every surface, every bed, every threshold, and every item in our possession. I anoint them by covenant decree and declare that they are instruments of wellness, not of disease.

Let the blood drive out every invisible affliction lingering in the air. Let the climate of our homes shift to reflect heaven's health. Where the blood speaks, sickness must flee. Where the blood is sprinkled, angels are stationed. Where the blood flows, healing is permanent.

In Jesus' name, Amen.

PROSPERITY

BLOOD-MARK ON MY LABOR

> "Yahweh was with Joseph, and he was a prosperous man. He was in the house of his master the Egyptian. His master saw that Yahweh was with him, and that Yahweh made all that he did prosper in his hand."
> — Genesis 39:2-3 WEB

Lord, my Covenant Partner, I declare that the same blood that redeemed my soul also rests upon the work of my hands. Just as You caused Joseph to prosper in a strange land, so I decree that everything I touch—my job, my business, my investments—is marked for increase because of Your presence and favor.

I thank You that because of the blood of Jesus, my labor is not in vain. I am not bound by economic systems or company politics—I operate under the influence of divine success. Let those around me see Your hand on my life. Let my results provoke recognition, honor, and reward. The blood of Jesus is my seal of excellence, productivity, and unstoppable advancement.

May this same covenant blessing rest on my family. Let every endeavor of my spouse and children flourish. Let our house be filled with testimonies of supernatural results and undeniable prosperity. We are not common—we are covenant-marked. And because the blood is on our hands, our labor will always yield more than enough.

In Jesus' name, Amen.

PEACE

Peace Sealed by the Blood

> "Moses took the blood, and sprinkled it on the people, and said, 'Behold, the blood of the covenant, which Yahweh has made with you concerning all these words.'"
> — Exodus 24:8 WEB

O Covenant-Keeping God, I stand beneath the crimson covering of the blood of Jesus and declare that my peace is not fragile—it is sealed by the eternal Word and the unbreakable covenant of the cross. Your blood has spoken a better word over me and my household, silencing every storm, breaking every chain, and marking us as untouchable to the adversary.

Today, I decree that the same voice that thundered at Sinai and confirmed Your promises through the shedding of blood now resounds over my life. My mind will not be tormented. My emotions will not be tossed by the winds of fear. My relationships will not be fractured by the schemes of the enemy. We are anchored in the covenant of peace that cannot be annulled.

Let every storm in my home bow to the blood. Let every anxiety dissolve in the assurance of Your oath. We walk in the safety of Your unshakable word, our hearts resting in the security of Your promises. Our peace is not a temporary feeling—it is a divine inheritance sealed forever by the blood of Christ. In Jesus' name, Amen.

DAY 52

PARDON

APPEAL TO GOD'S MERCY

> "Have mercy on me, God, according to your loving kindness. According to the multitude of your tender mercies, blot out my transgressions."
> — Psalm 51:1 WEB

Merciful Father, I cry out to You from the depths of a heart humbled by grace. You are the God of lovingkindness and compassion, and I run to You, not away from You. I do not come on the basis of my merit but on the basis of the blood—perfect, precious, and powerful—shed by Your Son.

Let the flood of mercy that flowed from Calvary wash over me and my family. Let every transgression be blotted out by Your divine eraser. Where the enemy tries to etch guilt into our minds, I appeal to Your lovingkindness to blot it out. Your mercy doesn't just overlook—it erases and restores. You are not reluctant to forgive but eager to restore.

Today I lift my family before You, covered in the blood, and cry for mercy over every area of sin, failure, or shame. Let the stronghold of condemnation be shattered, and let the grace of Your presence come rushing in like a river. May we live in the joy of those who are forgiven. In Jesus' name, Amen.

PROTECTION

Marked With Christ's Ownership

> "From now on, let no one cause me any trouble, for I bear the marks of the Lord Jesus branded on my body."
> —Galatians 6:17 WEB

Righteous Redeemer, I stand boldly under the eternal mark of the Lord Jesus Christ. The blood that was shed for me is a permanent sign of divine ownership. I am not my own. My family is not unclaimed. We are marked, labeled, and sealed by heaven's decree—set apart for Your glory, untouchable by the forces of darkness.

Let the blood-mark be visible in the spirit realm, announcing to every evil force that we belong to the Lord Most High. Let every demonic agenda break and shatter at the sight of this covenant mark. Our ears are tuned to heaven, our steps ordered by righteousness, our hands cleansed for holy service. Nothing unclean, cursed, or diabolical can stick to our lives or lay hold of our destiny.

Lord, when the enemy surveys for an open door, let him see only the blood. When trouble searches for a landing place, let it pass over us. We are covered, stamped, and branded with the authority of Jesus Christ. Let this mark speak for us in moments of battle, temptation, and judgment. We are blood-marked and spiritually guarded.

In Jesus' name, Amen.

PREVAIL

Victory Over the End-Time Beast

> I saw something like a sea of glass mixed with fire, and those who overcame the beast, his image, and the number of his name, standing on the sea of glass, having harps of God.
> — Revelation 15:2 WEB

Eternal God, I stand clothed in the victory of the Lamb who was slain. I decree that my household will not be deceived in these perilous days. The blood of Jesus marks our minds, our hearts, and our lives. We overcome the beast and every counterfeit system by the unshakable truth and triumphant blood of Christ.

Father, let the fire of discernment burn within me. Strengthen us to stand against the deception that floods this generation. I renounce the influence of every false god, lying spirit, and worldly seduction. I cover my family in the blood of the Lamb, and I declare that our hearts belong fully to the King of kings.

We are not among those who shrink back—we overcome. We are sealed with divine conviction and protected by covenant truth. As the storm of deception rages, we are anchored by the cross and sustained by the testimony of Jesus. Lord, give us the song of the overcomers—the harp of God in our hands, the victory of God in our mouths.

In Jesus' name, Amen.

PRESERVATION

HEALING MERCY ANSWERS MY CRY

"Yahweh, my God, I cried to you, and you have healed me."
— Psalm 30:2 WEB

O Merciful God, the covenant-keeping Healer, I lift my voice with gratitude and faith. When I cried out in pain and desperation, You didn't turn away. You came near and answered me with mercy. You laid Your healing hand on my household and turned our mourning into rejoicing. The blood of Jesus has sealed my healing and that of my family.

I declare that our cries have not been in vain. Every whispered prayer, every tear-soaked plea has moved heaven to respond. Your blood has become our answer. Where symptoms lingered, You have released the decree of healing. Where medical reports loomed like shadows, You have scattered them with light. The cry that once rose from fear now erupts with praise, because You, O Lord, have healed us!

Let the testimony of answered healing echo in our generations. Let it be said in our lineage: "They cried to the Lord, and He healed them." No sickness shall return. No condition shall regress. We have been heard, we have been healed, and we will never be the same again.

In Jesus' name, Amen.

PROSPERITY

Honoring the Blood Guarantee

> "How much worse punishment do you think he will be judged worthy of, who has trodden under foot the Son of God, and has counted the blood of the covenant with which he was sanctified an unholy thing..."
> — Hebrews 10:29 WEB

O Holy and Righteous God, I exalt the blood of the covenant that has sanctified me and guaranteed my access to divine abundance. I will not treat lightly what You have sealed with the highest price—Your Son's life. I honor the blood that speaks of better things: increase, favor, and overflow.

I declare that my provision is not a random occurrence but a right secured by the blood of Jesus. I am not at the mercy of circumstances; I live under a divine guarantee. Let heaven record today that I esteem the covenant. I believe it, I receive it, and I live by it. I will not reduce prosperity to chance or toil—it is the fruit of the covenant.

Let this reverence extend to my household. Let my family be known for honoring the blood, and let our lives reflect the wealth, peace, and security found in it. We are not beggars—we are believers. And the covenant we honor will overflow into every area of our lives.

In Jesus' name, Amen.

PEACE

GRACE TO LIVE PEACEABLY

"If it is possible, as much as it is up to you, be at peace with all men."
— Romans 12:18 WEB

Prince of Peace, You have empowered me by the blood of Your Son to walk in peace even in the most difficult places. My capacity to love, forgive, and remain calm in the midst of hostility does not come from my own strength, but from the victory of the cross that has already conquered every spirit of division and strife.

I declare that my home will be a sanctuary of peace, even when the world rages. You have given me grace to respond with gentleness, to disarm anger with kindness, and to pursue reconciliation as a living testimony of the gospel. I refuse to be drawn into the snares of offense or the traps of bitterness.

Lord, let the fragrance of Your peace saturate my speech, my actions, and my relationships. Even where others reject it, I will remain steadfast, because my peace flows from the blood that bought me. My family will be known as peacemakers, shining in a world desperate for rest. In Jesus' name, Amen.

DAY 53

PARDON

HEART-LEVEL REPENTANCE

> "Tear your heart, and not your garments, and turn to Yahweh, your God; for he is gracious and merciful..."
> — Joel 2:13 WEB

Gracious Redeemer, I don't just offer words—I bring my broken heart. I rend it open before You, God, not with outward display, but inward surrender. I return not with pretense but with passion, because I know You are gracious, slow to anger, and abounding in mercy.

Lord, let my repentance go beyond the surface. Let it be the cry of my soul and the posture of my life. I refuse to live a double life—draw me into true surrender by the power of Your blood. As I turn, turn my entire family toward You. Let generational guilt be lifted as we fall into Your grace.

Blood of Jesus, speak over every wound, every compromise, and every delay. Cleanse us thoroughly and lead us into new life. May our hearts burn once again for what burns in Yours. We return because You welcome us—not with wrath, but with outstretched arms.

In Jesus' name, Amen.

PROTECTION

Redeemed and Hidden by Blood

> "These are those who were not defiled… These were redeemed from among men to be first fruits to God and to the Lamb."
> —Revelation 14:4 WEB

Precious Lamb of God, I thank You for redeeming me by Your holy blood. My name is written in the Lamb's Book of Life, and my identity is sealed in Your sacrifice. I declare that I and my household are the redeemed of the Lord, separated from destruction and exempted from the curses of this world. We are not common—we are consecrated.

Let the blood declare our distinction wherever we go. When judgment passes, let us be hidden. When calamity rages, let us be sheltered. When systems collapse and hearts fail, let our redemption speak deliverance. We are not of this world; we are ambassadors, a royal priesthood, a protected inheritance in Christ. Let our lives bear the fruit of Your ownership—purity, power, and protection.

Father, redeem every area of our lives that has been under bondage. Let every family chain be broken, every soul tie severed, every generational pattern reversed. We stand as the purchased ones—redeemed, secured, and forever sheltered under the covenant of Your blood.

In Jesus' name, Amen.

PREVAIL

I Will Not Die But Live

> I will not die, but live, and declare Yah's works.
> — Psalm 118:17 WEB

O Lord, my Deliverer, I rise today in the resurrection power of the blood! I declare with boldness that death has no hold on me or my family. Every assignment of premature death, sickness, or disaster is overturned by the blood of Jesus. I shall not die, but live—to proclaim Your mighty works and glorify Your holy name.

I plead the blood of life over my body, my mind, and every member of my household. Where there has been a sentence of affliction, I decree healing. Where there has been fear of loss, I declare preservation. The blood of Jesus silences the voice of death and raises us into life overflowing.

Father, You have written the days of my life in Your book, and I declare that we shall fulfill every divine purpose assigned to us. No arrow of the enemy will prosper, no trap will prevail. I speak longevity, vitality, and fruitfulness into my family line. We are covered, we are preserved, and we will live to see generations proclaim Your glory.

In Jesus' name, Amen.

PRESERVATION

You Alone Heal and Preserve

> "See now that I, even I, am he. There is no god with me. I kill and I make alive. I wound and I heal…"
> — Deuteronomy 32:39 WEB

Sovereign Healer and Ruler of all, I exalt You as the only One with the power to wound and to heal, to take and to restore. You are God alone, and no force of darkness can overturn Your decree. I bring my family under Your dominion today. You have the final say over every health condition and every generational diagnosis. You alone can raise us from affliction.

By the power of Your blood, I declare that every wound is closing. Every place where the enemy sought to inflict harm is now a place of resurrection life. You have chosen us not for death, but for restoration. Not for decline, but for divine renewal. You hold the keys to our health, and You have decreed: "Live!"

Every other voice is silenced. The blood speaks louder than symptoms. You are not just able to heal; You have already acted in love. You are the One who governs every heartbeat, every breath, every system. Let my household live under Your healing sovereignty. You kill what was killing us. You heal what man cannot.

In Jesus' name, Amen.

PROSPERITY

TREASURED AND POSITIONED BY FAVOR

> "Now therefore, if you will indeed obey my voice and keep my covenant, then you shall be my own possession from among all peoples, for all the earth is mine."
> — Exodus 19:5 WEB

Majestic King, I praise You for making me—and my household—Your treasured possession through the blood of Jesus. You have chosen me out of all the earth, not because of my merit but because of mercy. I receive this favor not as flattery, but as fact, rooted in covenant truth.

You have positioned me for influence, placed me in strategic locations, and surrounded me with divine opportunities. I am not wandering—I am appointed. I am not invisible—I am set apart. Through the blood, I am qualified to dwell in places others only dream of, and to receive what others labor for without access.

Let this positioning extend to my family. May my children walk into divine assignments and favor-packed destinies. May my spouse receive honor and recognition in every sphere. We are not hidden—we are highlighted by heaven. And because we are treasured by the Most High, we shall never live beneath our inheritance.

In Jesus' name, Amen.

PEACE

Rescued from Inner Turmoil

> "He has redeemed my soul in peace from the battle that was against me, although there are many who oppose me."
> — Psalm 55:18 WEB

Redeemer of my soul, I lift my voice in triumph because You have not only redeemed me, but You have done it in peace. No battle within or without can steal the calm You have placed in my spirit. Though many may rise against me, they will stumble and fall, for the blood has purchased my freedom from inner war.

I release every weight, every anxious thought, and every unhealed wound into Your hands. The storms of the mind have been silenced by the voice that cried, "It is finished!" I declare that no accusation, no betrayal, no unseen warfare will unsettle my peace.

Today, my household and I stand in the quiet strength of Your covenant. The noise of the enemy is drowned out by the song of the redeemed. You have lifted me above the chaos, set me in a place of rest, and wrapped me in the stillness of Your presence. In Jesus' name, Amen.

DAY 54

PARDON

JESUS, OUR INTERCESSOR WHEN WE FALL

> "My little children, I write these things to you so that you may not sin. If anyone sins, we have a Counselor with the Father, Jesus Christ, the righteous."
> — 1 John 2:1 WEB

Heavenly Advocate, I thank You that even when I fall, I am not forsaken. You, Jesus, stand at the right hand of the Father, interceding on my behalf. When the accuser raises his voice, Your blood silences him. When guilt rises, Your advocacy rises higher still.

Thank You, Lord, that my sins don't surprise You, and they don't separate me when I run to You. You stand in the courtroom of heaven, not pleading for leniency but presenting the final verdict—paid in full. For every stumble, You offer strength. For every fall, You offer forgiveness.

Let this same intercession extend over my household. For every family member trapped in shame or struggling in silence, let Your advocacy rise. Pull them from the pit. Restore them by grace. May they know You not as judge but as the Redeemer who never stops fighting for us.

In Jesus' name, Amen.

PROTECTION

COVERED BY DIVINE SURVEILLANCE

> "As birds hovering, so Yahweh of Armies will protect Jerusalem. He will protect and deliver it. He will pass over and preserve it."
> —Isaiah 31:5 WEB

Lord of Hosts, I thank You that You hover over my home like an eagle over its young, never blinking, never retreating. By the blood of Jesus, I activate the supernatural surveillance system of heaven. Day and night, You scan the perimeters of my life, detecting threats before they arise and intercepting every arrow before it lands.

Let the eyes of the Lord shine around my household. Let the fire of divine presence be upon our walls and in our gates. Every unseen enemy, every silent danger, every coded curse—expose and destroy it, O God. Let the blood of Jesus function as an alarm system that cannot be hacked or disabled.

Father, I declare that nothing escapes Your attention—not even the smallest schemes of the enemy. You will protect, You will deliver, You will pass over and preserve. Your watchful care is our constant safety. Because of the blood, we do not fear the ambush. We do not fear the night. We are under constant divine surveillance.

In Jesus' name, Amen.

PREVAIL

THE LORD IS MY MAN OF WAR

> Yahweh is a man of war. Yahweh is his name.
> — Exodus 15:3 WEB

Captain of Heaven's Armies, I exalt You as the undefeated Warrior! The blood of Jesus is my banner, my defense, and my weapon. I declare that every battle concerning my family belongs to You. The Lord of Hosts arises for me, and every enemy must scatter in fear and defeat.

I surrender the hidden warfare—the battles no one sees but You. I release the burdens too heavy for me to carry and the giants too tall for me to slay. You are the God who split the sea and crushed the chariots. And now, by the power of the blood, I declare: the same victory flows through my veins.

I cover my house, my children, and my territory in the blood of the Divine Warrior. I declare a hedge of fire and a shield of vengeance around every area of my life. Lord, fight for me with sword and flame; roar from Zion and break the neck of every oppressor. I trust not in my strength, but in the might of the blood-covered King.

In Jesus' name, Amen.

PRESERVATION

RESTORED FROM LONG-TERM AFFLICTION

> "For I will restore health to you, and I will heal you of your wounds…"
> — Jeremiah 30:17 WEB

O Faithful Restorer, the wounds have been long and deep. The affliction has tried to label us, define us, and linger like a shadow. But today, by the power of the blood covenant, I declare that healing is not only possible—it is ours. You restore health to the wounded, and You mend even the places we forgot were broken.

I call forth restoration over every area that's suffered under chronic illness or long-term conditions. Whether in the body, the mind, or the emotions—let Your healing sweep through my family like a holy river. Every wound from trauma, every scar from sickness, every silent ache—we bring it under the blood. Restore vitality to our days, strength to our frames, and peace to our minds.

Where the years have been lost, let restoration come. Let this be the season of divine payback, where health returns stronger than before. Let not one trace of that sickness remain. I call my family restored, renewed, and radiant. You are the God who restores—not partially, but wholly.

In Jesus' name, Amen.

PROSPERITY

OVERTAKEN BY COVENANT BLESSINGS

> "All these blessings will come upon you, and overtake you, if you listen to Yahweh your God's voice."
> — Deuteronomy 28:2 WEB

Covenant-Keeping God, I open my life to be overtaken—not by trouble, not by fear, but by blessing. You have spoken, and I believe: because of the blood, I have the right to be pursued by Your promises. I decree that I don't chase blessings—blessings chase me.

Let favor follow me into every room. Let provision meet me before I know I need it. Let contracts, open doors, and divine connections overtake me, not by manipulation but by manifestation of covenant. I align my heart to Your voice, and the blessings flow without striving.

May my family be swept into this divine overtaking. Let our children be surrounded by good success. Let every generation run ahead of curses and straight into blessings. Because of the covenant, we live not at the back—but at the front of heaven's favor.

In Jesus' name, Amen.

PEACE

SURRENDERING TO PEACE

> "Acquaint yourself with him now, and be at peace.
> By it, good will come to you."
> — Job 22:21 WEB

Holy Father, I lay my will, my plans, and my anxious striving at Your feet. To know You is to know peace, and to walk with You is to walk in quiet strength. I choose agreement with Your Word over the noise of my own understanding.

I surrender the battles of my mind and the storms of my emotions. Your blood has given me access to a covenant where my soul can breathe again. In yielding to Your way, I find not loss, but abundance; not defeat, but blessing.

Let my home be a place where Your peace rules as King. Let my decisions flow from the counsel of Your Spirit. As I align my heart with Yours, let every area of my life be filled with the goodness that comes from walking hand in hand with the God of peace. In Jesus' name, Amen.

DAY 55

PARDON

SILENCING GUILT AND ACCUSATION

> "I heard a loud voice in heaven, saying... the accuser of our brothers has been thrown down..."
> — Revelation 12:10 WEB

Warrior of Heaven, I lift my voice in triumph today! The blood has already spoken, and the accuser has already fallen. No longer does guilt have a grip, and no longer does shame have a seat in my story. I declare: every accusing voice against my life and family is cast down by the authority of the blood.

Let the cry of heaven echo in my spirit—"Not guilty!" I refuse to rehearse what You've already redeemed. I renounce every whispered lie, every false identity, every guilt-laced memory that haunts the mind. The blood testifies better things than judgment—it proclaims freedom.

Lord, let the blood of Jesus silence the voice of every curse, every generational guilt, and every internal torment. We are not defined by accusation but by adoption. Today, I walk free—my head lifted, my spirit clean, my name written in the Lamb's Book of Life.

In Jesus' name, Amen.

PROTECTION

JESUS KEEPS WHAT'S ENTRUSTED

> "While I was with them in the world, I kept them in your name. Those whom you have given me I have kept."
> —John 17:12 WEB

Holy Shepherd and Guardian of my soul, I praise You for keeping power. I entrust my life and the lives of my loved ones into Your nail-scarred hands. Your blood is not only our covering—it is our keeping. You are faithful to guard what has been given into Your hands. Let no one be lost, no one snatched, no one broken beyond repair.

Lord, I declare that my children, my marriage, my calling, my destiny—all are kept by Your blood. No demonic snare, no worldly enticement, no spiritual decay will prevail against the ones You have claimed. Let Your blood seal every door against backsliding and despair. Let Your voice keep us from deception and danger.

Even when we walk through the fire, we will not be consumed. When we pass through the waters, we will not drown. Because You are with us, and Your blood has marked us, we are preserved, protected, and pursued by divine mercy. Jesus, You keep what the Father gives—and we are safe in You.

In Jesus' name, Amen.

PREVAIL

Covered Courage Under Covenant

> Don't be afraid, for I am with you. Don't be dismayed, for I am your God.
> — Isaiah 41:10 WEB

Faithful Father, I receive Your strength today! I arise from fear, anxiety, and discouragement. I declare that I am covered by covenant and shielded by the blood. You are with me, and because of that, no terror can paralyze me, no pressure can shake me. My courage is rooted in who You are and what Christ has accomplished for me.

By the blood, I reject every intimidation of the enemy. I rebuke every spirit of despair and cast down every lie that says I won't make it. You are my God—the One who lifts me up, strengthens my hands, and secures my steps. Your promises are my armor, and Your presence is my peace.

Let courage rise in my household! Let boldness be our portion and confidence be our testimony. I declare my children will walk in fearless faith, and my family will stand immovable in Your truth. We are not forsaken; we are fortified. We will not faint; we will flourish—because we are blood-covered and God-kept.

In Jesus' name, Amen.

PRESERVATION

Freedom From Every Infirmity

> "When Jesus saw her, he called her, and said to her, 'Woman, you are freed from your infirmity.'"
> — Luke 13:12 WEB

Delivering King, I stand in the presence of the One who still sees and still speaks. Just as You looked upon that bound woman and declared her freedom, I receive that same liberating word for myself and my family. Every spirit of infirmity, every demonic root of affliction, be loosed in the name of Jesus.

We are not bowed down, we are not bound—we are blood-marked and made whole. Where affliction has gripped our bodies, where cycles of pain have persisted, I declare: Freedom! Let every spine straighten. Let every hidden root of infirmity shrivel under the power of the cross. Your word has come. Your blood has spoken. And we are loosed!

No longer identified by the bondage, we rise into health. Our posture is changed, our perspective is lifted. Freedom is not a future hope—it is a present reality. Let our household walk in uprightness, in strength, and in the wholeness of the redeemed.

In Jesus' name, Amen.

PROSPERITY

TAUGHT TO PROFIT BY THE LORD

> "I am Yahweh your God, who teaches you to profit,
> who leads you by the way you should go."
> — Isaiah 48:17 WEB

Holy Instructor of Increase, I submit my mind and my plans to You. You are the God who teaches me to profit. You do not delight in waste or poverty, but You guide me into abundance, one strategy, one idea, one step at a time. The blood gives me access to divine instruction.

Open my ears to wisdom that multiplies wealth. Lead me in paths that turn effort into harvest. Give me supernatural insight for my business, career, and finances. I reject worldly striving—I embrace Spirit-led strategies. I am not led by trends—I am led by truth.

Let this anointing rest on my family. May my household be known for wise stewardship and innovative solutions. Let our table overflow not just with bread, but with brilliance. We are taught of the Lord, and therefore, we cannot help but prosper.

In Jesus' name, Amen.

PEACE

Peace Through the Living Word

> "This is my comfort in my affliction, for your word has revived me."
> — Psalm 119:50 WEB

Faithful Shepherd, in the valley of trouble, Your Word breathes life into my soul. The blood of Jesus has unlocked every promise, making it my right to stand in unshakable peace. Though afflictions may press on every side, Your living Word revives my hope and strengthens my heart.

I refuse to feed on the lies of fear or the whispers of defeat. Instead, I feast on the truth that cannot be broken. Your voice stills my anxious thoughts, and the revelation of the cross drives out every shadow.

In my family, Your Word will be our anchor. We will speak it, pray it, and stand on it until peace overflows in every room. We are not defined by what we see, but by what You have spoken. In Jesus' name, Amen.

DAY 56

PARDON

COMING BOLDLY FOR MERCY AND GRACE

> "Let's therefore draw near with boldness to the throne of grace, that we may receive mercy…"
> — Hebrews 4:16 WEB

King of Grace, I come running—not crawling—into Your presence today. By the blood of Jesus, the veil has been torn and the throne has been opened wide. I come boldly because the price has been fully paid. I bring my weaknesses, my needs, and my family to You.

Let Your throne be a fountain of mercy for us. Let Your grace pour into every dry place. For every weary soul in my household, I ask for renewal. For every hidden fear, I ask for peace. For every lingering sin, I ask for cleansing. You don't turn us away; You invite us closer.

Father, I declare that we are a family marked by bold access. We are not orphans—we are blood-washed children. Let the atmosphere of heaven break into our home. Let mercy reign over condemnation. Let grace triumph over struggle. Let us live in the joy of constant communion with You.

In Jesus' name, Amen.

PROTECTION

SHIELDED FROM END-TIME CALAMITY

> "Because you kept my command to endure, I also will keep you from the hour of testing…"
> —Revelation 3:10 WEB

Almighty God, in a world shaking with chaos, I take refuge in the blood of Jesus, my eternal Passover. You promised to keep those who endure in faith from the hour of great trial. I plead the blood over my family and all we possess. Let the blood build a wall of preservation in days of disaster, and let divine endurance anchor our hearts in peace.

Father, shield us from the judgments that fall on rebellion. Let our obedience place us under divine exemption. The blood cries louder than any plague or famine. When economies fail and nations tremble, let our covenant stand as our safety net. Let us be as Goshen was in Egypt—lit while others are in darkness, protected while others are struck.

Lord, You are not only our Savior, but our Shelter in the storm. Let every global shaking only deepen our security in You. We are marked, sealed, and hidden from wrath through the precious blood of the Lamb.

In Jesus' name, Amen.

PREVAIL

Faith in the Blood Prevails

> Whatever is born of God overcomes the world. This is the victory that has overcome the world: your faith.
> — 1 John 5:4 WEB

Father, I proclaim my blood-born identity as an overcomer! I was not born of the flesh alone, but by the Spirit and the covenant blood of Jesus. Therefore, I walk in overcoming faith. I believe in the power of the cross. I trust in the voice of the blood. And by that unshakable faith, I rise above the world's chaos and corruption.

Today, I renounce every fear and declare my victory over every worldly system, demonic cycle, and generational oppression. The blood of Jesus is the substance of my faith. I don't just hope—I believe. I believe my family is protected. I believe our future is preserved. I believe we are victorious in every battle we face.

Let this overcoming faith arise in my spouse, in my children, in my household. Let us live by faith, fight by faith, and win by faith. We will not bow to the pressures of this age. We are more than conquerors—because our faith is in the blood that speaks better things.

In Jesus' name, Amen.

PRESERVATION

RESTORATION OF SOUL AND SPIRIT

> "He restores my soul…"
> — Psalm 23:3 WEB

Lover of my soul, I come under Your gentle shepherding. In the quiet places of the heart, where trauma echoes and sorrow lingers, You speak peace and restoration. I declare over myself and my family that our souls are not forsaken—they are being renewed by the blood of Jesus.

Let emotional wounds be healed. Let the fractured places of our memories be gathered and made whole. Restore joy where there has been weeping. Restore confidence where there has been despair. Let every mental burden, every heavy cloud, lift now by the power of the covenant. You lead us beside still waters, and You are restoring our innermost being.

Where we've been emotionally exhausted, renew us. Where spiritual discouragement tried to rob our passion, reignite us. We are not hollow—we are whole. The Good Shepherd has laid down His life, and His blood speaks peace into our minds and spirits.

In Jesus' name, Amen.

PROSPERITY

God's Investment Must Prosper

> "Take heed, therefore, to yourselves...to shepherd the assembly of the Lord and God which he purchased with his own blood."
> — Acts 20:28 WEB

Righteous Redeemer, You have purchased my life—not with silver or gold, but with Your own blood. I am not cheap, not forgotten, not random—I am Your costly investment. And because You paid the highest price, I know You will ensure that I prosper, fulfill purpose, and bring You glory.

I will not treat my life as common. I am a divine asset, bought for impact. Let my days produce fruit, my efforts yield results, and my walk reflect worth. I refuse to squander what heaven has paid dearly for. I arise today with dignity, responsibility, and authority.

Let my family walk in this same revelation. May we never underestimate ourselves or each other. May our value be seen in how we speak, live, and serve. We are Your possession, paid in full, and You will ensure that Your investment bears eternal return.

In Jesus' name, Amen.

PEACE

Cleansed for Mental Stability

> "They washed their robes, and made them white in the Lamb's blood."
> — Revelation 7:14 WEB

Spotless Lamb, I thank You that my identity is no longer stained by the past, but washed and made pure through Your blood. Because I am clean, my mind is no longer bound by the shame, confusion, and torment that once ruled me.

I declare that every lie of unworthiness is broken, every voice of condemnation silenced. Your blood has given me a new name, a new mind, and a new peace that nothing can shake. My home will not be a place of mental torment but of renewed thoughts anchored in truth.

Let the clarity of heaven fill my heart. Let the confidence of being fully forgiven steady my emotions. As I walk in this cleansed identity, I will not return to the garments of guilt, but remain clothed in the white robes of righteousness and peace. In Jesus' name, Amen.

DAY 57

PARDON

REDEEMED FROM JUDGMENT

> "Christ redeemed us from the curse of the law, having become a curse for us…"
> — Galatians 3:13 WEB

Redeeming Lamb of God, I stand in awe of the exchange made at Calvary. You didn't just forgive my sins—you became the curse so I could walk in blessing. You absorbed the judgment that was meant for me. I declare: my family and I are no longer under the curse—we are covered by the cross.

Every form of judgment—spiritual, emotional, or physical—was broken the moment Your blood was shed. I cancel every generational curse, every legal claim of the enemy, and every lingering shadow of the past. By the blood, we are redeemed from failure, sickness, poverty, and shame.

Let the blessing flow, not just over me, but over my lineage. I plead the blood over my children, their destiny, and their dreams. Let every curse stop with me. Let a new cycle of grace begin. We walk in the blessing—not by effort but by inheritance.

In Jesus' name, Amen.

PROTECTION

GUARDED FROM SATANIC AMBUSH

> "But the Lord is faithful, who will establish you and guard you from the evil one."
> —2 Thessalonians 3:3 WEB

Faithful God, I lift my voice and decree: No ambush, trap, or demonic scheme will prevail against me or my family. For the Lord is our strong tower, and the blood of Jesus is our impenetrable fortress. Let every plan of the enemy fail before it begins. Let every snare be revealed and overturned before we step into it.

Lord, establish our feet on holy ground. Let the blood neutralize every spiritual surveillance and demonic tracking. Frustrate the enemy's blueprints, intercept his whispers, and dismantle his weapons. We are guarded not by flesh, but by the faithfulness of a covenant-keeping God whose blood speaks louder than our fears.

Strengthen us in the inner man, and let divine discernment sharpen our senses. We declare: No premature death, no tragic event, no satanic manipulation will take root in our lives. The evil one cannot touch what the blood has secured. Guard our minds, our health, our homes, and our lineage.

In Jesus' name, Amen.

PREVAIL

Freedom Through the Blood's Law

> For the law of the Spirit of life in Christ Jesus made me free from the law of sin and of death.
> — Romans 8:2 WEB

Righteous Redeemer, I exalt You for the higher law—the law of the Spirit of life in Christ Jesus! By the authority of the blood, I declare my complete release from every bondage. The grip of sin, the shame of the past, and the sentence of death are broken by the blood's decree.

I proclaim liberty over my mind, my emotions, and my relationships. The chains of guilt are shattered. The curse of addiction is crushed. The spirit of death is rebuked. Every member of my family walks in the newness of life, because the law of the blood has overruled every verdict of the enemy.

Let Your life flood my home. Let Your Spirit breathe over every dry place. Where there has been torment, let there now be peace. Where there has been oppression, let there now be release. I declare, the blood has written a new law over me—one of grace, power, and freedom.

In Jesus' name, Amen.

PRESERVATION

Living in a Healing Atmosphere

> "The inhabitant won't say, 'I am sick.' The people who dwell therein will be forgiven their iniquity."
> — Isaiah 33:24 WEB

Holy God, I declare that my household is a place where the confession of sickness no longer has dominion. We dwell in the land of covenant covering. Because we are forgiven by the blood, we are also healed. Let every mouth in my family speak the language of divine health, not of chronic decline.

No more will we partner with the enemy through negative confessions. No more will "I am sick" be spoken under our roof. We will say what You say: "We are healed." I release a new atmosphere over our home—one of faith, one of life, one where symptoms cannot take root. Where the blood covers, the tongue must align.

Let every thought, every word, every declaration in our family support the truth of wholeness. We dwell under grace, not under sickness. We inhabit the shadow of the Almighty, where no disease dares abide. We will live and speak as the healed of the Lord.

In Jesus' name, Amen.

PROSPERITY

Barns Filled, Vats Overflowing

> "So your barns will be filled with plenty, and your vats will overflow with new wine."
> — Proverbs 3:10 WEB

Lord of the Harvest, I receive Your promise today: my barns shall be filled, and my vats shall overflow. By the covenant blood of Jesus, I declare that I am not meant for just enough—I am destined for overflow. My storage will not be empty, and my supply will not run dry.

Because I honor You with my substance, I receive the fullness of Your Word. Let every account, every business, every project in my hand be filled with divine provision. Let new wine—fresh opportunities, fresh creativity, fresh resources—overflow into every area of my life.

I speak the same over my family. We do not live from paycheck to paycheck—we live from provision to provision. Our barns are full, our homes are blessed, and our joy is complete. We are stewards of the overflow, because the blood has made room for more.

In Jesus' name, Amen.

PEACE

HEALING FROM EMOTIONAL PAIN

> "Surely he has borne our sickness and carried our suffering…"
> — Isaiah 53:4 WEB

Man of Sorrows, acquainted with grief, I worship You for carrying what I could not bear. Every weight of anxiety, every crushing sadness, every silent pain has been nailed to the cross. Your blood speaks healing over the wounds no one sees.

I choose to release my grip on pain and embrace the wholeness You purchased. You did not only take my sin, You took my sorrow. You bore the heaviness so my heart could be light. You carried the weight so my family could be free from cycles of fear and depression.

Let Your peace saturate every memory that once brought torment. Let Your presence breathe life into the places within me that felt dead. From this day forward, I will walk in the joy and rest that are my inheritance in the blood. In Jesus' name, Amen.

DAY 58

PARDON

Complete Salvation In Christ

> "...he is able to save to the uttermost those who draw near to God through him..."
> — Hebrews 7:25 WEB

Great High Priest, I exalt You today for a salvation that knows no limits. You don't just save partially—you save completely. You save my past, redeem my present, and secure my eternal future. You save my whole household to the uttermost.

No situation is too far gone, no soul too stained. By Your eternal priesthood, You stand before the Father with blood that never loses its power. I call upon that saving power for every family member—those near, those far, those wandering, those weary. Let Your blood reach and rescue.

God of total restoration, I declare salvation over our minds, emotions, habits, and relationships. Rescue us to the depths of our being. Make us trophies of grace, shining with the evidence of a salvation that never ends.

In Jesus' name, Amen.

PROTECTION

Standard Against Flood Attacks

> "So shall they fear Yahweh's name from the west, and his glory from the rising of the sun; for when the enemy comes in like a flood, Yahweh's Spirit will lift up a standard against him."
> —Isaiah 59:19 WEB

God of Battle, I raise the banner of the blood high over my household. When the enemy rushes in like a flood—through fear, through chaos, through sudden assault—let the blood of Jesus rise as a standard. Let it be a wall he cannot penetrate, a floodgate he cannot breach.

I decree that my family will not drown in emotional overload, spiritual weariness, or financial pressure. When trials increase, Your glory increases all the more. The blood stands as proof that the enemy's access is denied. Let every flood meant to overwhelm be turned into a wave of breakthrough.

Father, make our dwelling a high place—above floodwaters, above panic, above demonic manipulation. The blood of Jesus is our high tower. When the enemy overreaches, You overrule. Raise up angels to fight on our behalf, raise up favor to counter attack, raise up victory to cancel sorrow.

In Jesus' name, Amen.

PREVAIL

TRAINED HANDS, BLOOD-ANOINTED WARFARE

> Blessed be Yahweh, my rock, who teaches my hands to war, and my fingers to battle.
> — Psalm 144:1 WEB

Lord of Armies, I bless You for divine training and supernatural strategy! You do not send me into battle unprepared. By the anointing of the blood, You have equipped my hands for war and sharpened my senses for victory. I am not a casualty—I am a conqueror.

I declare that my hands are sanctified by the blood and empowered to destroy every work of darkness. I decree that my fingers carry prophetic fire to strike down every demonic resistance. You are my Rock—immovable, unshakeable—and You've made me a warrior in Your image.

I raise a battle cry over my family. I release arrows of intercession and throw down altars of iniquity. By Your teaching, I war wisely. By Your blood, I war victoriously. I do not fight aimlessly; I fight with heaven's force, and I win every time.

In Jesus' name, Amen.

PRESERVATION

Sickness Taken from Among Us

> "You shall serve Yahweh your God, and he will bless your bread and your water, and I will take sickness away from among you."
> — Exodus 23:25 WEB

Blessed Healer, covenant God, as we serve You with our lives, You have promised not only to bless our provision but to remove sickness from our midst. I take You at Your word. Let this promise reign over my home: sickness has no place here. Disease has no permission to dwell in our company.

We sanctify our bread and water with thanksgiving. Every meal, every bite, is a vessel of healing. Let what we consume be transformed into medicine by the blood. Let divine immunity rise in our bodies. Remove every trace of disease, every foreign invader, every affliction masquerading in silence. You didn't say You would manage it—you said You would remove it.

Let this promise define our family culture. We serve You, and You protect us. We worship You, and You preserve us. Sickness may roam, but it will not stay. Because You walk among us, healing is permanent, and deliverance is our reality.

In Jesus' name, Amen.

PROSPERITY

Increase Upon Increase

"May Yahweh increase you more and more, you and your children."
— Psalm 115:14 WEB

God of Increase, I thank You for the blood of Jesus that unlocks generational multiplication. I declare that my life is not stagnant. I am increasing—more and more. Not just me, but my children after me. The covenant speaks multiplication, and I receive it now.

Let every area of my life rise to new levels: my income, my wisdom, my influence, my opportunities. I am not diminishing—I am enlarging. I declare that the cycle of decrease is broken. I expect growth because I am joined to a God who cannot fail.

Let my family be swept into this divine current. May our children go further, rise higher, and shine brighter. May every generation outdo the last in wisdom, wealth, and worship. You are the God of more and more, and we say yes to the increase.

In Jesus' name, Amen.

PEACE

PEACE AND RIGHTEOUSNESS UNITED

> "Mercy and truth meet together. Righteousness and peace have kissed each other."
> — Psalm 85:10 WEB

God of Covenant Harmony, I thank You that in the blood of Jesus, righteousness and peace are forever joined. Because of the cross, I am not striving for acceptance; I live from it. Peace is the fruit of knowing I am justified in Your sight.

I declare that the rule of righteousness brings stability to my thoughts, unity to my family, and calm to my relationships. There is no separation between my standing before You and the rest of my soul—You have made them one.

May my home be an expression of this divine union, where truth is spoken in love, mercy flows freely, and peace reigns without end. In Jesus' name, Amen.

DAY 59

PARDON

Christ Came to Save, Not Condemn

> "For God didn't send his Son into the world to judge the world, but that the world should be saved through him."
> — John 3:17 WEB

Father of Mercy, I thank You for sending Jesus—not to point a finger but to open Your arms. You did not come to condemn me, You came to claim me. Your love has rescued me from wrath and brought me into the safety of salvation.

I reject every voice that says I am unworthy, disqualified, or forsaken. Jesus, You came to heal what was broken, not to punish. Let that truth ring in my ears louder than every lie. I receive Your saving grace with joy and reverence. Let my family know this love too—fully and forever.

May our home be a dwelling place of mercy, not condemnation. Let every child, every spouse, every loved one feel the warmth of Your saving light. We are not condemned—we are celebrated as those brought near by the blood.

In Jesus' name, Amen.

PROTECTION

SHIELDED BY GOD HIMSELF

> "But you, Yahweh, are a shield around me, my glory, and the one who lifts up my head."
> —Psalm 3:3 WEB

O Shield of My Life, I declare that You are not only near me—you are around me. Encircle my family like fire. Surround my home like wind. Let the blood of Jesus form an unbreakable circumference of protection, so that no harm can penetrate.

Be our glory when shame tries to creep in. Be our lifter when heads hang low. I speak over every member of my household: The Lord is your shield! You are surrounded with favor, soaked in mercy, and defended by divine fire. Nothing formed against us shall stand.

Lord, as we go out and come in, let the shield of Your presence go before us. Let it block what we don't see and destroy what we can't hear. Let every ambush dissolve before it manifests. We rest tonight and rise tomorrow with heads lifted high—not by our strength, but because of the shield of the blood.

In Jesus' name, Amen.

PREVAIL

FINAL END TO ALL TROUBLE

> What do you plot against Yahweh? He will make a full end. Trouble will not rise up the second time.
> — Nahum 1:9 WEB

O God of vengeance and justice, I thank You that the blood of Jesus not only delivers—it ends cycles. Today, I prophesy the full end of every recurring trouble in my life and family. Cycles of fear, sickness, financial strain, and generational bondage are brought to final ruin under the power of the blood.

You are not the God of delay—you are the God of the final word. By the blood, I decree that what tried to rise will rise no more. What tormented my family in the past will torment us no more. The blood is speaking finality, closure, and divine reversal.

I establish this word over my children, my legacy, and my entire bloodline. Trouble ends here. The torment stops now. The cycle is broken permanently. I celebrate the power of final victory—the kind only You can secure.

In Jesus' name, Amen.

PRESERVATION

Healing to the Uttermost

> "Therefore he is also able to save to the uttermost those who draw near to God through him…"
> — Hebrews 7:25 WEB

Mighty Intercessor, seated at the right hand of the Father, I draw near by the blood that grants me access. You are able—fully, completely, eternally—to heal and save to the uttermost. I bring every broken place in my family before You and trust that not one is too far, too deep, or too long for You to restore.

Save to the uttermost! Heal to the core! Let every hidden sickness, every buried grief, every inherited dysfunction be redeemed. Reach into the depths of our genetics, our histories, our emotions. Your salvation is not surface—it is total. The same blood that redeems the soul restores the body.

No diagnosis is beyond Your reach. No shame or mental torment is outside Your healing scope. Uttermost healing means full recovery, full preservation, and full victory. You are our Eternal Priest, and Your intercession guarantees our healing.

In Jesus' name, Amen.

PROSPERITY

Harvest from Blood-Bought Seed

> "Don't be deceived. God is not mocked, for whatever a man sows, that he will also reap."
> — Galatians 6:7 WEB

Covenant God, I declare today that every seed I have sown is returning with increase. You are not unjust, and You do not forget. The blood of Jesus has marked my seed, protected it, and guaranteed its harvest. What I sow in faith, I shall reap in fullness.

I sow my time, my tithes, my service, my obedience—and I declare, by blood covenant, that my harvest is inevitable. I reject fear and embrace faith. I call forth every delayed harvest. I summon every seed sown in tears to return with joy.

Let my family walk in this revelation. Let every act of kindness, every offering, every sacrifice made in faith come back pressed down, shaken together, and running over. We are not sowing in vain. The blood has blessed our ground.

In Jesus' name, Amen.

PEACE

WALKING IN THE GOSPEL OF PEACE

> "How beautiful are the feet of those who preach the Good News of peace…"
> — Romans 10:15 WEB

Lord of the Harvest, thank You for calling me to carry the message of peace, not just in words, but in the life I live. Through the blood, I have received this peace, and now I am commissioned to spread it wherever my feet go.

I declare that my steps will not bring confusion, but clarity; not strife, but reconciliation. My family and I will walk as living testimonies of the peace purchased by Christ, becoming vessels of healing in a fractured world.

Let our presence bring calm to chaos, and our words be rivers of life. May the fragrance of the gospel be evident in every interaction, opening hearts to the One who made peace through the blood of His cross. In Jesus' name, Amen.

DAY 60

PARDON

Praise For National and Personal Pardon

> "You have forgiven the iniquity of your people. You have covered all their sin."
> — Psalm 85:2 WEB

Forgiving Father, I lift my hands in gratitude. You have not only forgiven me personally, but You have covered the iniquity of an entire people. I join in that ancient song of deliverance and declare: blessed is the nation, the family, the soul whose sins are covered by the blood.

Lord, let Your mercy flood every area of our land and every heart in our home. From the leaders of our nation to the youngest child in our family, let the power of the blood bring cleansing. Revive us again, O Lord, and let Your forgiveness be the foundation of our future.

Today I praise You not only for what You have done, but for what You are doing—restoring the broken, reviving the weary, and rebuilding what was torn down. We are a forgiven people. We are a redeemed generation. We are a family marked by grace.

In Jesus' name, Amen.

PROTECTION

THE BLOOD, MY STRONGHOLD

> "Yahweh is good, a stronghold in the day of trouble;
> he knows those who take refuge in him."
> —Nahum 1:7 WEB

Rock of Ages, I run into You, my stronghold in every storm. I declare that the blood of Jesus is not only my shelter—it is my spiritual bunker. When trouble rages and threats multiply, I will not fear. You know my name. You know my voice. You know my family. We are known and covered by the blood.

Lord, let every day of trouble meet the power of the blood. Let every dark forecast be reversed by divine goodness. Raise up walls around us made not of stone, but of Your promises. Let our home be a fortress where peace rules, angels dwell, and deliverance is standard.

When the winds howl and the earth shakes, we will not be moved. We dwell in the secret place of the Most High. The blood has spoken: We are not forsaken. We are fortified. We are hidden. We are loved. And the Lord is our stronghold, forever faithful.

In Jesus' name, Amen.

PREVAIL

INHERITANCE OF THE OVERCOMER

> He who overcomes, I will give him these things. I will be his God, and he will be my son.
> — Revelation 21:7 WEB

Heavenly Father, I rejoice in the promise that belongs to the overcomer. I am not forgotten; I am favored. I am not defeated; I am destined. Through the blood of Jesus, I step into the fullness of my eternal inheritance. You are my God—and I am Your child.

Every battle I endure, I endure with this end in mind: inheritance. I press through storms not as a victim but as an heir. I resist the enemy not as a servant but as a son. The blood has qualified me, and Your love has claimed me. Therefore, nothing the enemy sends can disinherit me from my promise.

I declare over my family that we are not wanderers—we are heirs. We do not live beneath—we reign above. I receive houses I didn't build, vineyards I didn't plant, and crowns I didn't earn—because the Lamb overcame for me. And now I overcome through His blood.

In Jesus' name, Amen.

PRESERVATION

Healing Through Faith and Blood

> "...the prayer of faith will heal the sick, and the Lord will raise him up..."
> — James 5:15 WEB

Great Physician, I release the prayer of faith over my family right now. I join hands with heaven and declare that healing is not only possible—it is promised. The blood of Jesus backs every word I speak in faith. You are raising us up from affliction, from weariness, from beds of pain and despair.

Let faith rise in every heart. Let the whispers of doubt be silenced. I speak over my loved ones: rise up! Be restored! Be made whole! Let our bodies align with divine truth, and let strength return to every muscle, organ, and cell. This prayer is not empty—it is saturated in the power of covenant blood.

As we believe, we receive. As we declare, we are restored. Let every sickness crumble under the weight of faith-filled intercession. The Lord is lifting us even now. The Lord is raising us in wholeness and might. We walk not in fear, but in faith that heals.

In Jesus' name, Amen.

PROSPERITY

Final Inheritance, Fully Secured

> "He said to me, 'I am the Alpha and the Omega, the Beginning and the End. I will give freely to him who is thirsty from the spring of the water of life. He who overcomes, I will give him these things. I will be his God, and he will be my son.'"
> — Revelation 21:6-7 WEB

Alpha and Omega, my Beginning and my End, I worship You for the inheritance You've secured by Your blood. You have not left me to wander—I have a guaranteed future. I thirst for You, and You fill me with life, purpose, and eternal reward.

I declare that I am an overcomer. Every battle I face is already settled in Christ. I don't just survive—I inherit. The spring of life flows through me and into everything I touch. My inheritance is not in man's hands—it is sealed in heaven and revealed in the earth.

Let my household walk in this final assurance. We are sons and daughters of God, destined to overcome and receive what the blood has paid for. We are heirs of every promise, partakers of every blessing, and recipients of every reward.

In Jesus' name, Amen.

PEACE

Resurrection Peace Every Day

> "When therefore it was evening, on that day, the first day of the week, and when the doors were locked... Jesus came and stood in the middle, and said to them, 'Peace be to you.'"
> — John 20:19 WEB

Risen Lord, I welcome You into the locked places of my life. Your blood has opened the way for You to step into every room of my heart, every hidden fear, and every closed-off relationship, declaring, "Peace be to you."

I receive that peace now—peace that does not depend on circumstances, peace that cannot be stolen by threats or storms. Just as You breathed it over Your disciples, breathe it over my family and me today.

Let Your resurrection life displace despair. Let Your presence dismantle fear. May every day begin and end with the assurance that You stand among us, and where You stand, peace reigns unchallenged. In Jesus' name, Amen.

Epilogue

The journey you've just completed is not the end; it's the beginning of a new way of life. You have prayed the Word. You have declared the covenant. You have applied the Blood of Jesus over every area of your life.

Every battle you face from this day forward has already been addressed in the victory of the Cross. You are not fighting *for* victory—you are fighting *from* victory. And the Blood is your evidence.

When the enemy whispers condemnation, point him to the Blood that has pardoned you. When fear tries to invade, stand under the Blood's protection. When you feel the weight of the fight, remember you prevail through the Blood. When sickness or weakness comes, proclaim your preservation through the Blood. When lack knocks at your door, release prosperity through the Blood. And when chaos swirls, anchor yourself in peace through the Blood.

Keep this book close. Pray these prayers again and again. And never forget—the Blood of Jesus is eternally fresh, eternally powerful, and eternally speaking on your behalf.

You are an overcomer. And the Blood still speaks.

In Jesus' name, Amen.

Encourage Others with Your Story

If this prayer guide has strengthened your faith, deepened your intercession, or helped you stand in the gap, would you consider leaving a short review on Amazon? Your feedback not only encourages others but also helps more believers discover this resource and join in the prayer movement. Every review—just a few sentences—makes a difference. Thank you for being part of this movement.

MORE FROM PRAYERSCRIPTS

COMMAND YOUR DESTINY SERIES

Command Your Morning:
30 Days of Prayers and Declarations to Seize Your Day and Shape Your Destiny

There is a battle over every morning—and every believer must choose to either drift into the day or command it.

Command Your Night:
30 Days of Prayers and Declarations to Secure Your Rest and Shape Your Tomorrow

Every night is a spiritual battlefield—what you do before you sleep can determine the course of your tomorrow.

Command Your Evening:
30 Days of Prayers and Declarations to Release the Day and Reclaim Intimacy with God

There is a battle over every transition—and evening is one of the most spiritually neglected.

SPIRITUAL WARFARE SERIES

Scriptures & Prayers for Deliverance from Trouble:
40 Days of Prayer for When Life Feels Overwhelming

Are you walking through a season where life feels heavy and your prayers feel weak?

Scriptures & Prayers for Deliverance from Evil:
50 Days of Prayer to Overcome Darkness and Find God's Protection

When darkness presses in, how do you pray?

Scriptures & Prayers for Engaging the Enemy:
70 Days of Prayer to Rebuke the Enemy and Release God's Power

You weren't called to run from the battle—you were anointed to win it.

Scriptures & Prayers for Combating Spiritual Wickedness:
50 Days of Prayer to Overthrow Wicked Plans and Stand in God's Victory

Are you facing opposition that feels deeper than the natural? You're not imagining it—and you're not powerless.

THE BLOOD COVENANT SERIES

Pardon Through the Blood:
60 Days of Prayers for Total Forgiveness and Freedom

Guilt is a prison. The blood of Jesus holds the key.

Protection Through the Blood:
60 Days of Prayers for Living Untouchable Under Christ's Blood

You are not helpless. You are not exposed. You are covered—completely—by the blood of Jesus.

Prevail Through the Blood:
60 Days of Prayers for Spiritual Mastery Over the Enemy

What if every scheme of the enemy against your life could be dismantled—by one unstoppable weapon?

Preservation Through the Blood:
60 Days of Prayers for Divine Healing and Wholeness

Unlock Lasting Healing and Wholeness Through the Blood of Jesus

Prosperity Through the Blood:
60 Days of Prayers for Unlocking Heaven's Wealth and Walking in Covenant Increase

You were redeemed for more than survival—you were redeemed to prosper.

Peace Through the Blood:
60 Days of Prayers for Resting in the Covenant of Unshakable Peace

Are you ready to silence every storm of the mind, heart, and home—once and for all?

ONE NATION UNDER GOD SERIES

Standing in the Gap for Covenant Awakening:
30 Days of Prayer for National Repentance, Righteous Leadership & God's Sovereign Rule

What if your prayers could help turn the tide of a nation?

Standing in the Gap for Divine Defense:
30 Days of Prayer for National Guidance, Guarding & Glory

When the foundations of a nation feel as if they're shaking, prayer is the strongest fortress you can build.

Standing in the Gap for National Healing:
40 Days of Prayer for Reconciliation, Righteousness, and Restoration

What if your prayers could help heal a nation? What if God is waiting for someone—like you—to stand in the gap?

Standing in the Gap for The President:
50 Days of Prayer for Leadership, Loyalty, and Lifeline

When a nation's leader is under spiritual siege, will you answer the call to stand in the gap?

www.ingramcontent.com/pod-product-compliance
Lightning Source LLC
Chambersburg PA
CBHW060105170426
43198CB00010B/780